SKETCHING TECHNIQUES FOR ARTISTS

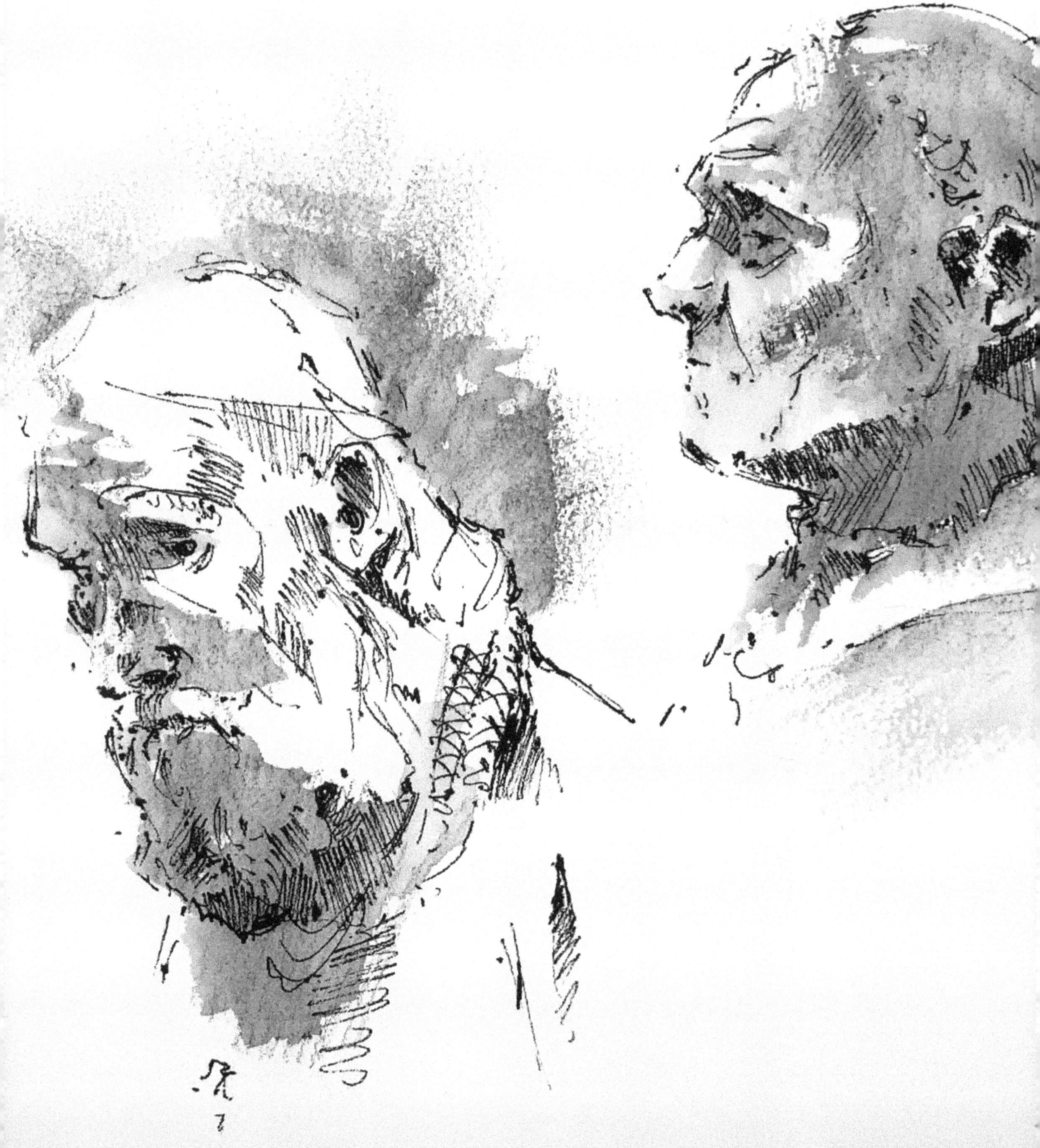

ALEX HILLKURTZ

SKETCHING TECHNIQUES FOR ARTISTS

In-Studio and Plein-Air Methods for Drawing and Painting Still Life, Landscape, Architecture, Faces and Figures, and More

ROCKPORT

Quarto.com

First published in 2021 by Rockport Publishers, an imprint of The Quarto Group,
100 Cummings Center, Suite 265-D, Beverly, MA 01915, USA.
T (978) 282-9590 F (978) 283-2742

EEA Representation, WTS Tax d.o.o.,
Žanova ulica 3, 4000 Kranj, Slovenia.
www.wts-tax.si

Rockport Publishers titles are also available at discount for retail, wholesale, promotional, and bulk purchase. For details, contact the Special Sales Manager by email at specialsales@quarto.com or by mail at The Quarto Group, Attn: Special Sales Manager, 100 Cummings Center, Suite 265-D, Beverly, MA 01915, USA.

ISBN: 978-1-63159-923-1

Digital edition published in 2021
eISBN: 978-1-63159-924-8

Library of Congress Cataloging-in-Publication Data is available.

Page Layout: Megan Jones Design

▸ Cairoli Castello, Milan in the rain.
Ink and graphite.

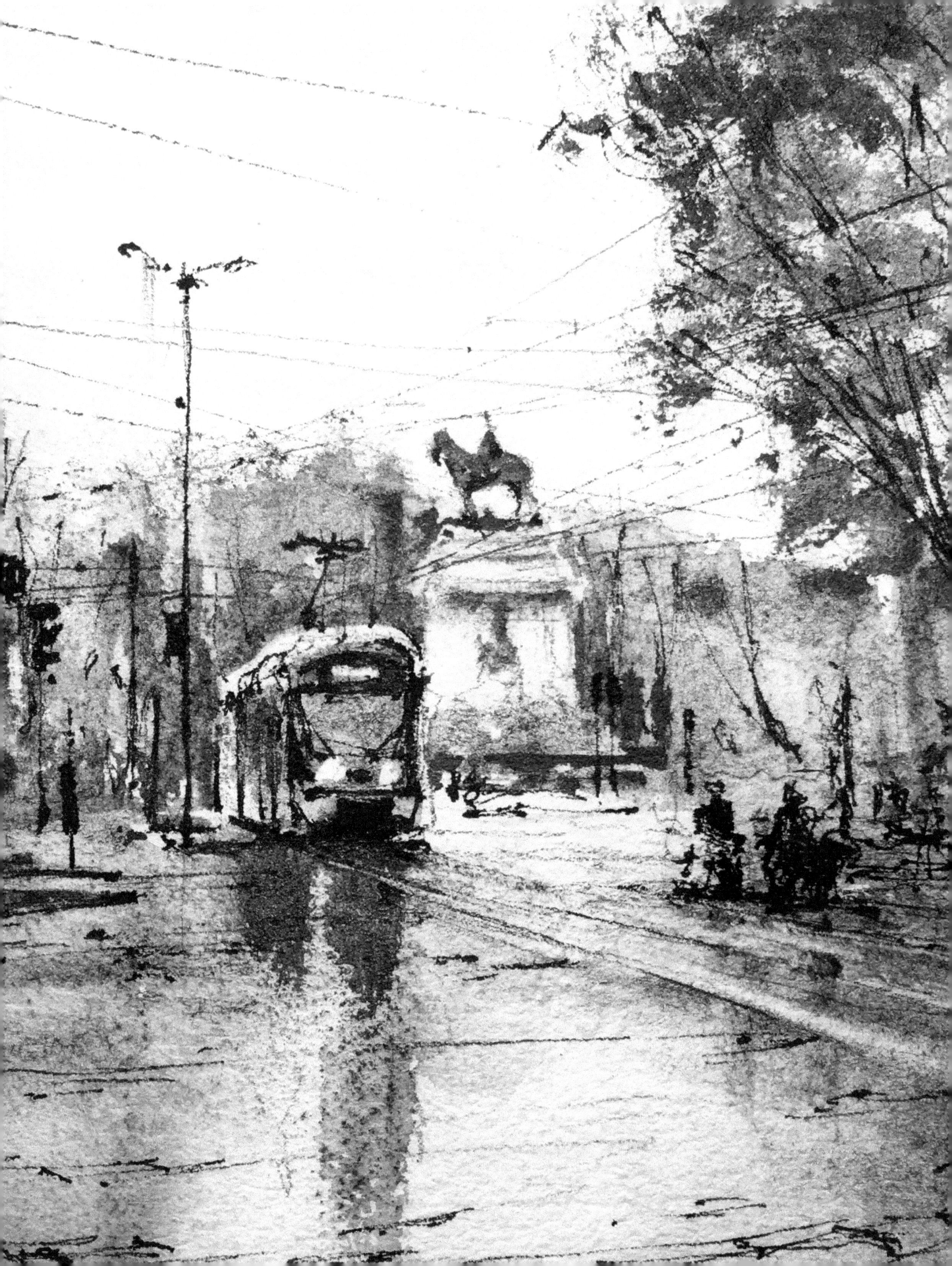

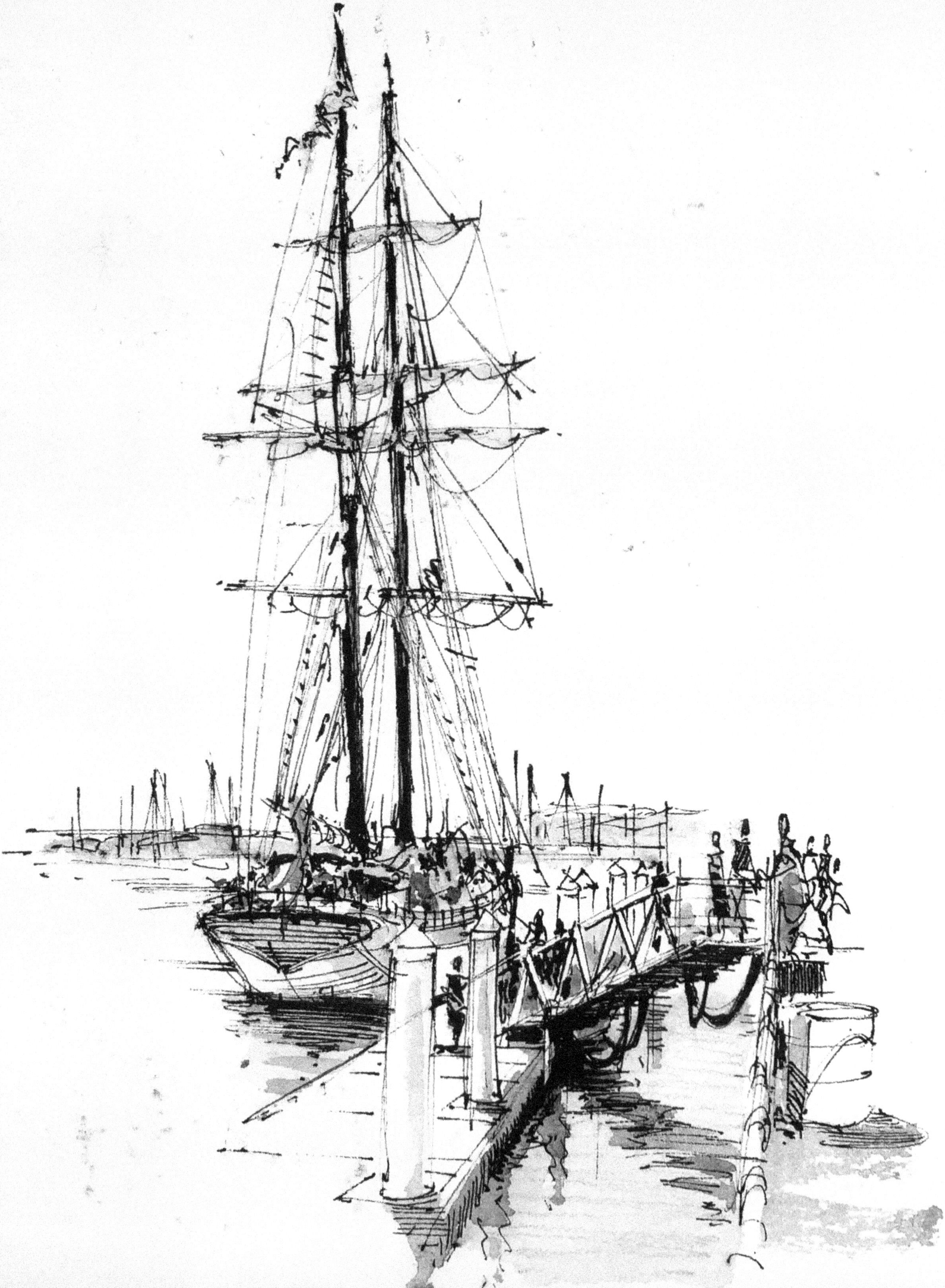

CONTENTS

◂ Marina Del Rey, California.
Ink and graphite.

INTRODUCTION

A sketch is an elusive animal. Sketches can duck and weave. They can hide in plain sight. They can taunt us when our vision exceeds our ability. Even when things are going well, just when we think we've got one captured, one false move on our part and they slip away, leaving us bewildered and frustrated.

A sketch is a memento. A quick jot to remember a place, listen to the birds, feel the breeze, let conversations wash over us in a language we may not yet know.

A sketch can be many things, and sketching can open doors to new experiences and places. I'd like to share some of what I've learned over the years about sketching. I'll offer tips and techniques, favorite materials, and also why I do certain things, and the thought processes behind them.

I come from a background in storyboarding and illustration for film. I've always been fascinated with what happens behind the scenes. Every time I watch a movie or TV show, every time I see a concert, sporting event, or any sort of production, I want to know what's going on behind the scenes. How did the spectacle before me come into being?

I feel the same way about painting and sketching. I love looking at great art. I love leafing through sketchbooks of friends' travels. And I'm always curious about what it took to create what I'm seeing. Why did the painter use this particular color? What about this location caught someone's eye? What was going on behind the scenes that allowed this creation to see the light of day?

I'd like to take you behind the scenes of my sketches and paintings. I'll show you how I achieve my results, and I'll explain the choices I made along the way. Sketches for me are like scenes in a movie. This book is the "making of," and it's my hope that shedding light on the process will be just as enjoyable as the final outcome.

▸ Venice Canal. Ink and watercolor on handmade paper.

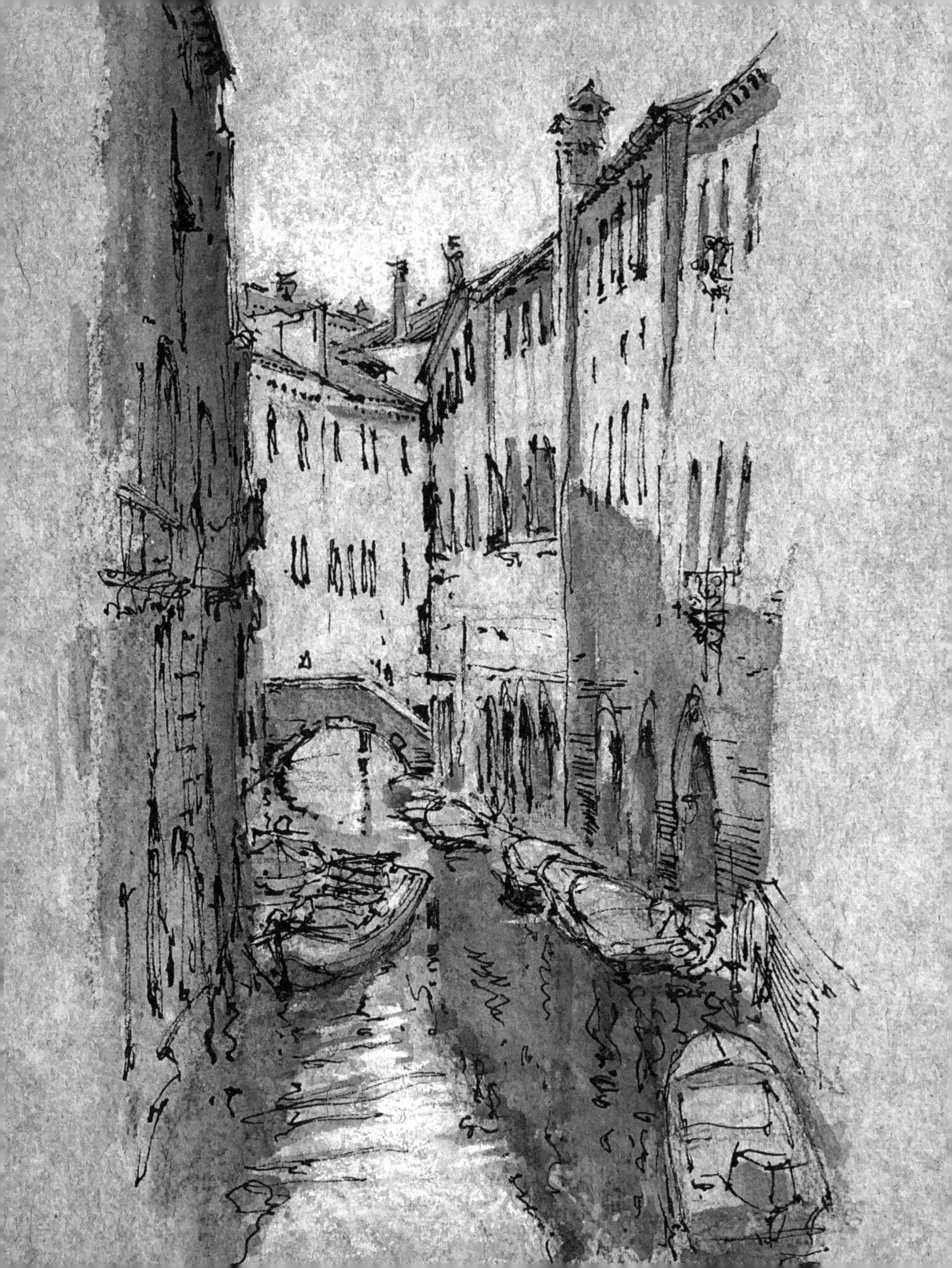

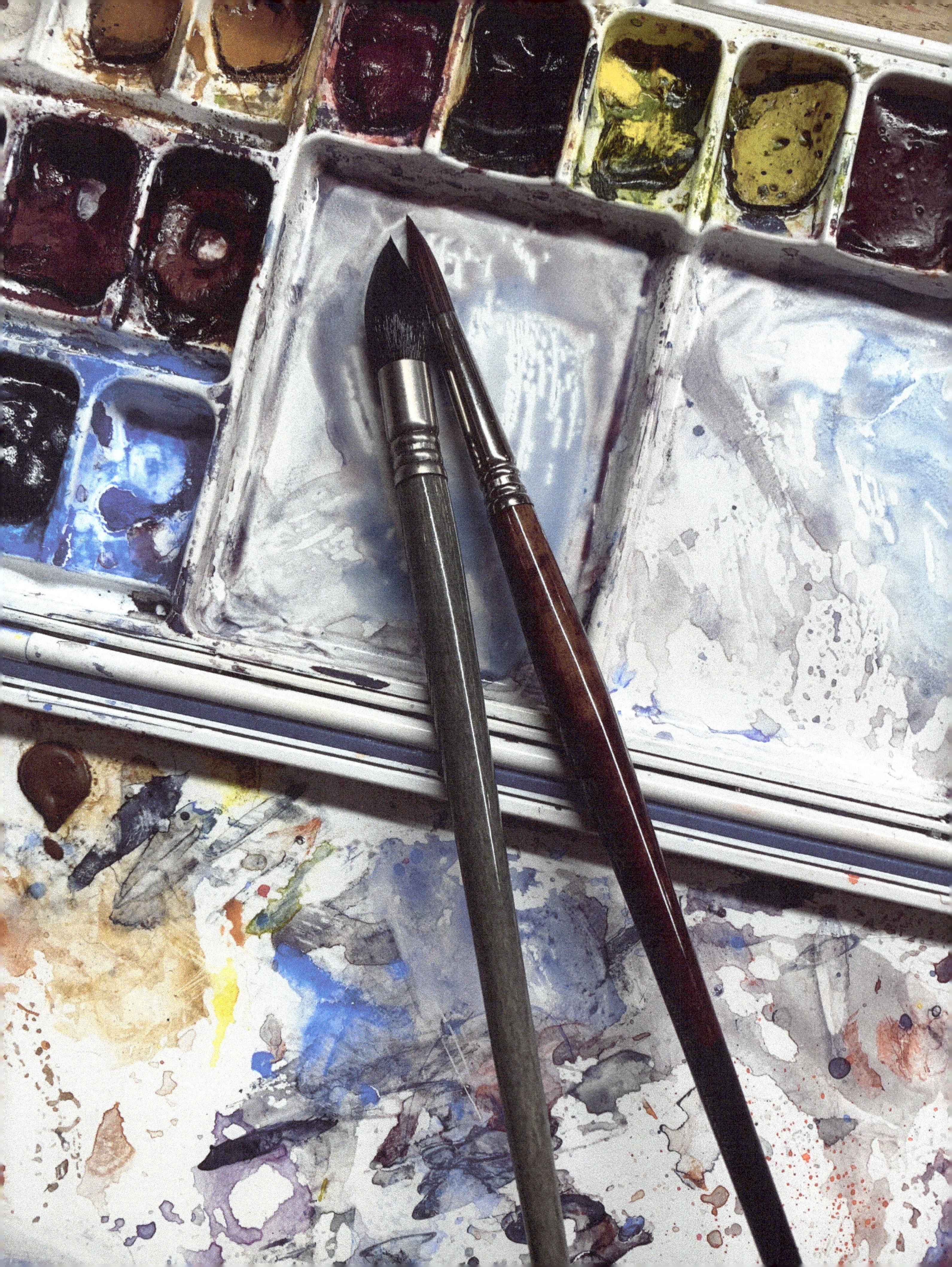

1

MATERIALS AND TOOLS

Pencil, ink, and paint can be applied to a page in many ways, each with its own purpose and personality. Tools are an extension of your hand, your arm, your imagination, and your soul. We could paint with our fingers, but an endless variety of art supplies have been invented to enhance our abilities and fine-tune our expression. It's worth spending time playing with these tools and getting used to the way they feel and perform.

A PERSONAL CHOICE

Tools used to express creativity can be a very personal choice. As you become more comfortable with different tools, you'll find ones that best express what you want to say. For some, a cheap pen with a steel nib is sufficient. Others prefer something more expensive and stylish. Like most art supplies (and tools in general), you get what you pay for. Remember, the best brush is the one you have with you. The best set of paints is what you have with you. You can do a lot with minimal materials.

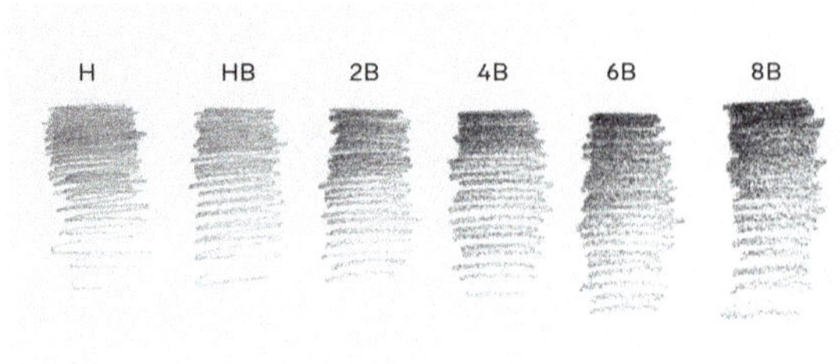

Pencils, Pens, and Inks

Making marks on paper is at the root of all sketching. Here are some of my favorite tools that get my sketches off to a good start.

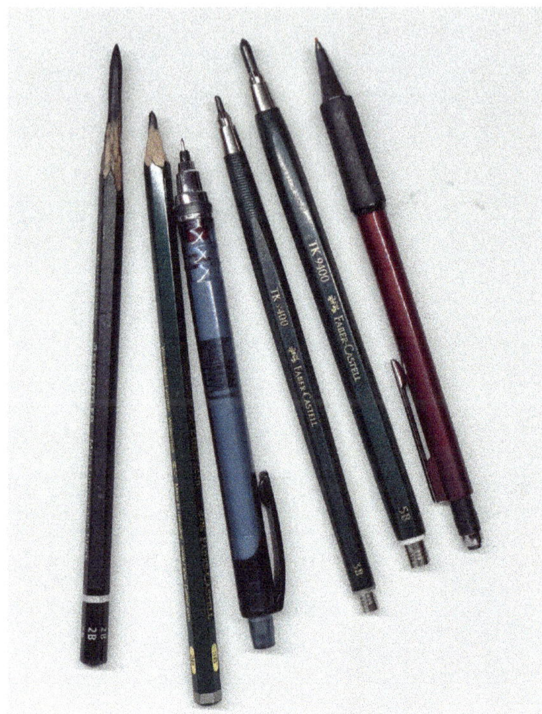

PENCILS

I have a soft touch while sketching so I prefer a darker lead. For me, 4B and 6B pencils are best. Because these leads are soft, I use a mechanical pencil to maintain a fine line without constant sharpening. For highlights, I use a white Conté à Paris sketching pencil. For quickly applying shadows, I like the dark wash (8B) Derwent water-soluble sketching pencil and ArtGraf graphite sticks.

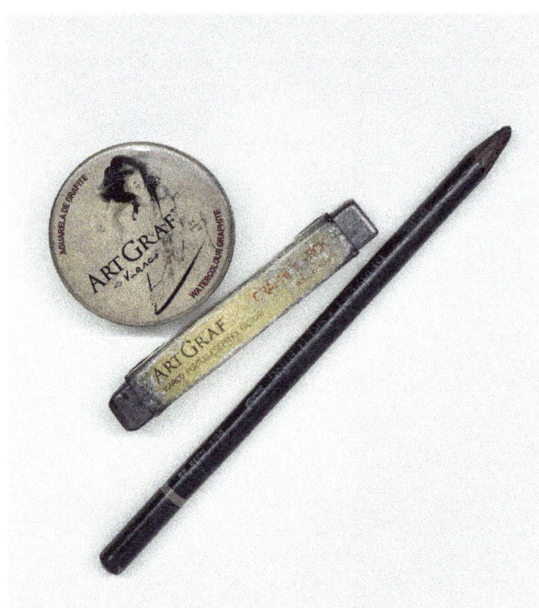

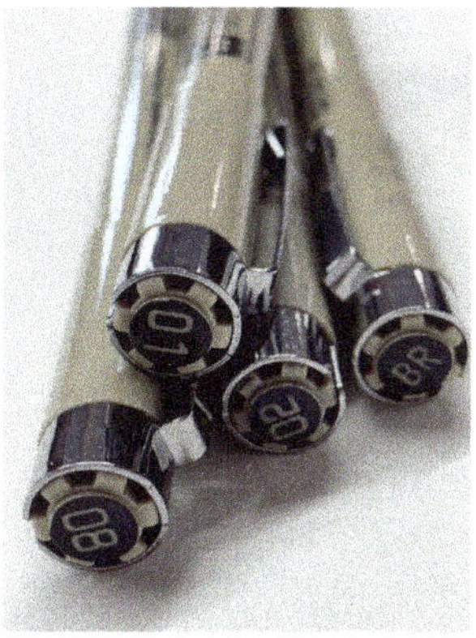

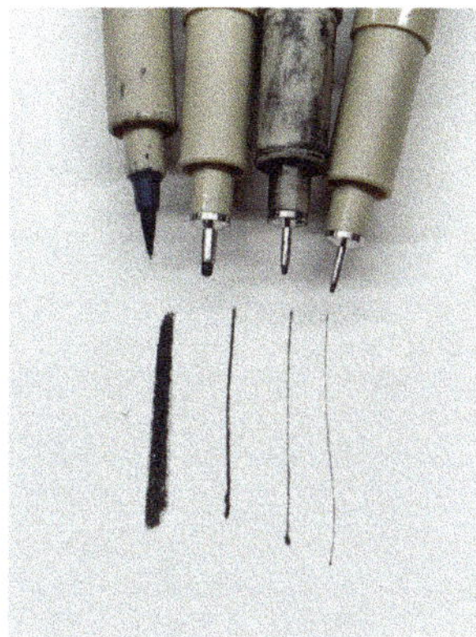

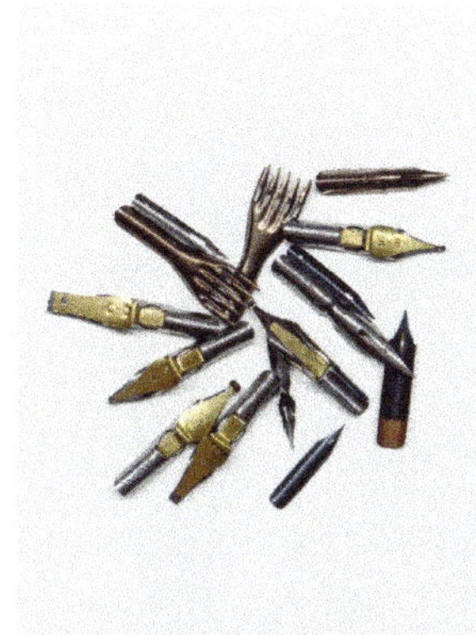

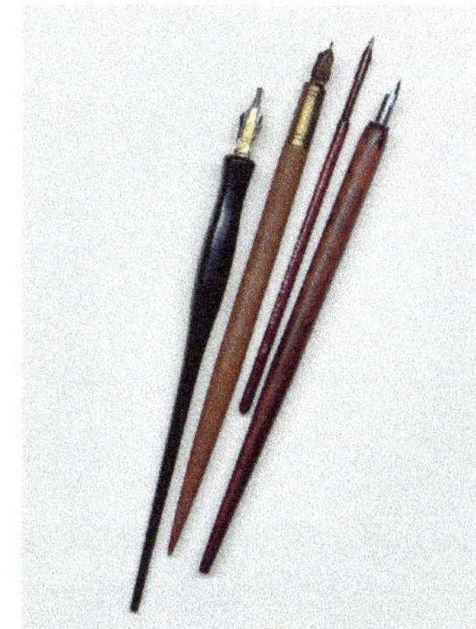

INK PENS

Fine liners, fountain pens, dip pens, and bamboo sketching pens—each tool is unique in its feel and application. I carry many options with me when I paint and sketch, so I always have what I need, depending on my mood and the subject I'm drawing.

FINE LINER PENS

Fine liner pens are felt-tip markers that come in multiple widths, so it's easy to apply variety to your sketch. They're a wonderfully simple tool for applying a clean, dark line. I use thicker pens for objects in the foreground, and thinner lines for those in the distance. By varying the line weight in this way, you create a sense of atmospheric perspective while using only black ink. Fine liners typically use waterproof ink, so adding washes of color later won't smudge your line. Sakura Pigma Micron pens sizes 05, 03, and 01 are my favorite.

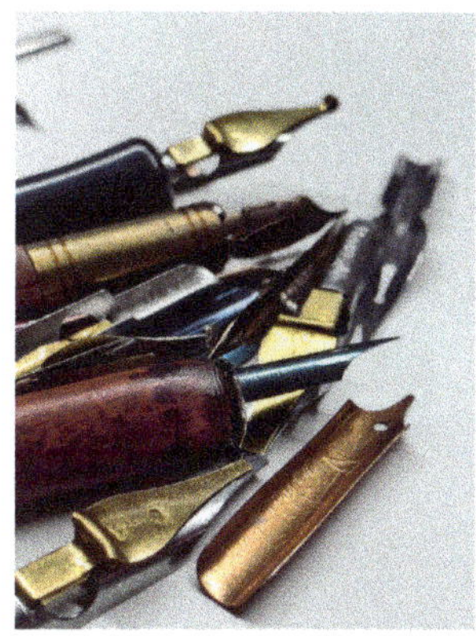

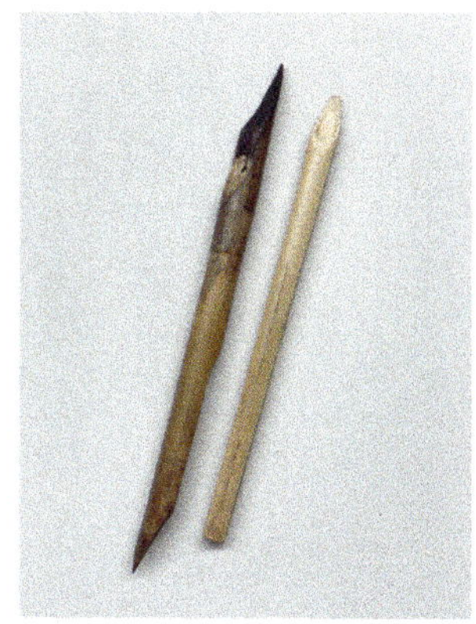

DIP AND BAMBOO PENS

Dip pens and bamboo sketching pens give a much more dynamic variety of line. These types of pens have been used for thousands of years, and I can't help but feel the pull of history when sketching with such traditional tools. I use dip pens in the studio as it's cumbersome to carry a bottle of ink while sketching outdoors. For me, the risk of one unfortunate spill isn't worth it.

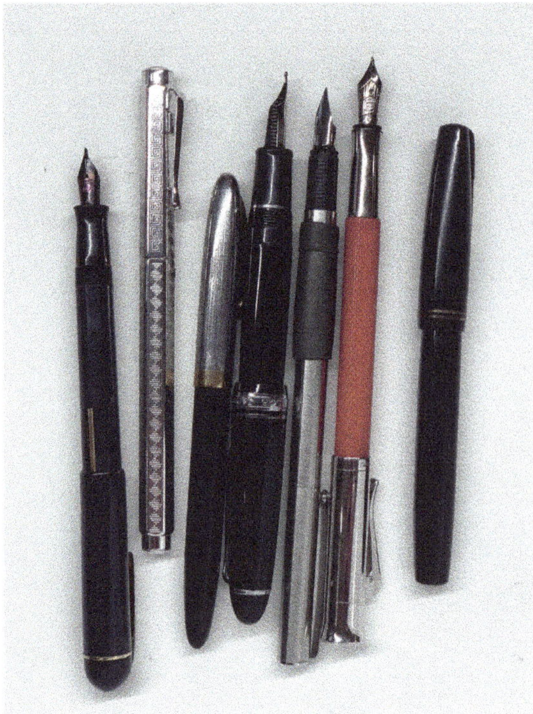

FOUNTAIN PENS AND INKS

My favorite tool for sketching is a fountain pen. These pens are compact, easy to use, and if used properly, won't leak. I've always been drawn to the appeal of fountain pens, with their elegance and artistry of construction.

GET A GRIP

Practice variety in your grip. Just like tennis players have many ways to get the ball over the net, you can build a variety of ways to hold pencils and brushes.

Holding a pencil as if you're writing a letter is perfect for fine detail, as you use your fingers and wrist to coordinate precise movements. For larger shapes, try an overhand position. This allows the use of your entire arm and shoulder. Your movement will be freer and more expressive. This can feel alien at first, so practice by drawing simple circles.

If drawing at a desk or table, try standing up. This gives you a better perspective on your page that diminishes distortion, and it also engages your whole body in the creative process.

You can choose from an endless variety of fountain pens, so it's best to experiment and find what suits you. I found my best pens by taking watercolor paper to my favorite pen shop and showing them what I do. I'm not writing calligraphy on wedding invitations, so what I need in a fountain pen differs greatly from most. I've tried many pens from different manufacturers, with all kinds of different nibs, drawing on my own paper, in my own style, to see what worked for me and what didn't. I need ink to flow evenly from the nib, and I love a flexible nib that allows for a variety of line widths. But I also enjoy how my pen skips across rough paper, adding randomness and vitality to my sketches. By trying different pens, you find what fits your hand and style.

I use a Graf von Faber-Castell Guilloche fountain pen with an F (fine) nib. I also have a Sailor 1911 Silver, a Lamy ST with an F (fine) nib, and a few vintage fountain pens from the 1940s: Waterman, Sheaffer, and Eversharp.

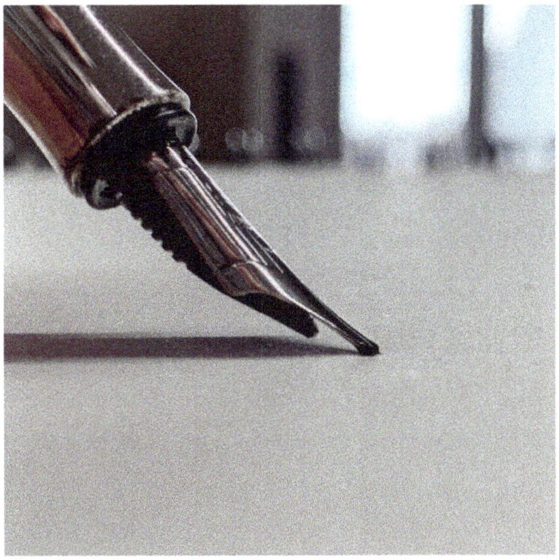

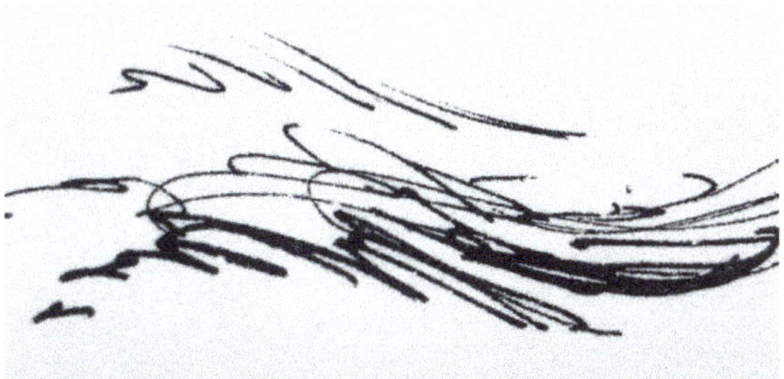

The variety of line widths that can be achieved with a single nib is impressive.

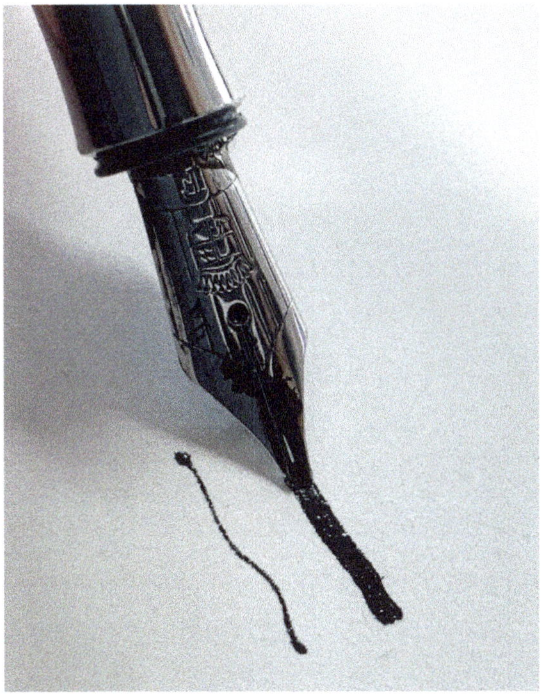

Draw a hairline bead of ink with a light touch. Apply more pressure for a thicker line.

For Lefties Only

I'm left-handed, and I first found fountain pens impossible to use. A fountain pen nib is meant to be pulled across paper, releasing a bead of ink in its path. Lefties push pens to write, so nibs stick and catch, making writing impossible. But with sketching there's no need to draw from left to right, as we do when writing. We are free to draw in any direction we chose. While sketching, the dogmatic rules of writing don't apply. When I discovered this, the world of fountain pens was suddenly available to me.

I use refillable cartridges for my fountain pens that I fill with Noodler's Ink Polar Black ink. This waterproof ink won't smudge when I wash over it with watercolor. De Atramentis Document Ink is also a very good waterproof ink and comes in a variety of colors.

Water-soluble inks can offer different effects. One I like is Diamine ink in Earl Grey. This is a dark gray ink that, when hit with water, releases purple, red, and aqua tones for some surprising results, like the ones seen in the sketch below of Amsterdam.

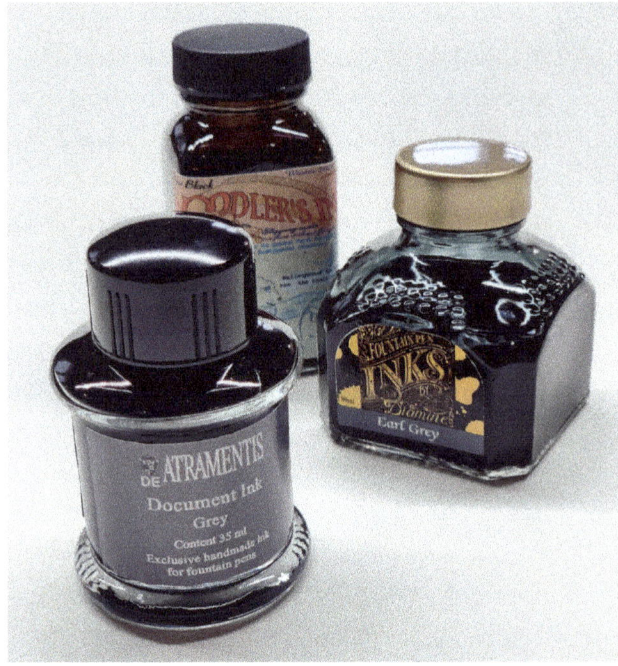

Fill 'Er Up

The ink that comes with fountain pens can be of varying quality, so I prefer to fill my pens with my own ink. For this you'll need a cartridge converter. This is a re-fillable cartridge that fits in your pen. Make sure you use ink that is designed for use in fountain pens.

Amsterdam. Water-soluble ink on paper.

Paper and Sketchbooks

Paper is perhaps the most important aspect of sketching and watercolor painting. Paper quality has a dramatic effect on the outcome of your work. I recommend 100% cotton paper.

These are some of my favorites:

- ARCHES Aquarelle 300gsm cold press
- L'Aquarelle Canson Héritage 300gsm cold press
- Sennelier watercolor 300gsm cold press

I like using paper in blocks for smaller sketches, so I don't need to stretch or mount the sheets. If I'm painting a larger piece, loose sheets are best.

Can you ever have too many sketchbooks? Like my paper, I have many books for different moods and settings. A basic sketchbook, suitable for thumbnail sketches and watercolor exercises, is never far from my side.

Here are some of my favorites:

- Strathmore 400 series sketchbook (22 × 28 cm)
- Soft leather covered sketchbook by Moulin de Larroque, France (17 × 22 cm)
- Ruscombe Paper Mill MGX Ivoire 160g (17 × 26 cm)
- Maxgoodz Aquarelle Light (18 × 27 cm)
- Charvin Carnet accordéon d'aquarelle sketchbook
- Clairefontaine naturel A5, 250g paper

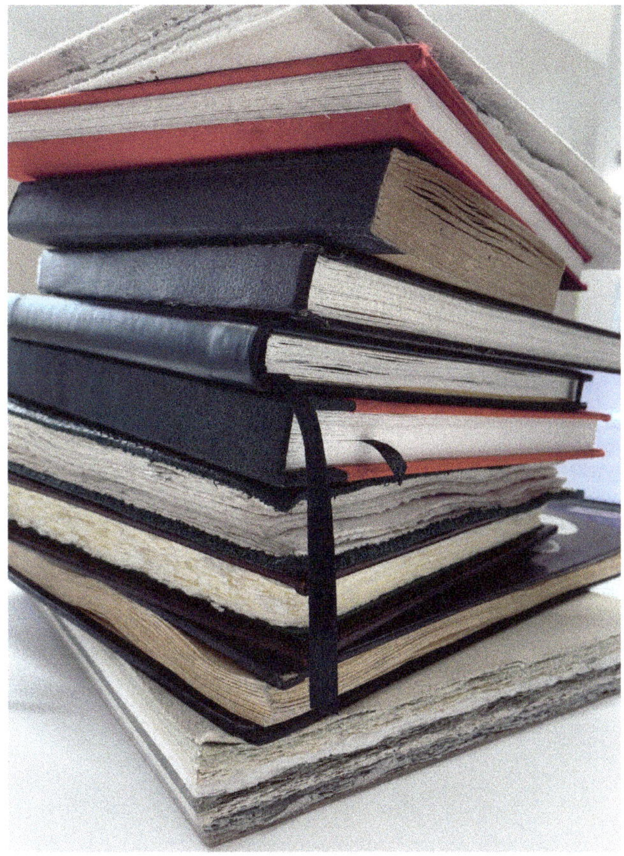

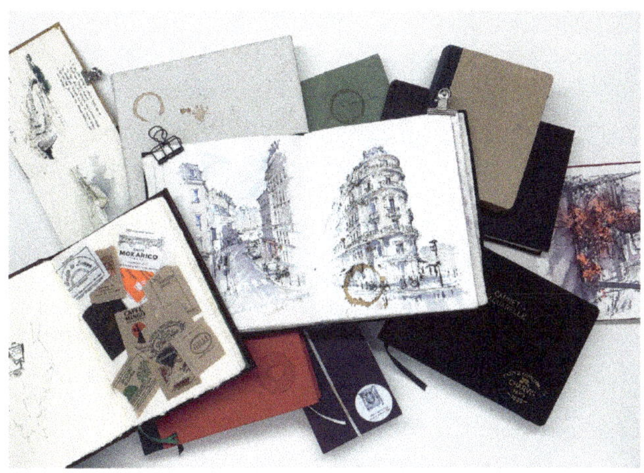

Brushes

I have an addiction to brushes. I can't leave an art store without some new brush I'm convinced I need. But while sketching, most of my work can be done with three simple brushes: a medium-sized round, a flat, and a mop.

Round brushes, such as an Escoda Perla size 10 or a Van Gogh size 8, provide a nice sharp point for details, while also allowing painting of larger areas.

Flat brushes, such as a Da Vinci Casaneo 30 or Raphaél series 915 size 18, are perfect for large washes of color.

Mop brushes, such as an Escoda Último size 14 or Raphaél series 803 petit gris size 5, are great for initial washes of color.

Another useful brush is a dagger brush, which has bristles cut at an angle to create a knife-like appearance. They can be used to create wonderfully expressive brushstrokes, from incredibly fine hairlines to larger washes. I use my dagger to paint thin tree branches and curly banister railings.

These different types of brushes allow for an immense variety of brush marks. But I always feel it's better to have a few tools that you know very well than to have a vast array of things you don't know how to use.

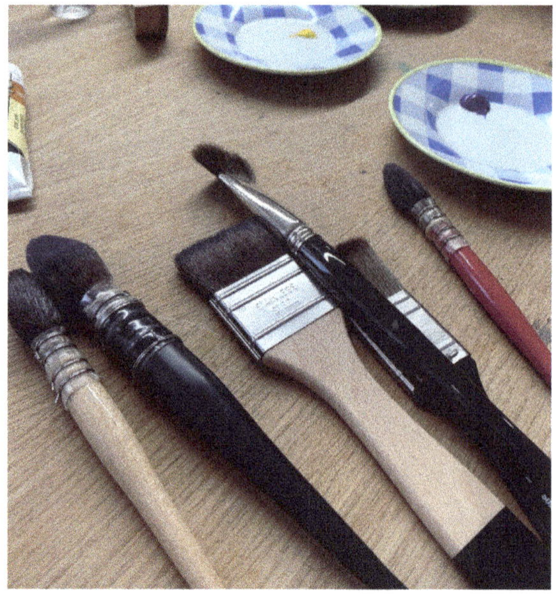

A selection of round, mop, and flat brushes.

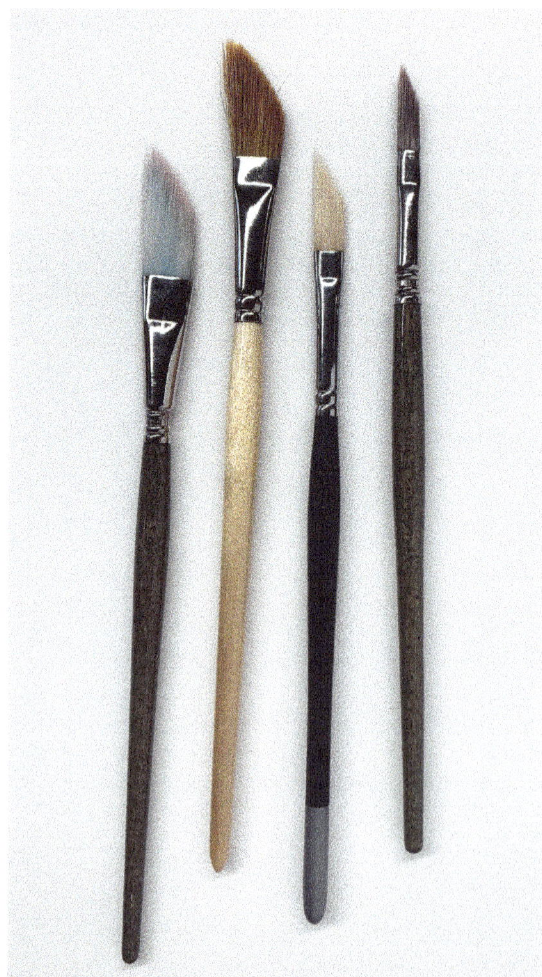

Dagger brushes come in a variety of sizes and bristle types.

Watercolor Paint

I primarily use Daniel Smith and Rembrandt paints, but most brands are suitable for what we'll be doing. I painted for many years with a student-grade set of half pans, so use what you have.

I paint with a fairly limited palette. As with brushes, I'm a real believer in being proficient with fewer materials, rather than having a vast array of things you're not familiar with. Read more about how to paint with a limited palette in chapter 9 (page 133).

These are the colors I find myself reaching for most often:

- Cobalt blue
- Ultramarine blue
- Burnt sienna
- Raw sienna
- Quinacradone sienna
- Pyrrol scarlet
- Organic vermillion
- Indian red
- Yellow ochre
- Hansa yellow
- Phthalo blue (green shade)

I have a few other specialty colors I keep close, but these are the colors I use the most.

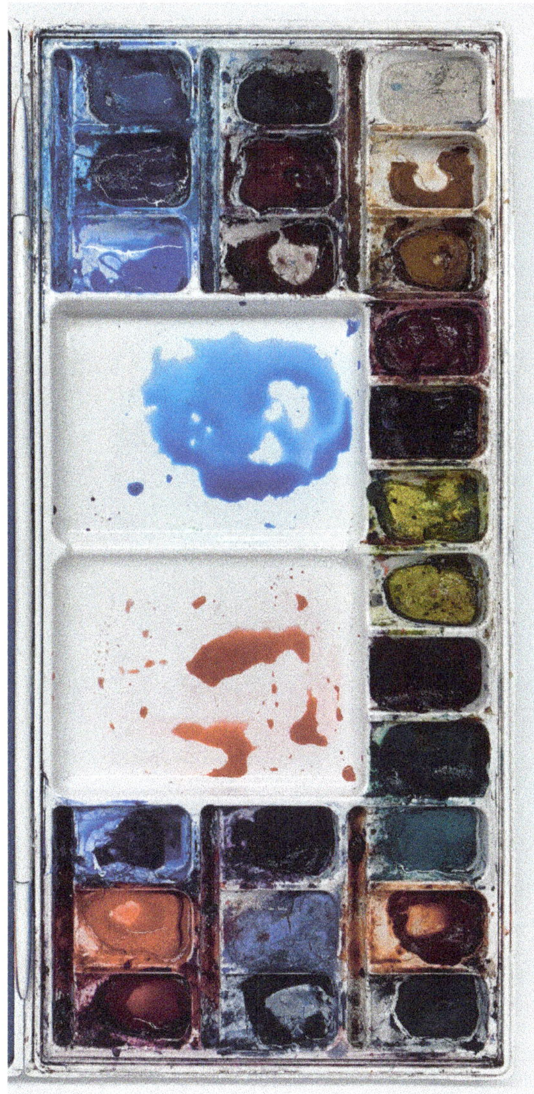

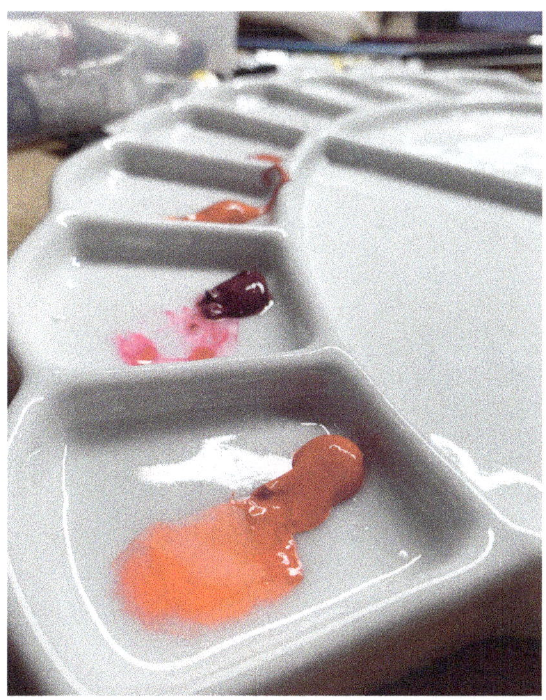

Miscellaneous Tools

I'm always finding new items to add to my sketching kit, and I'm sure you will too. With each sketch, I discover things I wish I had. Here are suggestions for a few additional items to bring with you while sketching.

- Paper towels
- Eraser
- Water container and water

A Layer of Protection

Since I'm left handed, I'm used to smudging ink when writing. Drawing and painting are different because I'm free to draw in any direction I like. I often start at the upper right corner of a page and work my way down to the left. Since we're not writing words that have to appear in a specific sequence, we are free to adjust the direction of our hand and the flow of our pen and brush to suit our needs.

If you need to lay your hand over your drawing, place a clean sheet of paper or paper towel down first to prevent smudging.

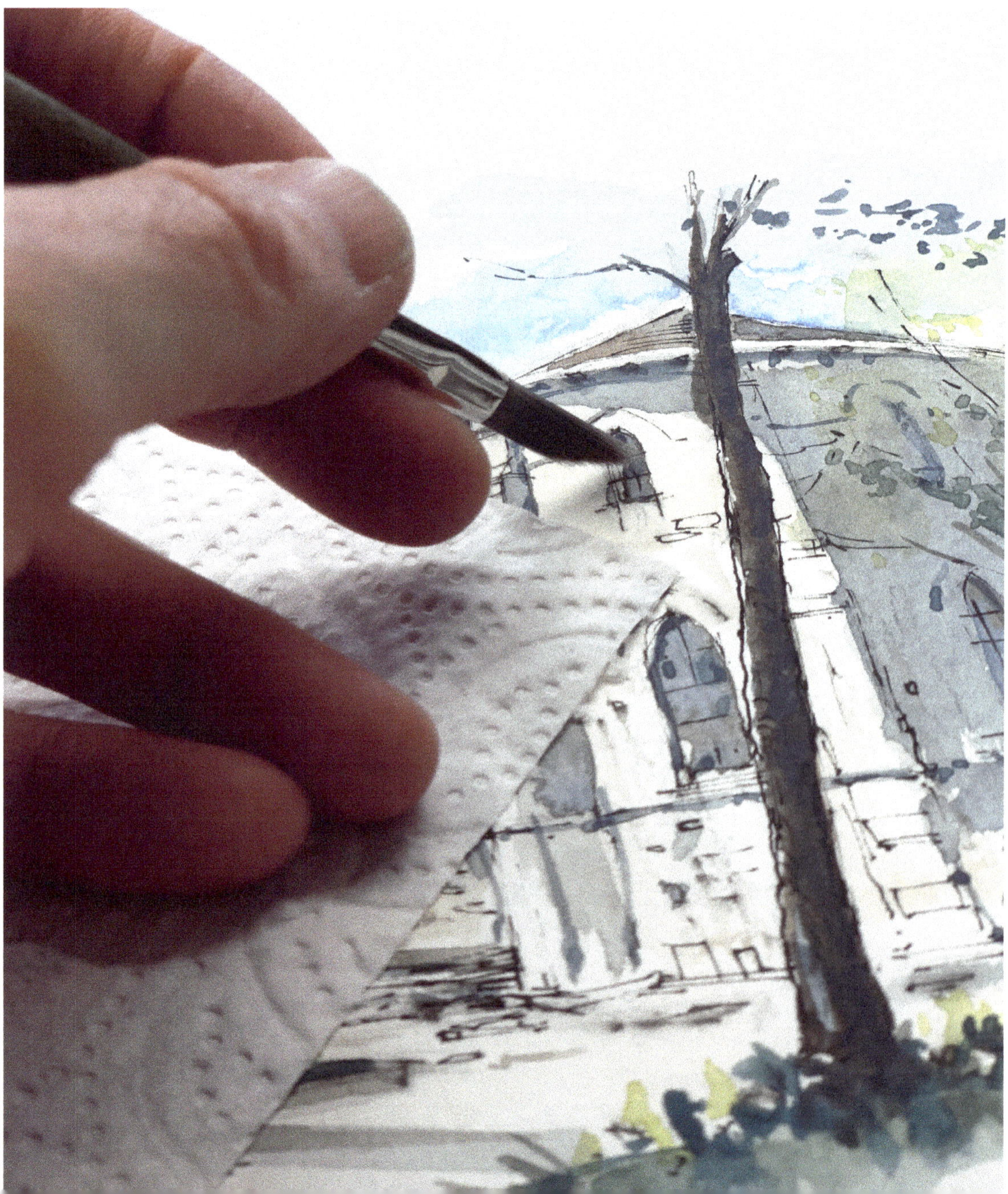

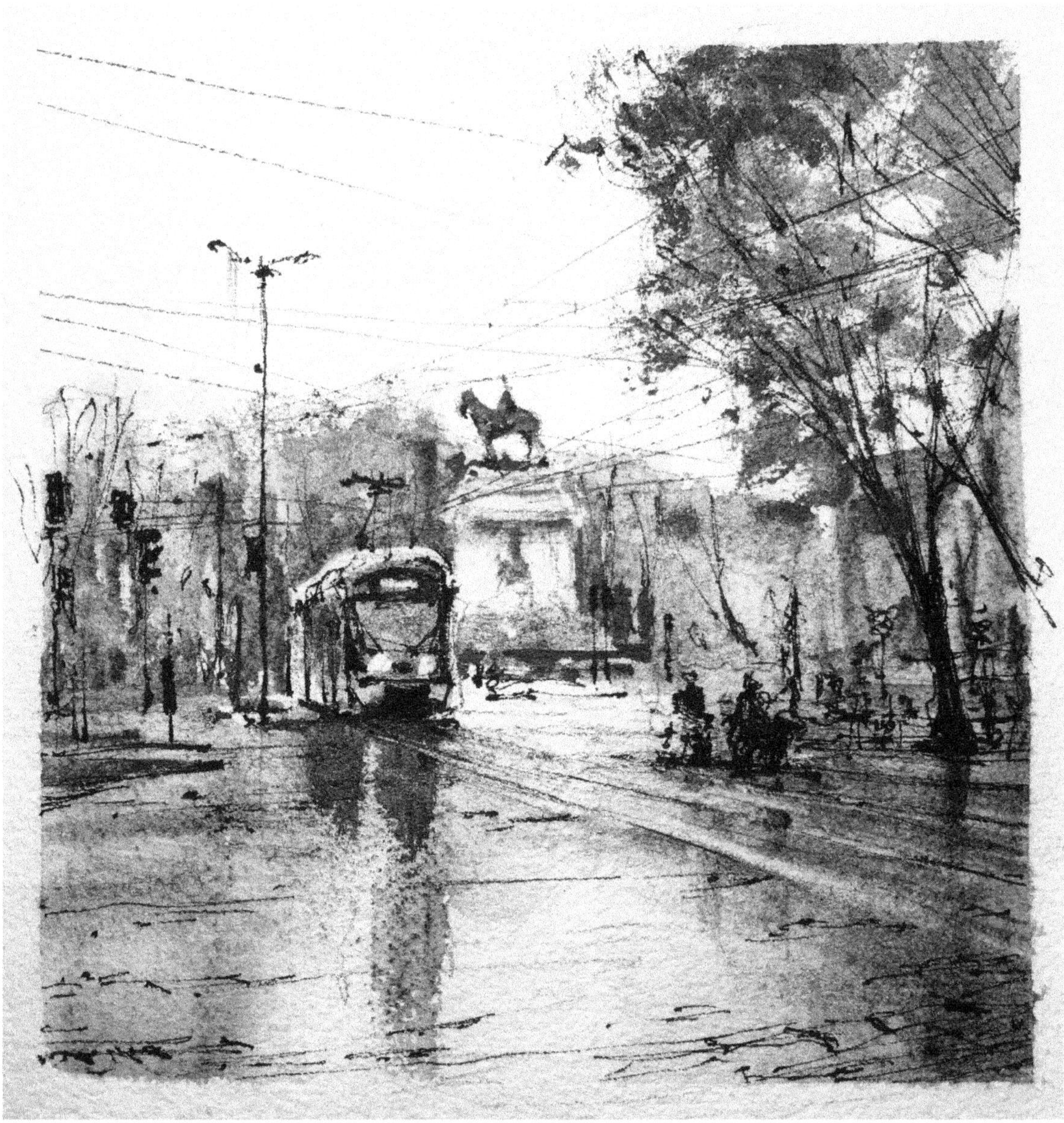

Cairoli Castello, Milan in the rain. Ink and graphite.

Each artist will develop his or her own unique set of tools and additional items to make sketching more enjoyable. When sketching outside, we are limited to what we want to carry with us. Space and weight become a premium. I'm constantly revising what's in my sketch bag. If I find I haven't used a brush in a while, maybe next time it will stay at home. But I'm also guilty of bringing too much. I hate the feeling of needing a certain tool and not having it at hand. With practice and many outings, you'll find your perfect balance.

Of course, the most important tools are your curiosity, your sense of adventure, and your willingness to translate emotion into a sketchbook.

> ***"As music is the poetry of sound, so is painting the poetry of sight."***
>
> —JAMES MCNEILL WHISTLER

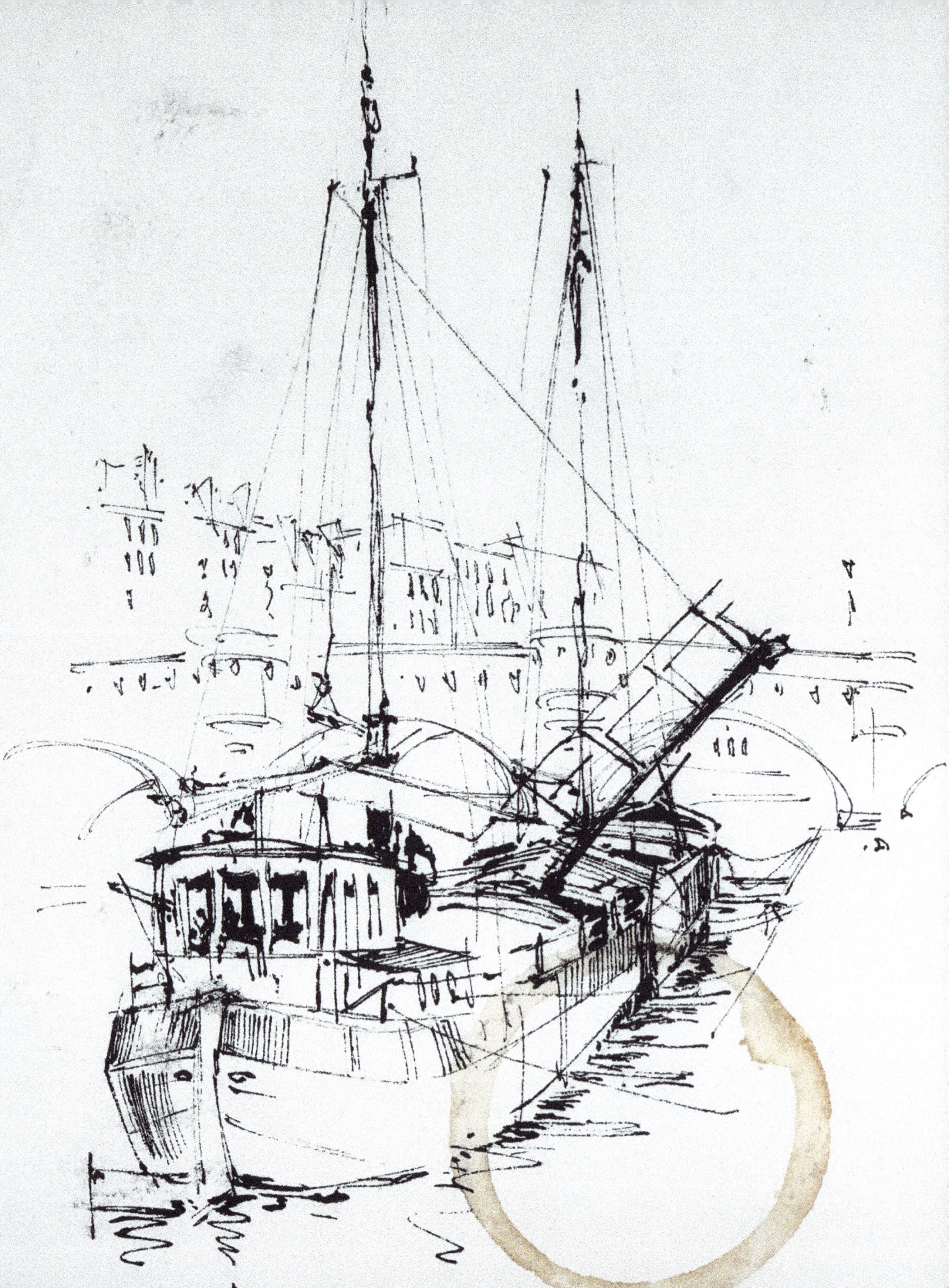

2

GENERAL SKETCHING TECHNIQUES

Everything you sketch tells a story: a story of a time and place, a memory, a dream, a mood. Sketches are an energy transfer. What you feel at the time of creation is translated directly onto the paper. It can be a mysterious process, but shining a light on this mystery gives clarity without diminishing its power. The techniques in this chapter will illuminate the stories we want to tell.

USING THE LANGUAGE OF FILM TO TELL A STORY

Sketches and paintings are like scenes from a film. Because I've spent many years storyboarding and illustrating films, I think in terms of camera angles and movie scenes. When I'm walking around my favorite neighborhoods looking for something to sketch, I imagine what a particular view would look like on a movie screen. I'm always looking for the most dynamic angle, the unexpected perspective, the unique vantage point from which to sketch. It's not enough to paint a pretty building. We're telling a story, and our choice of viewpoint says just as much as the subject itself. A viewer should lean in, wanting to know the story.

The style and techniques you use will differ depending on the story you want to convey. When I'm storyboarding a film, I vary my style depending on the genre. A romantic comedy has a very different visual language from a horror film.

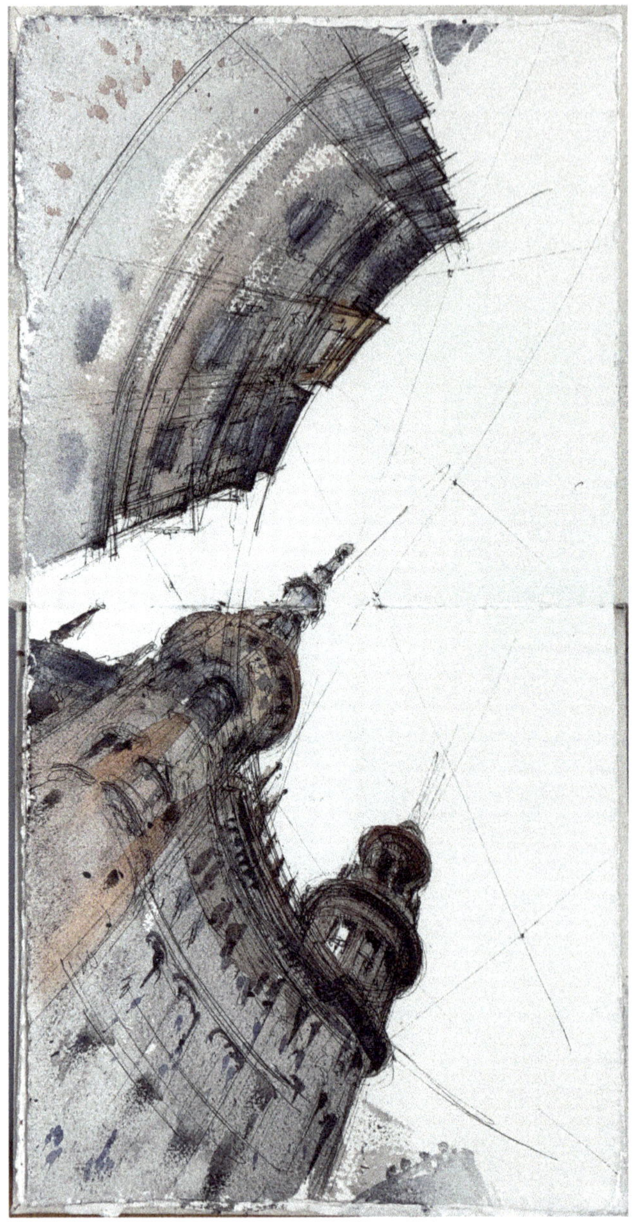

Find the unusual angles while sketching. Look for unexpected perspectives. Sometimes the most interesting view is looking straight up, as in this sketch from Madrid, Spain. Ink and watercolor.

1

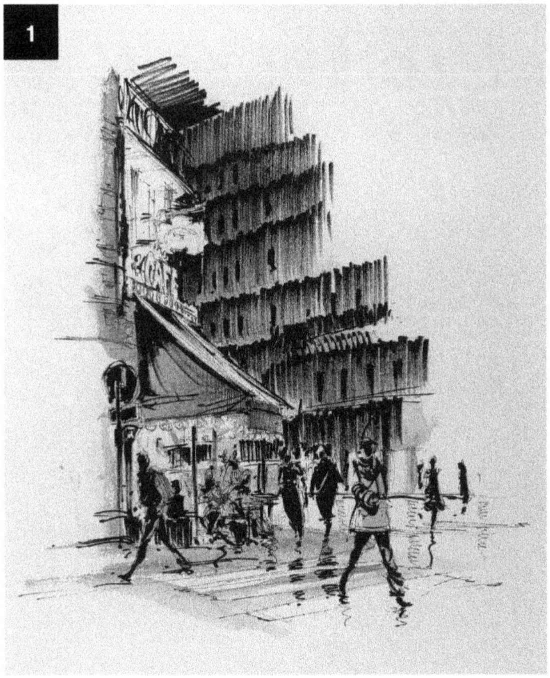

2

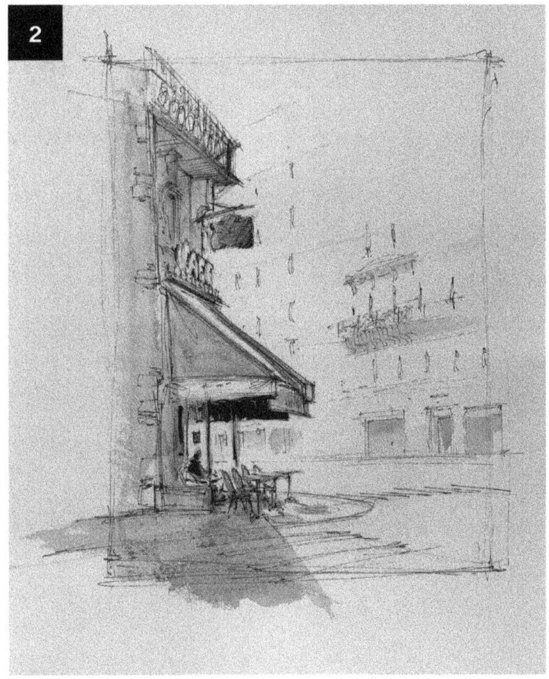

The types of shots, angles, and framing need to work in harmony with the story we're telling. These ideas of visual language translate directly into sketching. A Paris café on a bustling Saturday night (1) has a vastly different energy from the same café on a quiet Sunday morning (2). The way you move your brush, the colors you use, the mood you infuse into your painting, should all work together to enhance the story being told.

The language of film speaks to us on an emotional level. We may not consciously know it, but we certainly feel what's being conveyed. We see the world at eye level, but filmmakers love to vary the height of the camera to push emotional reactions to images. Using low angles, where the camera is lower to the ground looking up at an actor, gives characters added power or menace (3).

High angles, looking down on someone, makes them appear more vulnerable (4).

We can use some of these cinematic tricks in our sketches. Thinking in terms of camera angles can bring an added dimension to our paintings.

3

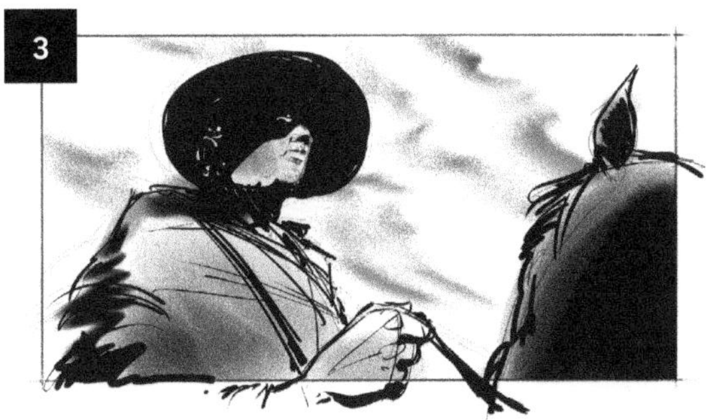

4

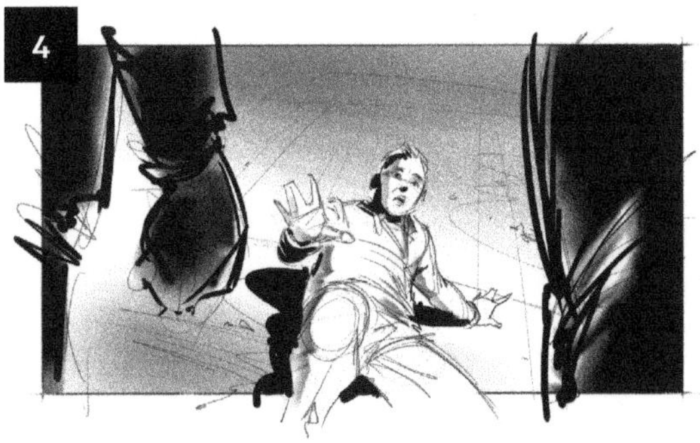

Low and high angles are used in film storyboards to denote strength or vulnerability.

SELECTING WHAT TO SKETCH

Choosing what to sketch can be tricky. Often, it's an unconscious decision. We're drawn to a certain view. Maybe it's the shape of a roofline, or the magical play of sunlight, or some detail that we're not quite aware of. So many elements speak to us and attract us to a subject that the process is shrouded in mystery.

Or, our location determines what we sketch. We happen to be sitting in a relaxing spot, a nice café, or the shade of a tree, and we sketch the view from there. And while a comfortable seat and a glass of wine are certainly enticing, in terms of a successful sketch, we're letting the tail wag the dog.

So, in the spirit of learning how to see, I want to shine a light into this mystery. Without diminishing the spontaneity of our decisions, or ignoring gut feelings, I'd like to steer you toward how to consciously find better sketches.

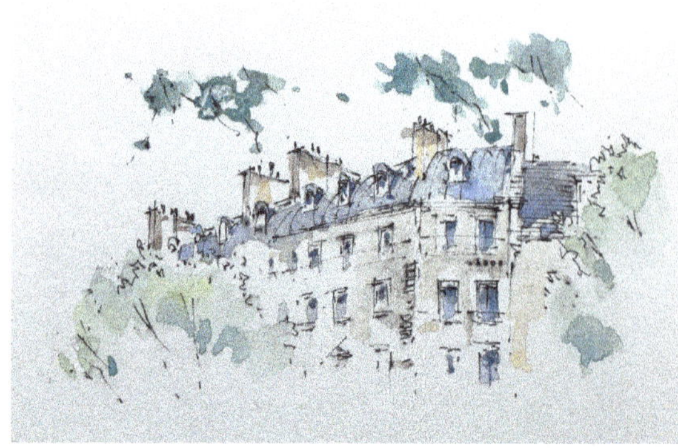

I chose this view because these springtime trees provide an organic frame for this glimpse of Paris rooftops. Ink and watercolor.

I think of sketching in terms of what, where, when, how, and who. Just as writers employ these questions to get to the heart of a mystery, we can use these questions to get to the heart of our sketches.

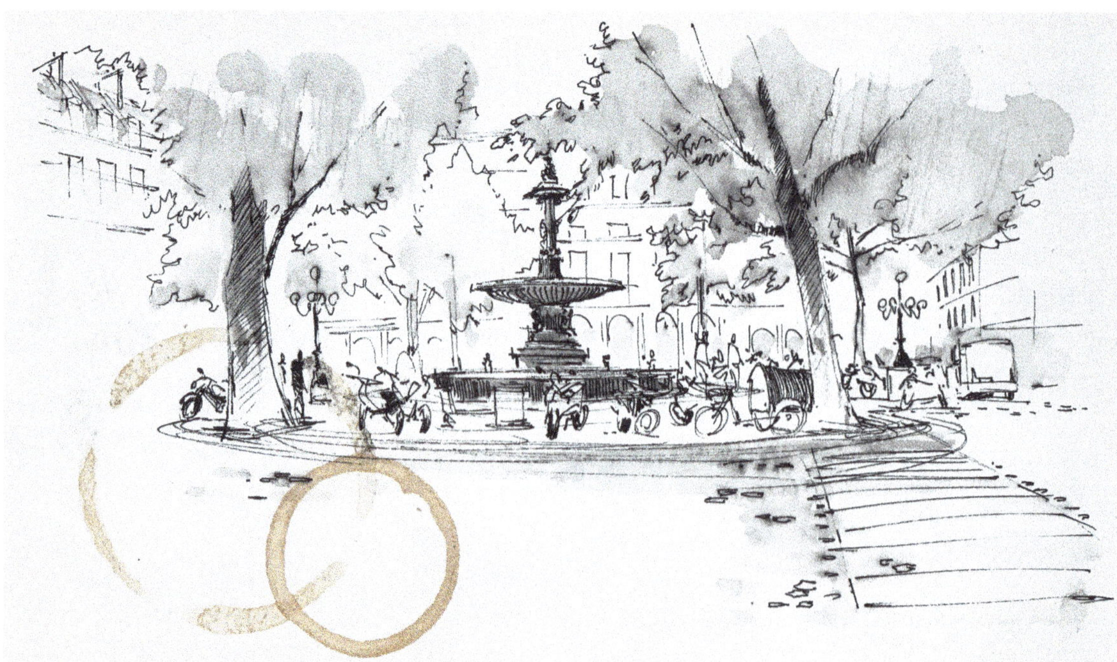

I love the depth in this simple sketch. The fountain is shaded by foreground trees, creating a silhouette against the sunlit background. Place André Malraux, Paris. Ink, watercolor, and coffee.

What

The "what" is the subject. What are we going to sketch? In a city like Paris, where I live, I'm spoiled with riches. At first glance, every street corner begs to be sketched. There are grand monuments, cathedrals, parks, and picturesque cafés at every turn. It's easy to get dizzy and overwhelmed by the abundance of choice.

But looking closer, not every street corner has the makings of a great sketch. Not all buildings are created equal. Some would make horrible sketches, and we need to know how to tell the difference before filling our sketchbooks with flat and boring images.

A quick view of a map holds clues to the history of this dynamic city—and also points to where the best sketches are to be found.

Like many European cities, Paris is a drunken spiderweb of streets. Its history and variety make for interesting corners and angles (1). It's not built on a grid like New York or Chicago. Paris is the nineteenth century laid on top of a medieval city, superimposed on a Roman town, built upon an ancient village (2). Maps on top of maps. And all this history is visible like a stack of transparencies that trace back through time.

1

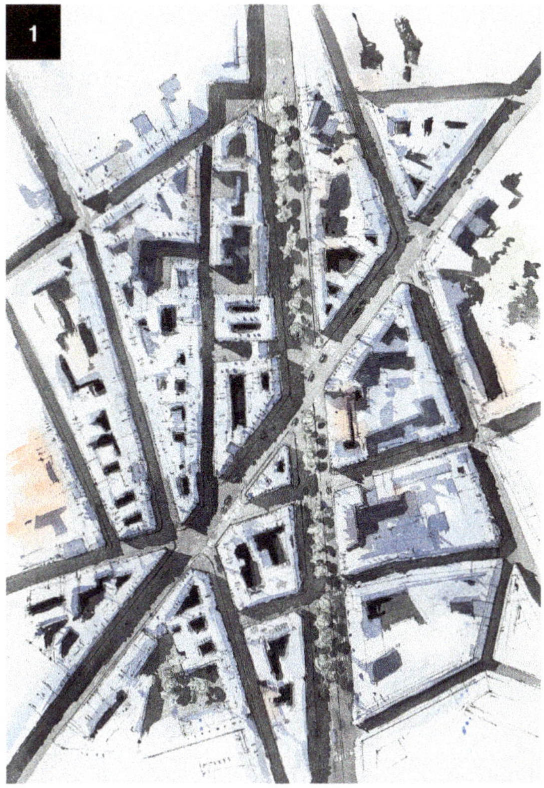

2

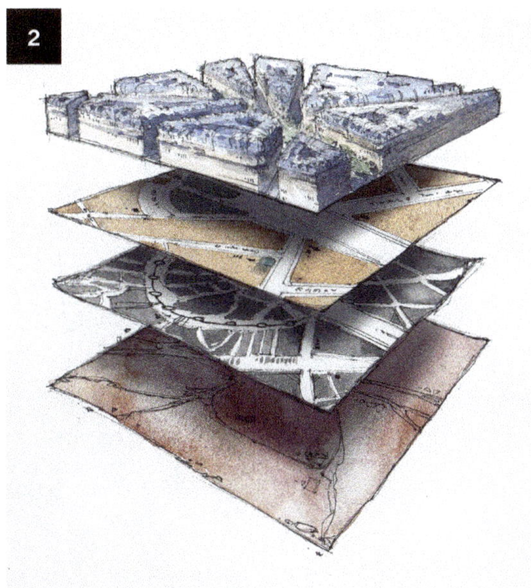

What this means for the here and now is a city with great angles. Grand boulevards connect the larger squares and monuments, train stations, and bridges but also slash through older sections of the city where streets dodge and weave, contract, then jig into hidden corners. All the while, the Parisian architecture fills the gaps where streets are carved. You can quickly see some corners are sharp, while others are flat (3).

If you're looking for interesting locations to sketch and to create the illusion of depth on your page, look for sharp angles on a map. It's these sharp angles that will give you a building protruding out into the intersection like the bow of the ship. There's going to be energy to that building.

When exploring a new city, I can look at a map for my initial inspiration as to where best to find potential sketches. It's these sharp angles—90-degree corners, 45-degree angles—that I aim for.

Flat angles are less dynamic. There might be interesting architectural details and great light, but as a sketch subject, you're fighting an uphill battle.

There's a reason everyone takes pictures of the Flatiron Building in New York. Its dynamic shape protrudes into the intersection. Nobody's taking photos of the square building next to it.

You don't have to be in a city to use this concept. You can apply this idea in your hometown, sketching your own house, or drawing cars or furniture. The idea is to create depth on your page. That is best done by finding the angle where part of your subject projects toward you and the rest recedes away.

3

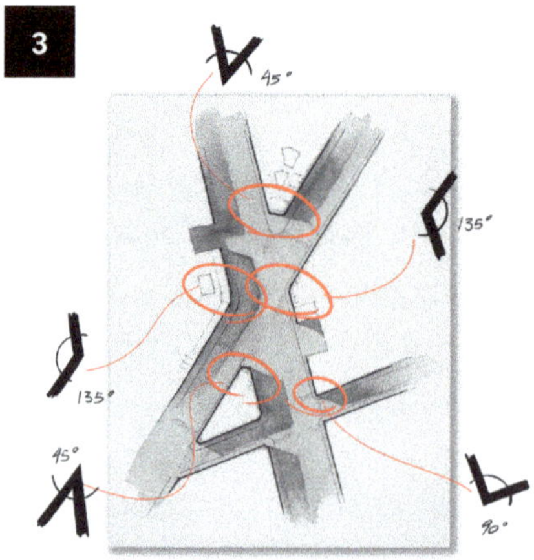

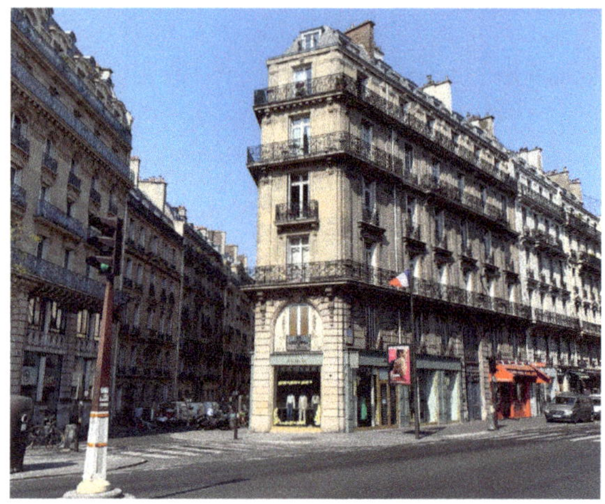

Buildings on sharp angled intersections make for dynamic sketches.

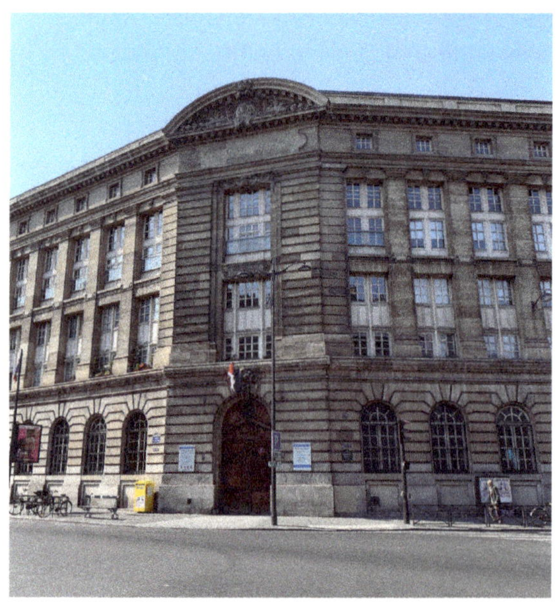

Buildings on wide angles on the map, like this 135° one, will make for a flat and uninspiring sketch.

Where

Once we've determined what we will sketch, we need to think about the where. The most important part of any painting happens before you touch your pencil to your paper. Your angle of view, where you chose to stand while sketching, is paramount. You can be a master of color and brushwork, you can be working with the best materials money can buy, but if your choice of view is flat and uninspired, your painting will fail to sing. The "where" of a sketch is where you chose to sit or stand to depict your subject. This isn't quite the same as composition, which we'll get to next. This is something even more fundamental.

Here's a building in Paris that I've sketched a few times.

I'm able to walk around the building and see it from many different angles: profile, head-on, etc. If I want to depict depth in my drawing and create the illusion of three-dimensionality, where I stand will have a dramatic effect of the outcome of my drawing.

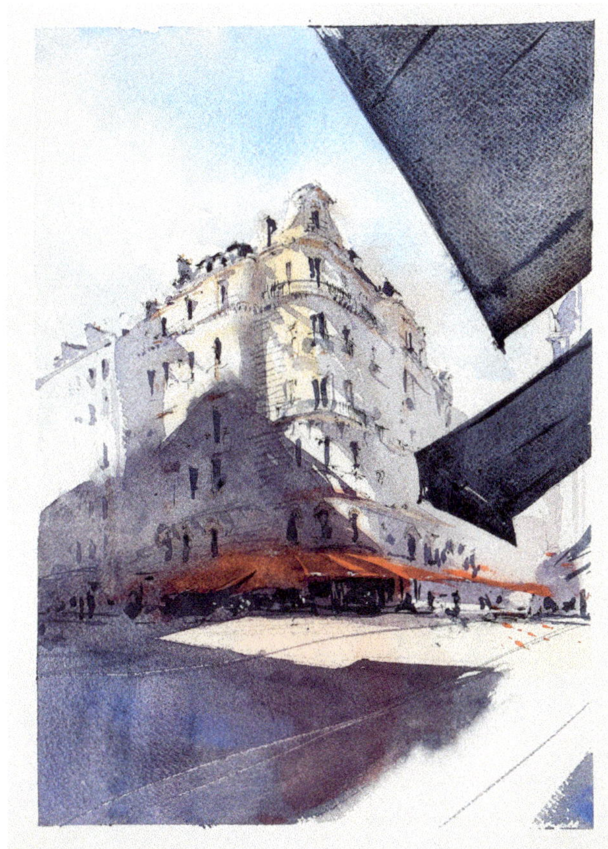

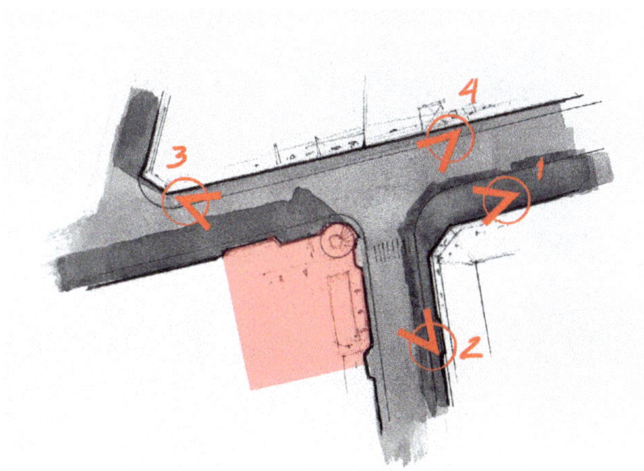

These red angle marks represent different places I can stand to see very different views of this same building.

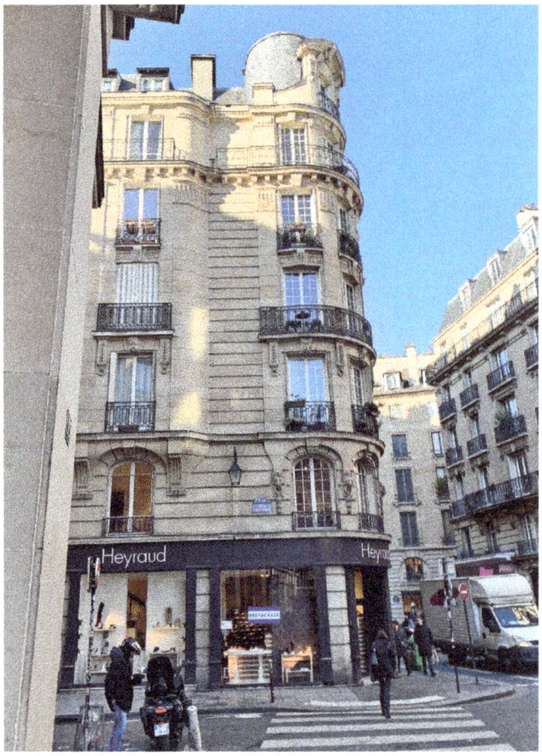

Angle 1 shows a profile view. While showing off some interesting details, this will make for a flat sketch.

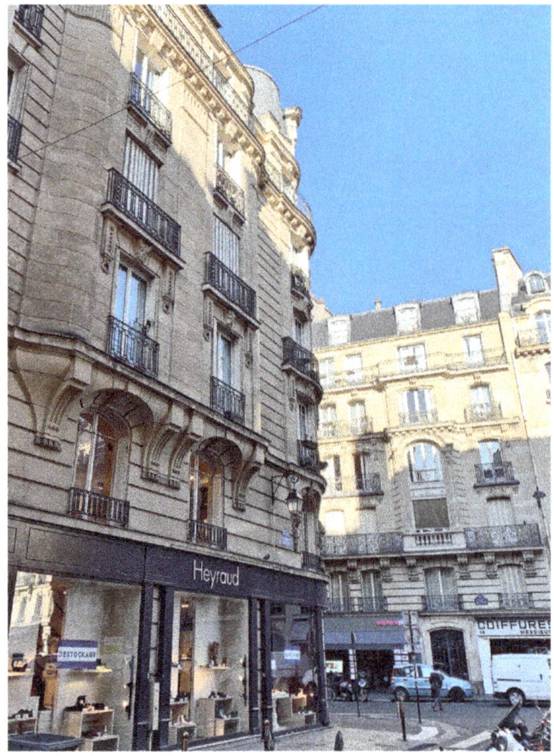

Angle 2 has some nice shadows, but it doesn't show off the main building at all.

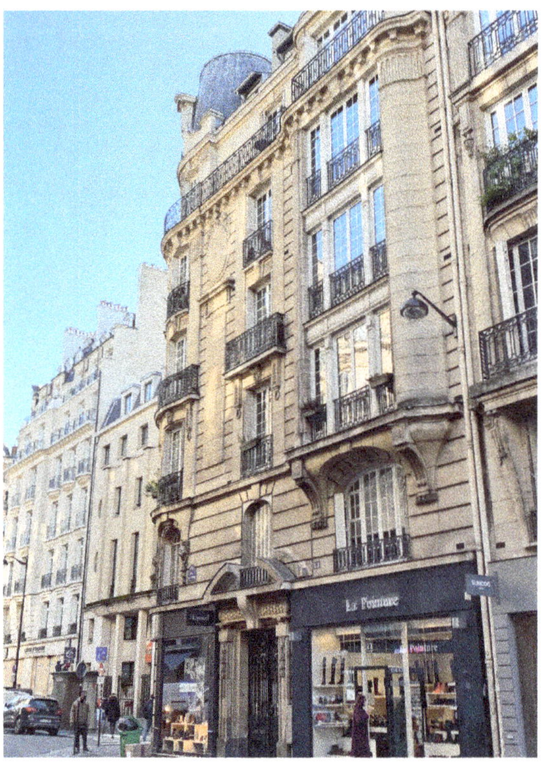

Angle 3 is raking down the back of the building. All light and shadow detail is lost, and our eye is drawn down and to the left, off the edge of our paper.

Angle 4 has everything I look for in a sketch. The building is shown off in a dynamic way protruding toward us. There's beautiful sunlight glancing the left side, while the right side is in shadow. Some foreground awnings add layers of depth.

This three-quarter view will translate directly onto the page, creating a painting that shows off the volume and character of this place.

When looking at a building, close one eye. This takes away our binocular vision and allows us to see how a subject will appear on a flat piece of paper. We're so used to seeing in three dimensions that we take it for granted. But our drawings are two-dimensional, so we must give ourselves every advantage when depicting the illusion of three dimensions.

Using Artistic License

Artistic license is a term that, unfortunately, has a lot of baggage attached to it. I love everything about the building I sketched on page 29—the angle, the light, the foreground awnings—but at street level, right where the center of focus will be, is a row of uninspiring shops. So, I used artistic license and added a café where there isn't one.

If we're creating representational sketches, there are laws of light, rules of perspective, and certain compositional forms that are innately more pleasing than others. But once we know these rules, we can bend them. We can move trees if they're in the way, remove ugly delivery vans, add people for more life, and yes, paint beautiful cafés.

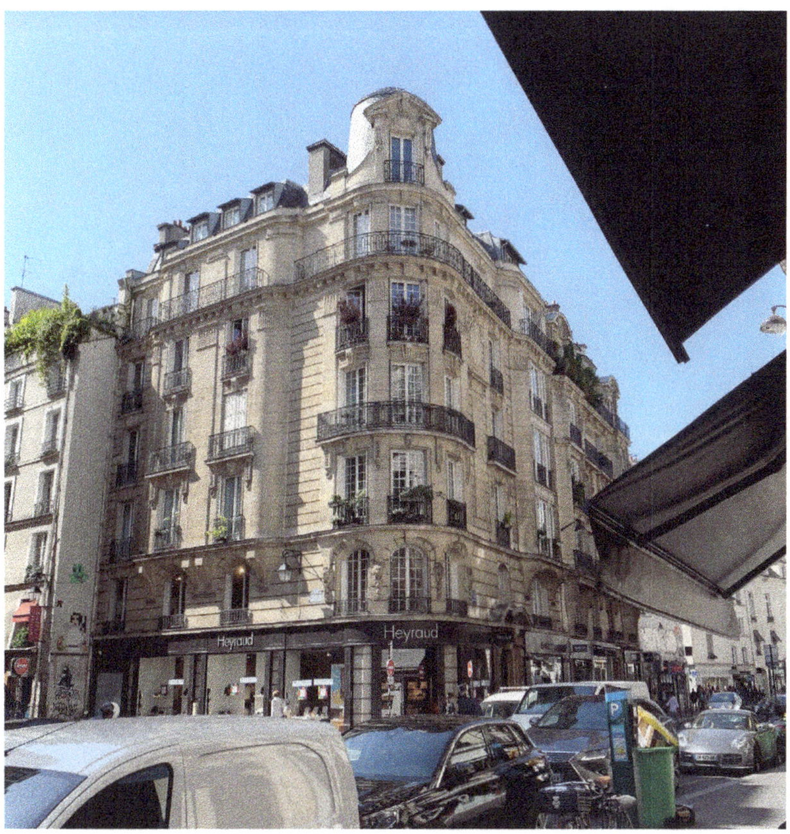

Angle 4

How

After the "what" and "where" questions, we need to think about "how" we will frame and compose what's before us. In Chapter 3, I will go into more detail about a few tools that can help us immeasurably. How you compose your sketch is one of the most important skills to learn. A great composition can make a sketch leap off the page.

You can frame your subject with your hands like a movie director. Some artists carry a card frame to use as a viewfinder and framing device. I like to do a quick thumbnail sketch and draw a frame around it to determine the composition. All these methods get us to the same place. We want to imagine how this subject before us will sit on our page. We have the ability to compose our image, to determine what to include and what to leave out. These are important choices, and it's in asking "how" that we start to find answers.

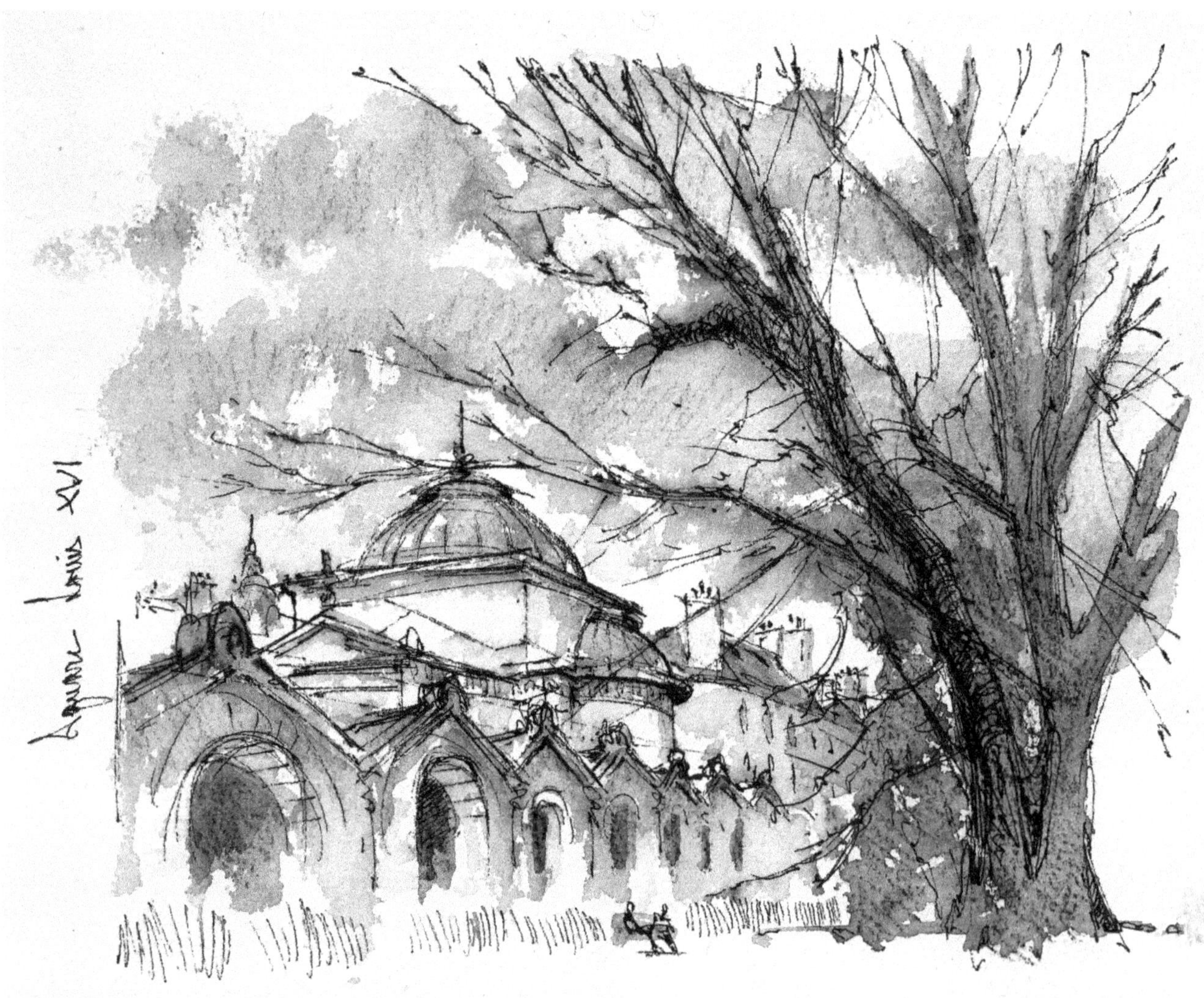

This imposing tree is a perfect complement to the squat and solid church. These two forces work well together, balancing horizontals and verticals as well as organic and formal structures. The composition is square, but asymmetrically balanced.

When

I've spent a lot of time behind the scenes on film sets. I love the process of filmmaking with its incredibly varied departments and hundreds of people, each with specialized skills. All this machinery and expertise is in the service of telling a story. Illusion is used to get at the truth. One trick to maintaining an illusion is controlling time.

Scenes take a long time to film. To maintain a consistent look, lights and shadows are carefully placed to freeze a moment in time. A beautifully slanting 4 p.m. light can be created on a sound stage and maintained for hours on end.

Controlling light and stopping time is a power unique to the gods (and cinematographers). Mere mortals like us with a pencil and sketchbook don't have sound stages and an army of film technicians at our disposal. But we can choose when to sketch.

As shown below, environments look very different at different times of the day. Early morning and late afternoon create the most dynamic shadows with angled, slanting light. Midday can be good for capturing the heat of sunlight and pools of shade under trees. Dusk and magic hour (just after sunrise and before sunset) have their own unique qualities.

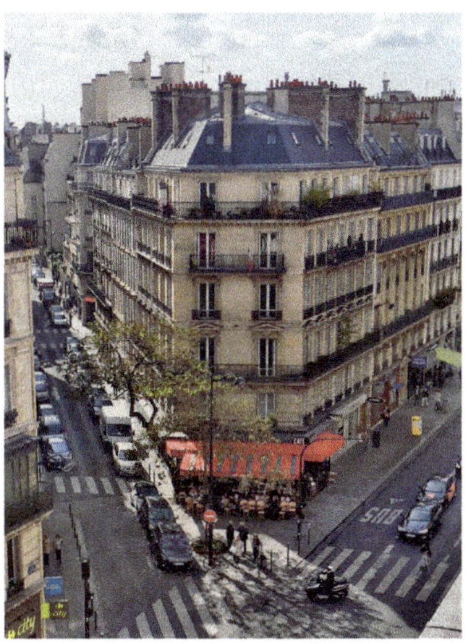

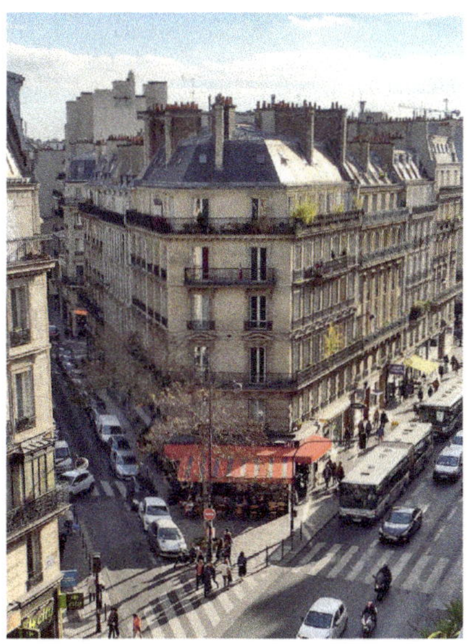

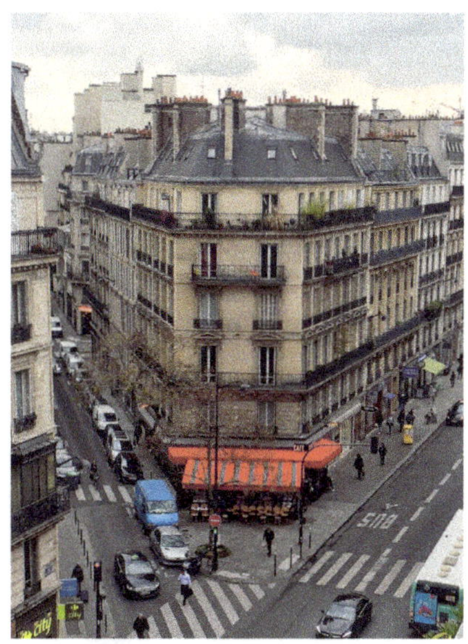

Try sketching the same subject at different times of the day. Notice how each sketch has quite a different feel to it.

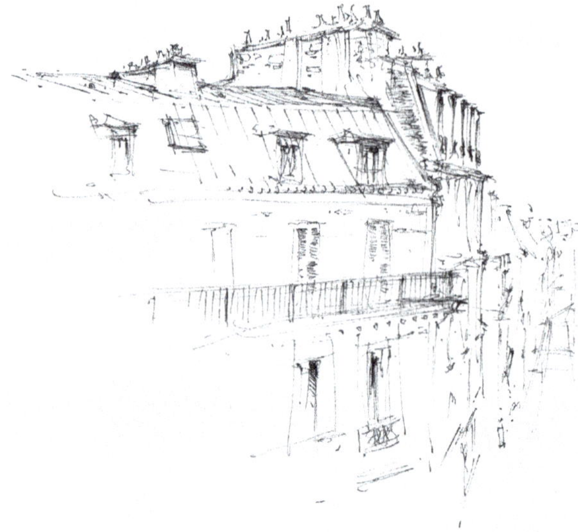

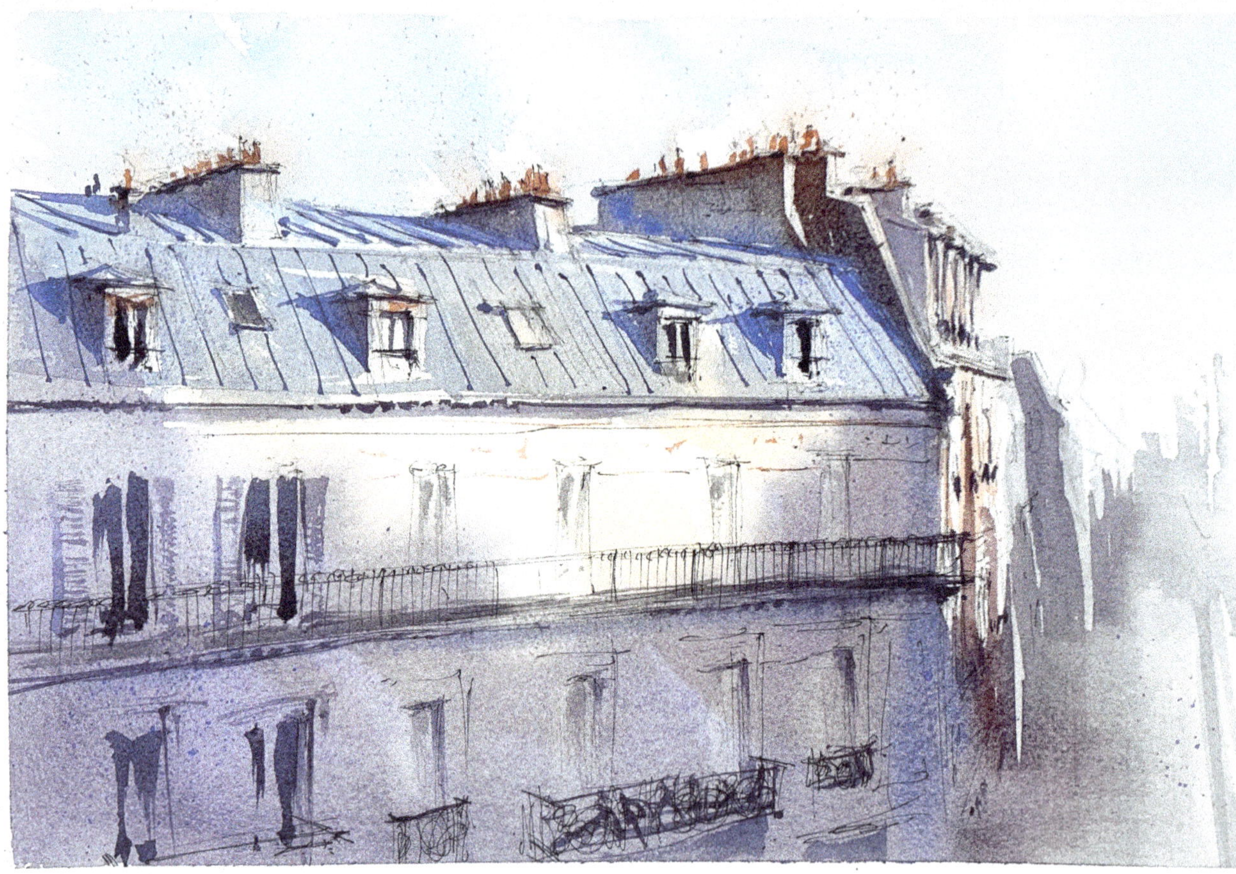

Who

I'd like to introduce the concept of thinking of inanimate objects as characters. With architecture, each building is a character with its own unique personality: old and grizzled, young and proud, coy and mysterious. Anthropomorphizing buildings is a wonderfully playful way to infuse life into your sketches. Once you start painting a personality rather than bricks, stone, and windows, your sketches take on new life. Each line, each brushstroke becomes imbued with the personality you are portraying. For more details about architecture as characters, see chapter 7 (page 103). For more on using this concept with still lifes, see chapter 5 (page 69).

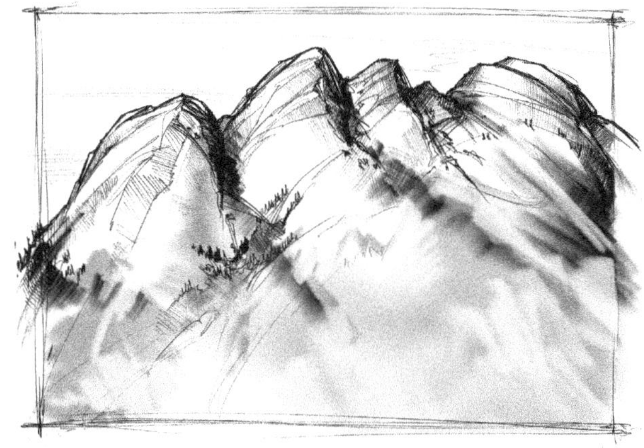

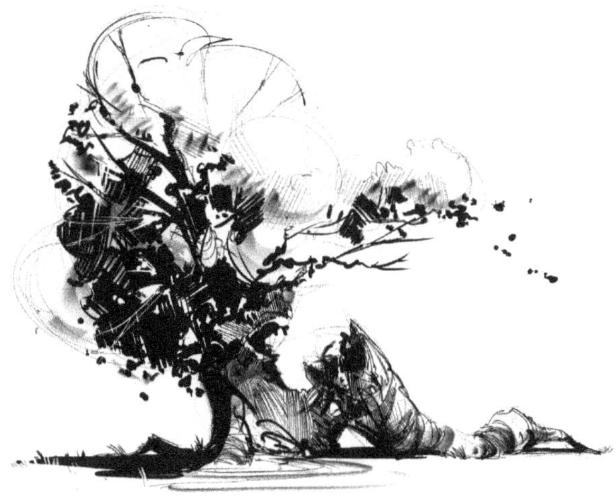

This idea can be applied to anything you sketch. Mountains famously look like sleeping giants, and trees have multiple personalities. The idea is to sketch these personalities, and to see everything around you as a personification with unique characteristics.

This set of questions is a powerful tool set. By becoming conscious of this process, you will get better at it. With practice, incorporating these questions into your process will elevate your sketches and paintings to new heights.

RENDERING LIGHT IN A SKETCH

While sketching, the lightest value available to us is often the white of our paper. In a black and white drawing, use the white of the paper to depict the brightest highlights and the jet black of the ink for the deepest shadows. Everything else in between can be varying shades of gray.

For shades of gray, different pencil weights are perfect for differing levels of shadow. Hard leads like H and 2H are perfect for light shadows, while softer leads such as 3B and 6B do the work of darkening areas of the page.

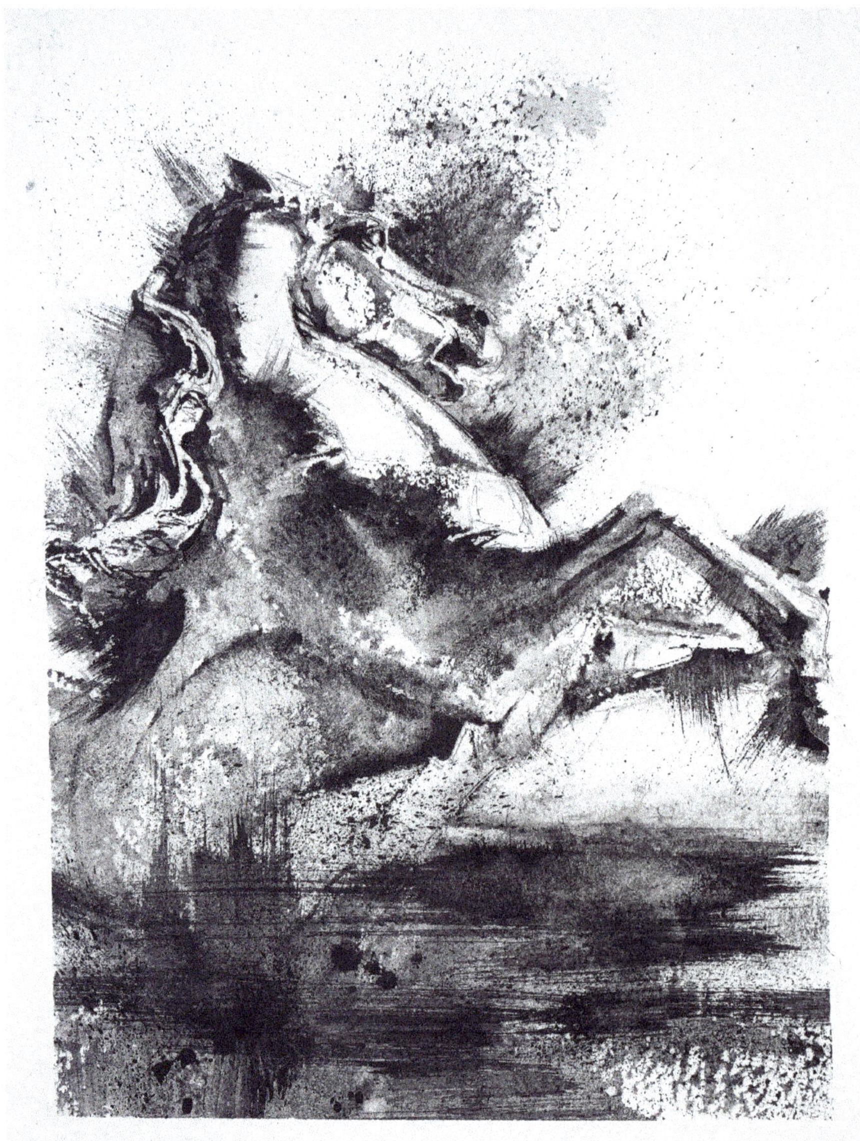

For this sketch of a *cheval marin*, I used a combination of ink and graphite.

Capturing Light

Painting light gives me goosebumps. This is where all the techniques discussed in the following chapters come together.

Because I'm always looking for ways to create the illusion of depth on a two-dimensional page, light and shadow are some of the most powerful tools we have, along with linear and atmospheric perspective.

When drawing a simple cube, it can look featureless and flat. But when we add a light source and create a shadow, suddenly there is the illusion of volume and depth.

The same is true in our sketches of more complex subjects. When sketching a building, we can beautifully define the perspective and vanishing points, add all the details we want, and have beautiful colors, but without a strong light source and shadow details, our sketch can still appear flat on the page. This last element is crucial because our eyes are attuned to perceive the shape and volume of objects largely based on light and shadow.

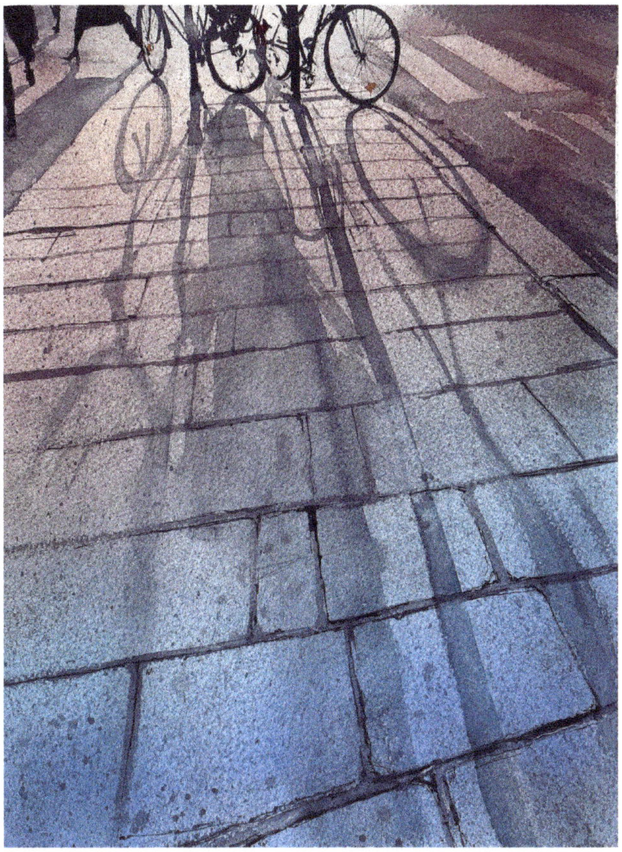

Gradations of warm and cool colors, combined with long winter shadows, are a wonderful way to depict light.

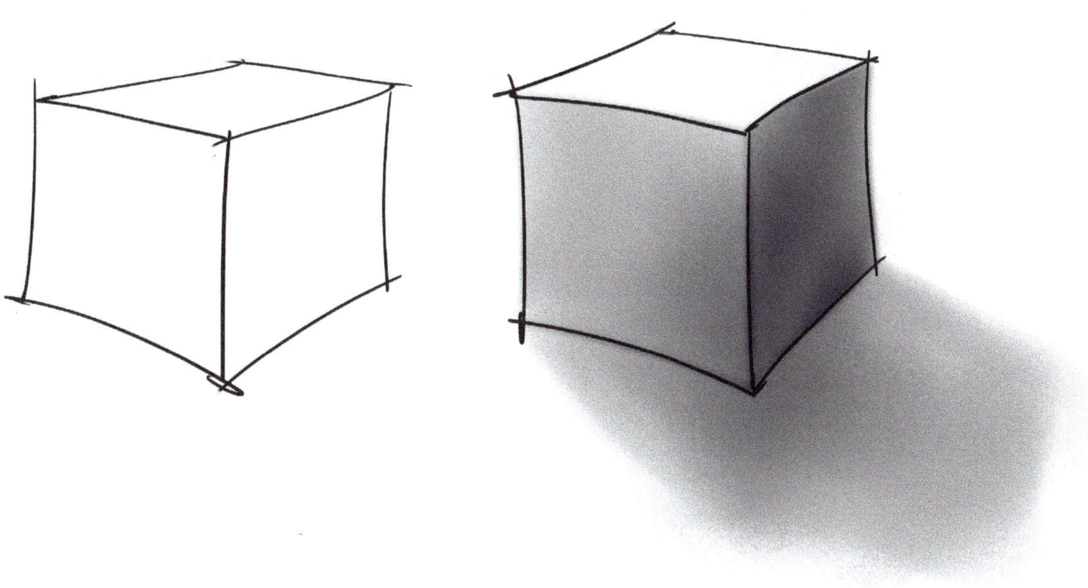

Cross-Hatching

Cross-hatching is the technique of creating a series of lines in a variety of directions and layers. It is a wonderful way to build and darken shadows with ink or pencil. Play with different techniques to see what suits your current sketch.

Use cross-hatching to create shadows around the trunk of a tree to build volume, or stretch lines across a street to enhance energy and direction of shadows.

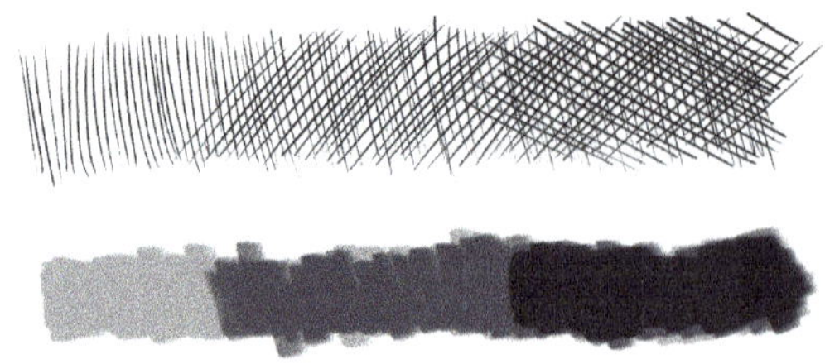

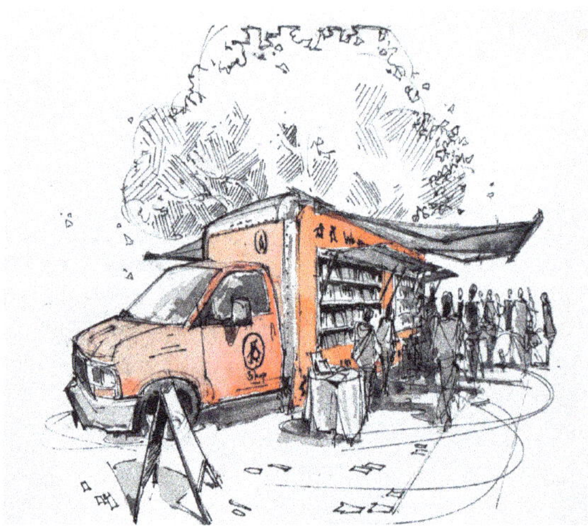

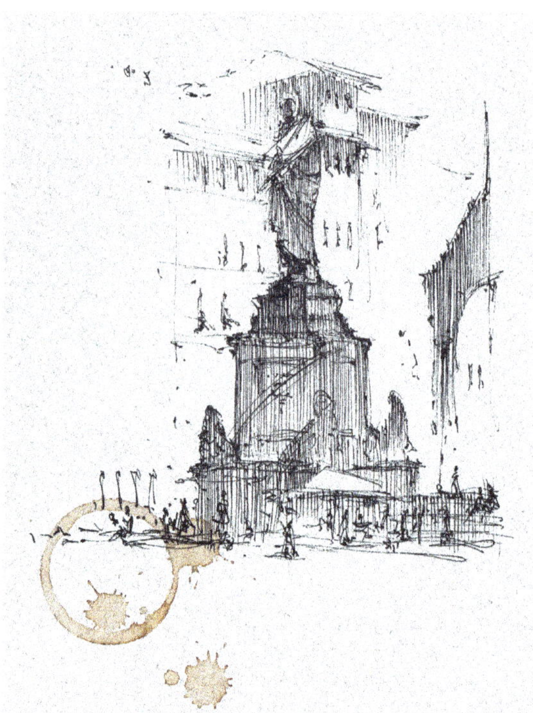

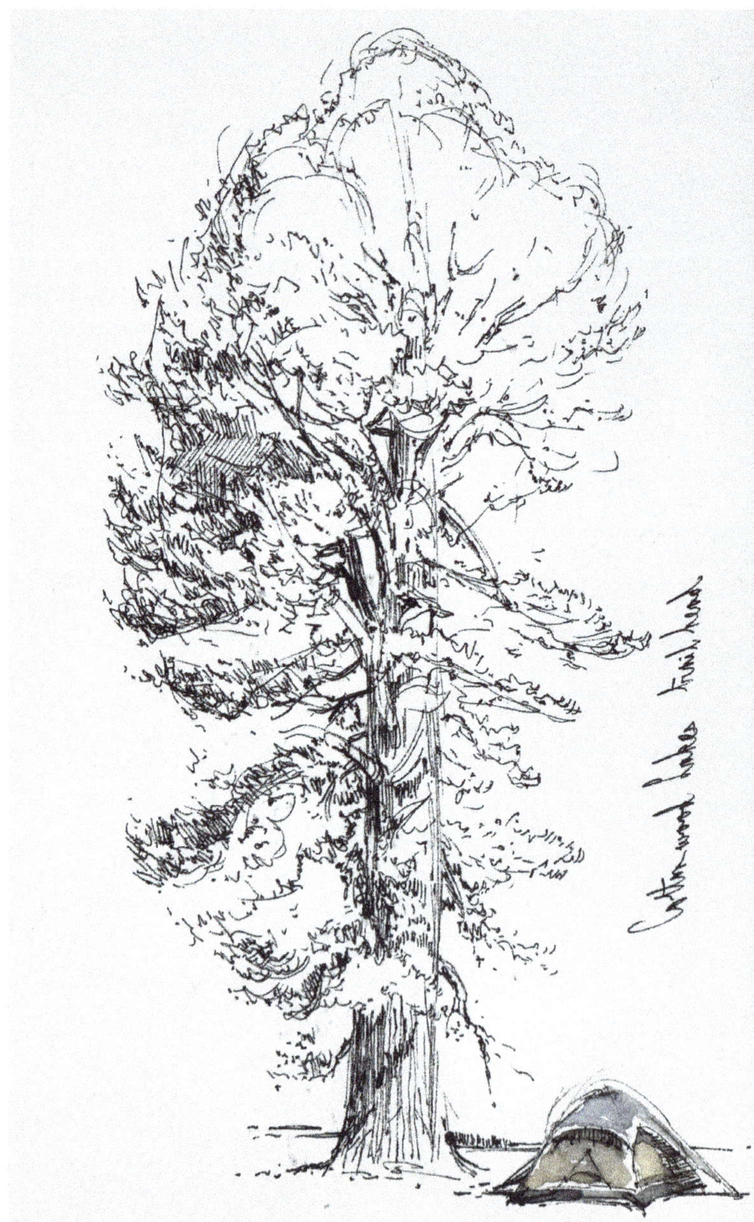

The Direction of Light

On a clear day sunlight comes from the same direction, and in turn, shadows all go in the same direction. Nothing makes your painting ring false like having shadows go in one direction for chimneys and another for people.

Making sure your shadows all point in the same direction seems obvious, but this is a common mistake. The sun moves, and the longer we stay in one place sketching a scene, the greater the risk of painting shadows that don't match each other.

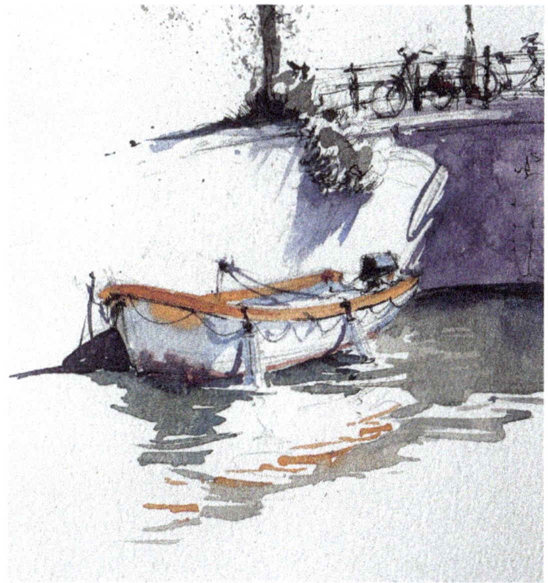

For this sketch of a quiet corner in Amsterdam, the sunlight comes from the upper right of the image. All shadows and highlights within the image must reflect this. Ink and watercolor.

I sketched this scene in Venice at sunset. A storm had just passed, and I waited for the sun to dip beneath a layer of clouds. I positioned myself so the shadows of the statue would be most dramatic.

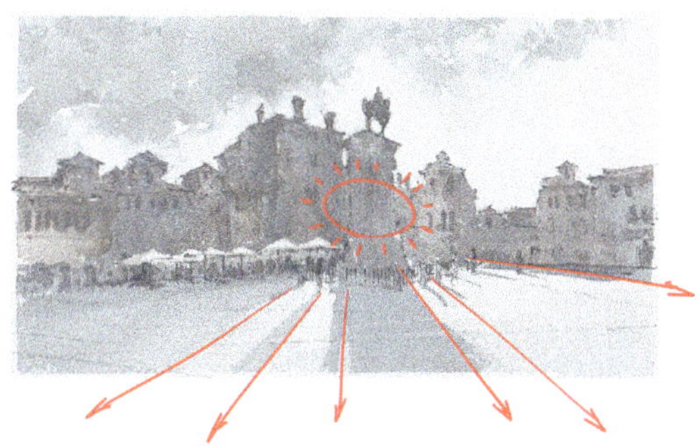

Shadows also follow the rules of perspective. In this view the shadows are all emanating from a single source, the sun.

> ***"Never lose sight of that first impression by which you were moved."***
>
> —JEAN-BAPTISTE-CAMILLE COROT

Photo Finish

Often what attracts me to a particular scene is the light. Before I get too deep into a sketch, I'll take a photo to freeze this moment of inspiration. I'm free to change and adjust as I go along, but with a snapshot of time, or a few snapshots, I have the freedom to choose when and how intense I want the shadows to be. These snapshots ensure the direction of light and shadows will be internally consistent.

DETAILS

How much to include and how much to exclude in a sketch? People get bogged down with the details and this question in particular. I used to be very precise in my drawings, including every little detail, measuring every angle. The more I sketched this way the more time it took and the less life my drawings had. I realized I didn't like the process and I didn't like the results, either.

The level of detail to include in any drawing is a matter of personal taste. While developing my style, I found that by loosening up, becoming more impressionistic, I invited life back into my drawings. Sketching became more enjoyable and the results danced on the page.

Rather than trying to sketch realistically, details are your chance to describe things in a calligraphic way, a poetic way.

Sketching Process

1 | Draw some simple squiggles on a page. These may seem meaningless on their own. But, like individual notes on a page, when they're in tune with each other, they describe a symphony.

> ***"It's not the notes you play, it's the notes you don't play."***
>
> —MILES DAVIS

1

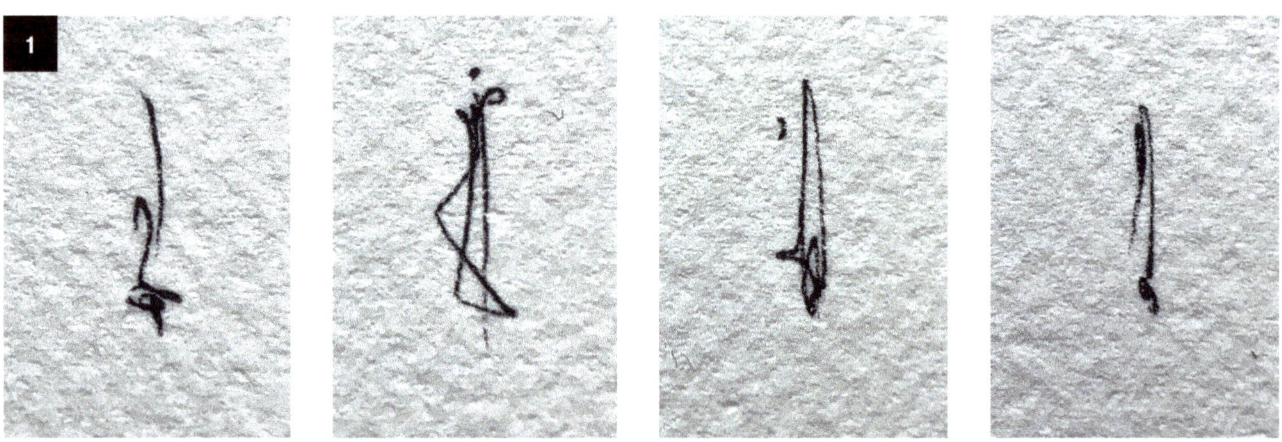

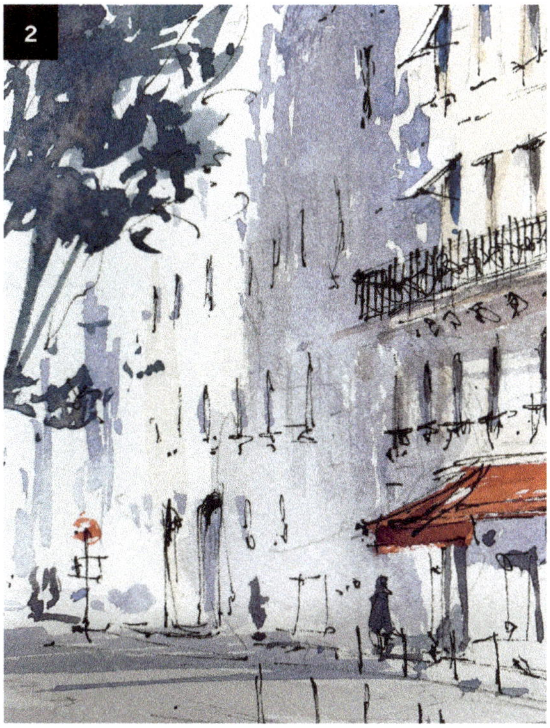

2 | When sketching architecture, we're inevitably faced with the challenge of how to depict rows and rows of windows on the side of a building. But windows don't need to be the perfect rectangle. As long as they are in the right place, a squiggle is enough, and the viewer's eye will read them as windows. Sketch a building and use rows of squiggles to indicate windows.

3 | Use this method to develop a shorthand for sketching objects. In this example, I've drawn the essence of a tree, without drawing every leaf. Allow yourself the freedom to suggest details, rather than dogmatically explain everything. Your sketch is a conversation, not a lecture.

3

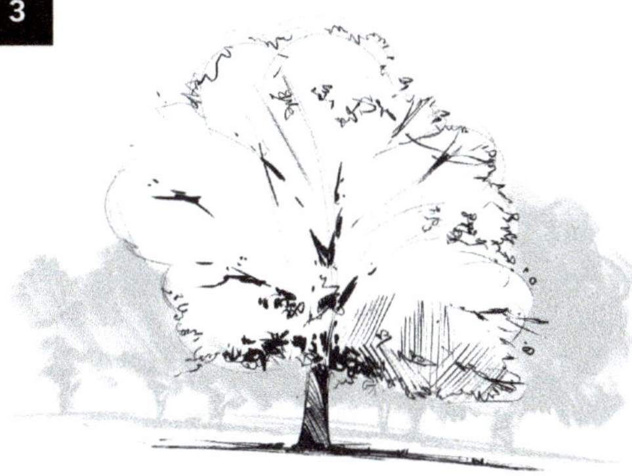

Shortcut Inspirations

Find your own handwriting, your own calligraphy for your sketches. I like to take inspiration from handwritten musical scores. Does what you're describing sound more like Beethoven or Chopin? Find the perfect language for the mood you're conveying. Find the music in your sketch.

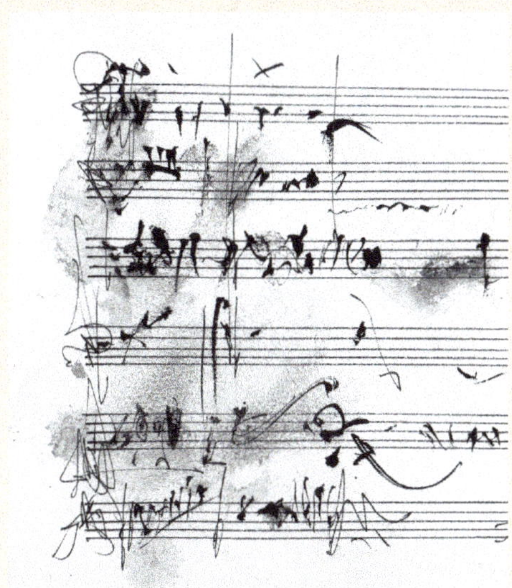

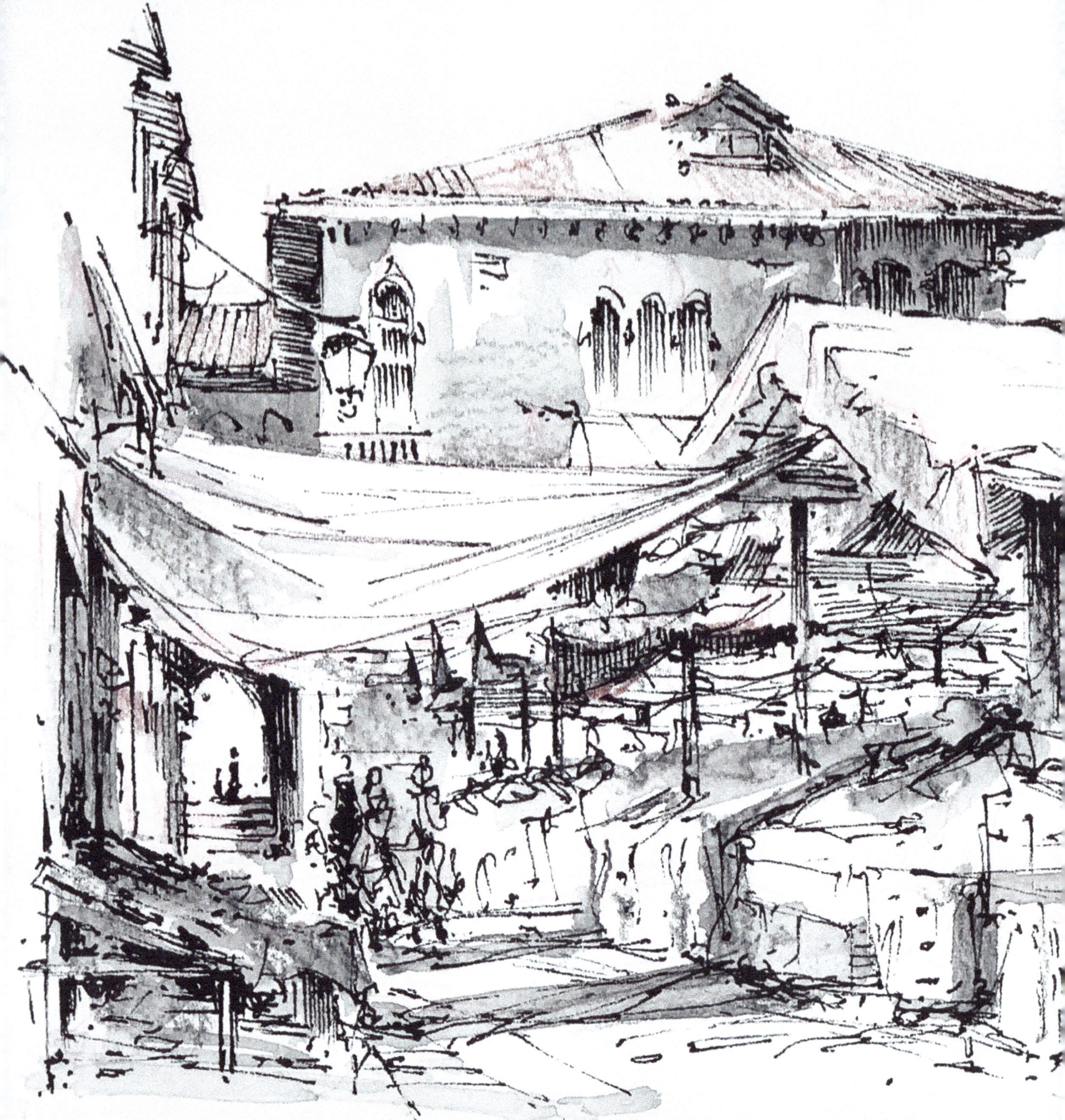

3

COMPOSITION

Composition is at the heart of what we do. It is balance and harmony, rhythm and flow. Composition in a sketch or painting is what catches your eye from across the room. It's what gently guides a viewer's eye around a piece, unfolding a story, revealing details. Creating a piece with real depth that invites the viewer in begins with a strong composition.

TELLING A STORY

Composition is a method of guiding a viewer's eyes into and through a piece. When we look at paintings, we don't take them all in at once. We read images in a certain order, like reading a book. Our eyes move in a dynamic sequence around a piece, seeing one area first, then moving on to secondary points of focus and lesser details, returning again to the main focal point. In truly great compositions, our eyes move around a painting, unfolding details, discovering secrets. We have the power to invite a viewer in and gently guide them around a piece.

There are two powerful tools that allow for endless variety and they will lift your sketches to another level. The first is the rule of thirds, and the second is using details and contrasts to define a center of focus. A story is being told, a conversation between painting and viewer is unfolding. Details that the painter has left out are filled in by the viewer, like old friends finishing each other's sentences.

First, we may notice the red awning of the café (1).

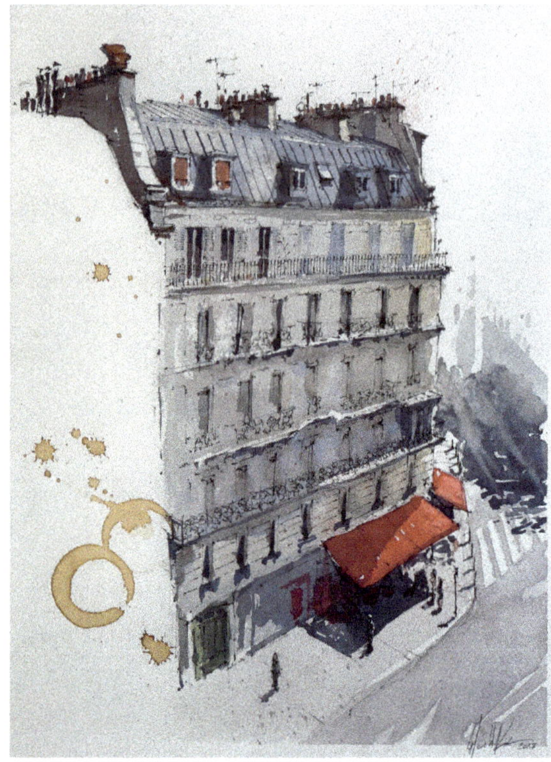

1

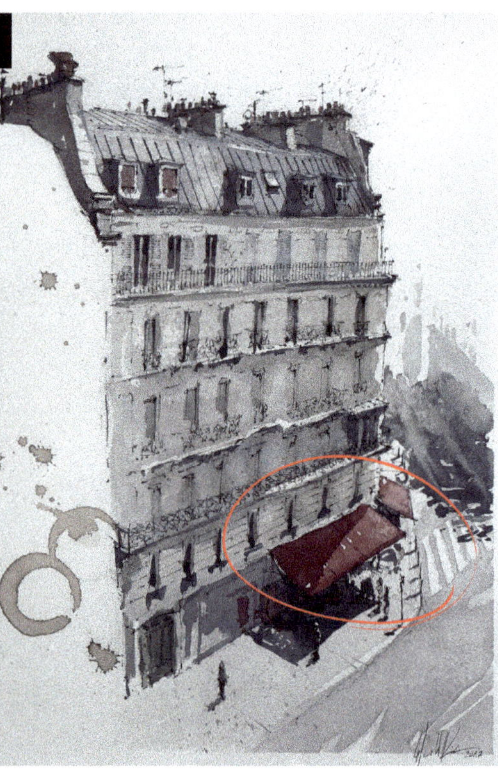

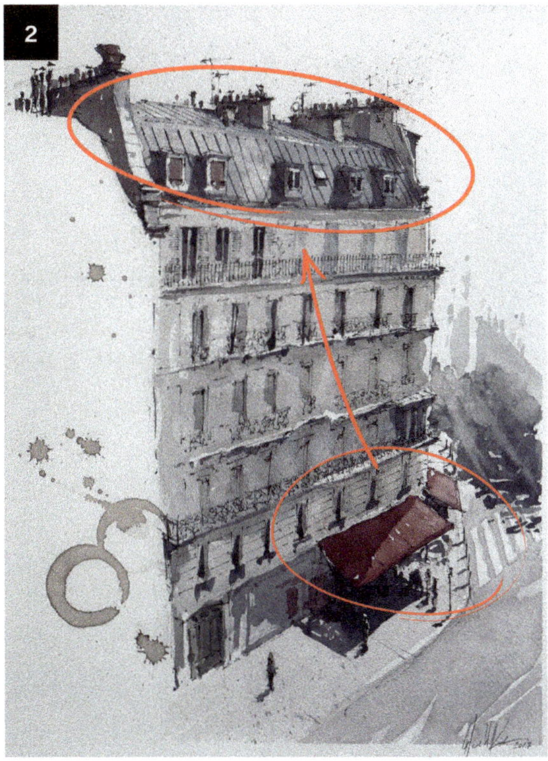

2

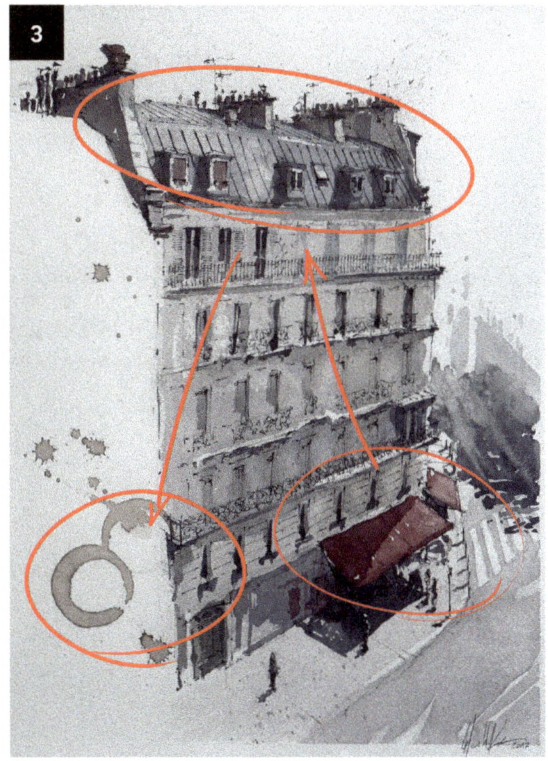

3

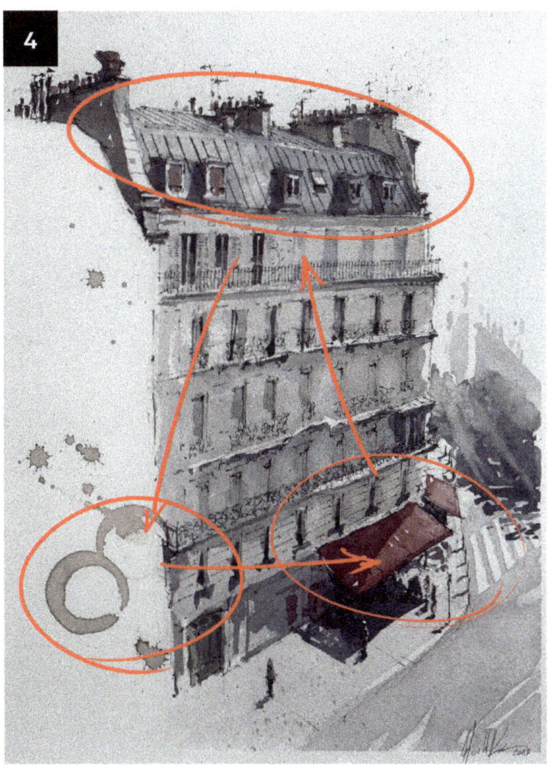

4

Then, we quickly move our attention to the rooftops (2).

Next we may wonder about the coffee stains (yes, these are intentional) (3).

Our eye movement forms a triangle, moving around the image. We come back to the café, noticing the people gathered there (4).

From here we take in lesser details: the windows on the facade, the street leading into the distance, the crosswalk, and the two orange windows near the top.

THE RULE OF THIRDS

The rule of thirds is a form of asymmetrical composition, meaning the center of focus will be off center, yet the piece will be balanced. We can divide our page into thirds both vertically and horizontally, creating four interesting points. Our center of focus, the main subject of our painting, should sit on one of these four points. This creates a naturally pleasing composition. Your eye will be drawn to this focal point, then have room to explore the rest of the page.

This type of asymmetrical composition creates a dialogue between painting and viewer, an easy movement that is harder to achieve in a symmetrical piece.

Once you become familiar with the rule of thirds, you will see it everywhere: in film posters, billboards, classic works of art, and photography.

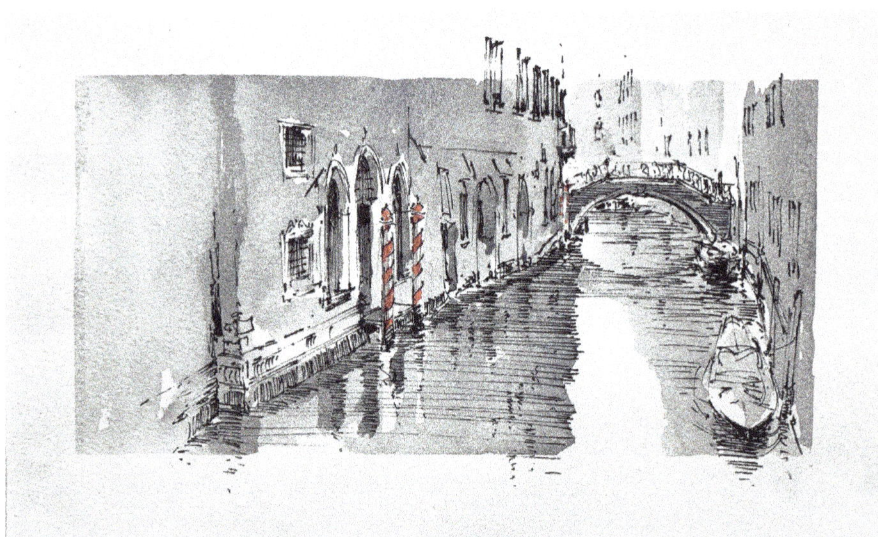

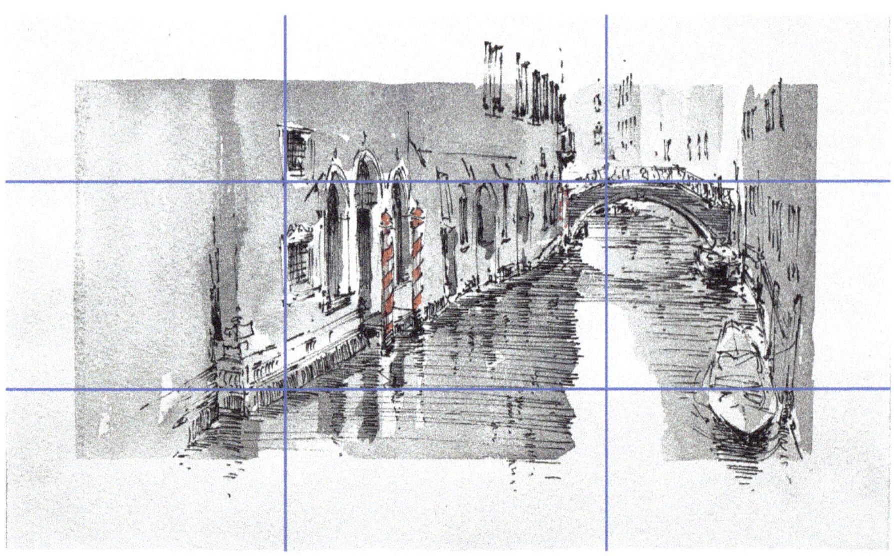

CONTRAST AND DETAIL

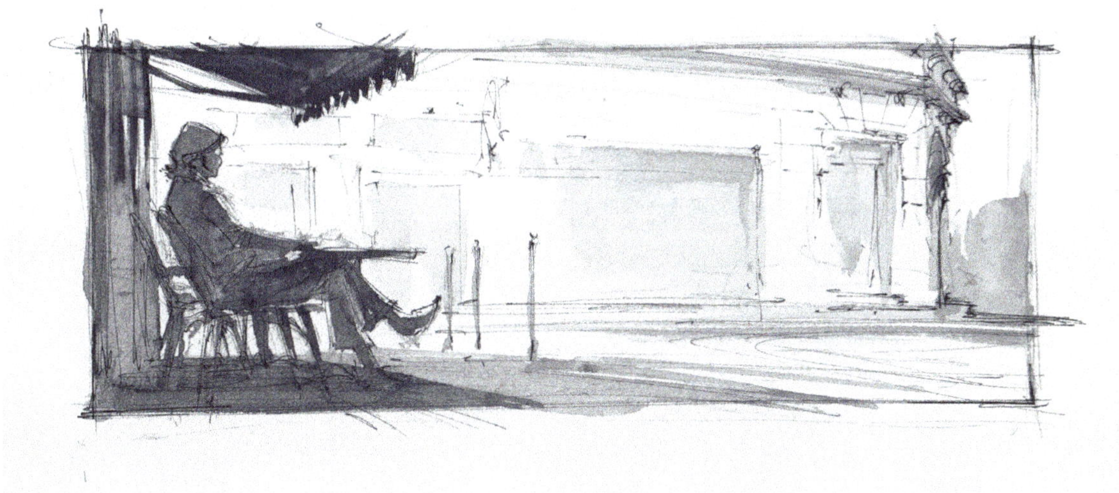

Another powerful compositional tool is the idea that your eye will be drawn to the area of a painting with the most contrast and greatest detail. If a sketch includes details from one edge to the other, top to bottom, your eye doesn't know where to settle. The piece becomes a jumbled mess. Choose one main focal point and concentrate all your details there. The rest of the piece can be less focused, more impressionistic.

You can use contrasts of light and dark, and also contrasts of color.

Details and dark shadows on the roof draw your eye in, while the background is muted and diffused.

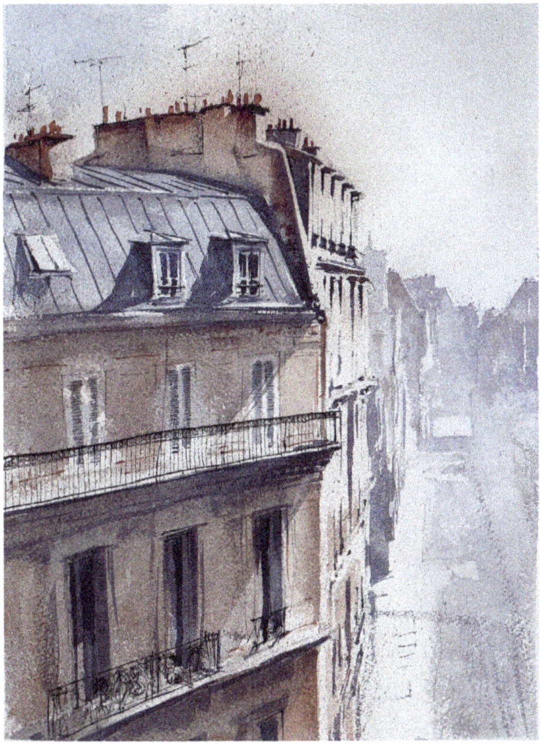

If we put these two ideas together and layer the rule of thirds onto contrasts and details, we begin to create truly dynamic compositions. These concepts work for a reason. They become a powerful means to infuse vitality and a true sense of story into our paintings. In chapter 6 (page 80), I discuss how these principles can be used to sketch a landscape.

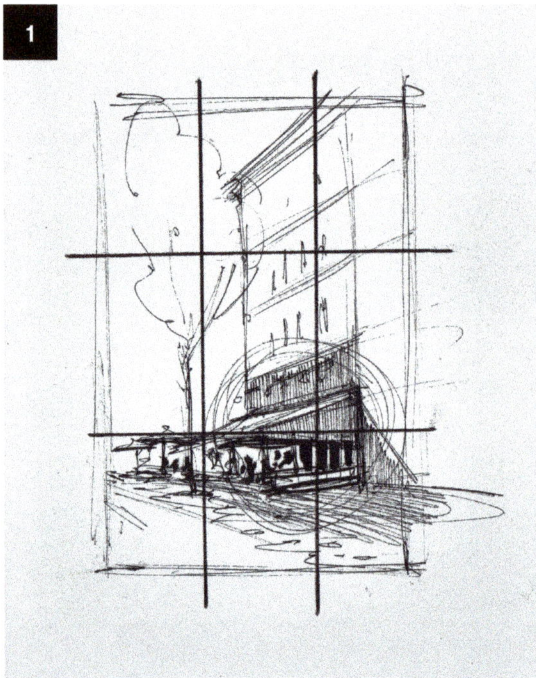

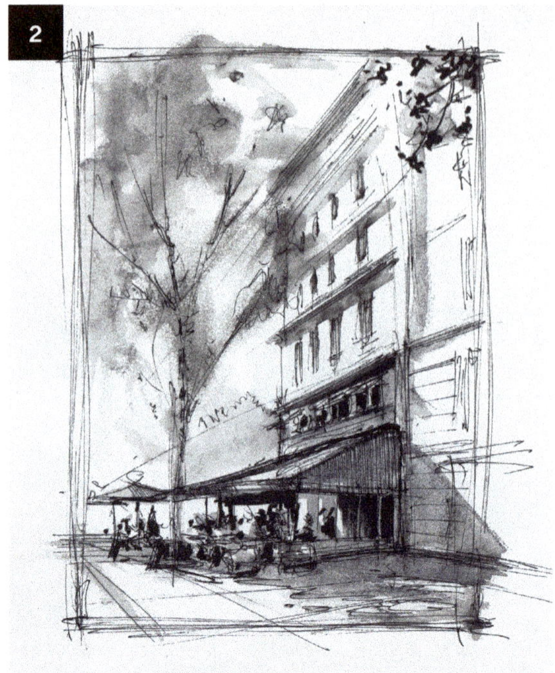

Sketching Process

1 | Take a few minutes to work out a composition in a quick thumbnail sketch. Create a rule of thirds grid. For my piece, I wanted the café to be the center of focus, so I placed it in the lower right portion of the composition. The tree occupies another intersection point, balancing the building nicely.

2 | In this more complete sketch, I'm thinking about where most of the details will be. I can afford to put lots of information under the awning of the café—people, tables, and chairs—all the activity of this busy place. I'll leave the rest of the composition less defined. I darkened the shadows around the café for emphasis. The awning will also be a brilliant red. These contrasts of tone and value will ensure the center of focus.

3 | The final painted sketch brings all the elements together. Using the rule of thirds to compose my piece and choose a focal area, as well as concentrating details and contrasts in the same space, ensures a strong center of focus and a well-composed image.

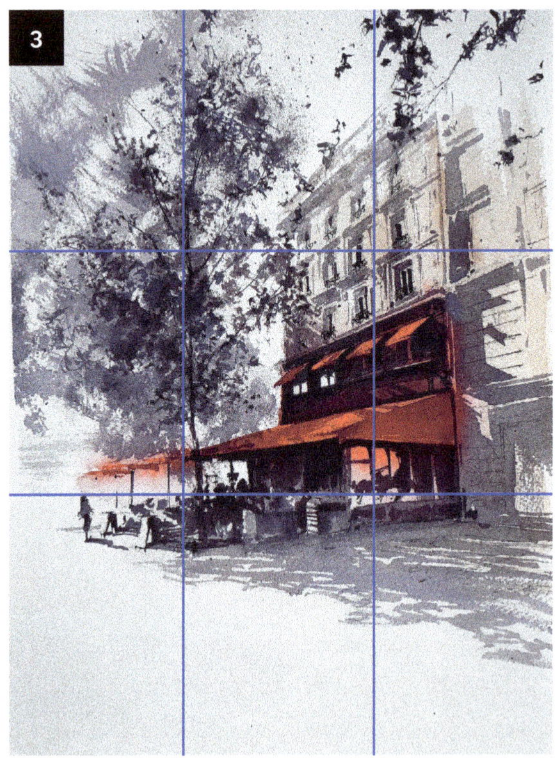

THUMBNAIL SKETCHES

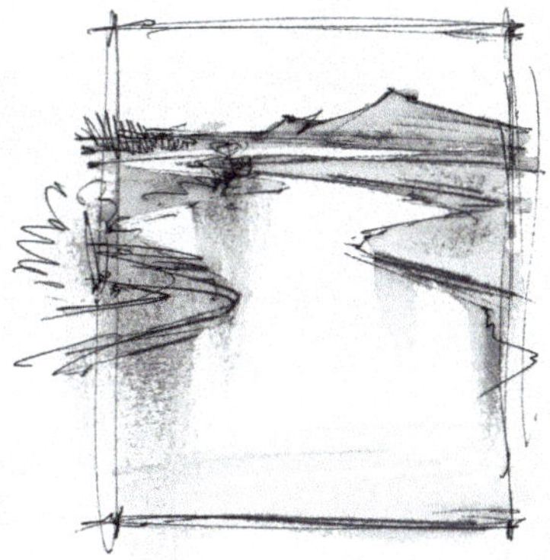

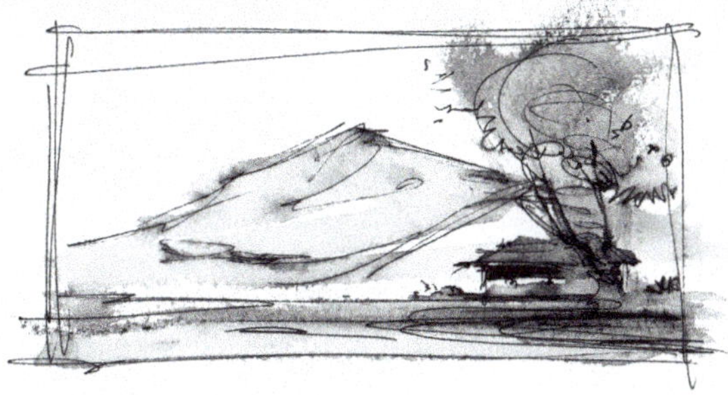

A thumbnail sketch is a small study used to work out many of the elements of what will become a larger piece. These are done quickly and are a wonderful way to get your head around a subject.

Thumbnails can be used in so many ways. They are a dress rehearsal, a visual thought process, and the first stages of a plan. They teach us volumes about our sketch in a few short minutes. We start to work out the composition, perspective, how light and shadows are defining the form of our subjects, and where to determine the center of focus. Because these sketches are done quickly, if we decide we don't like our composition or angle of view, we can easily start over.

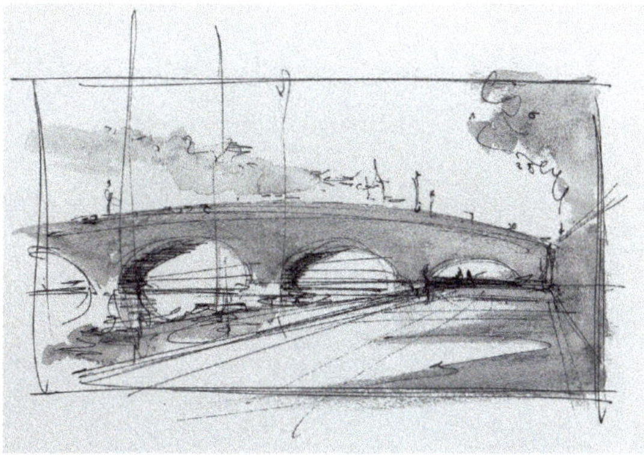

A common mistake in sketching is to bite off more than you can chew. You sit down to draw a scene, and without thinking you begin sketching the building next door, the people at the bus stop across the street, the row of trees trailing off your page. Before you know it, you've run out of paper. This is the artist's version of mission creep, and spending a few minutes doing a quick thumbnail sketch can put a stop to this.

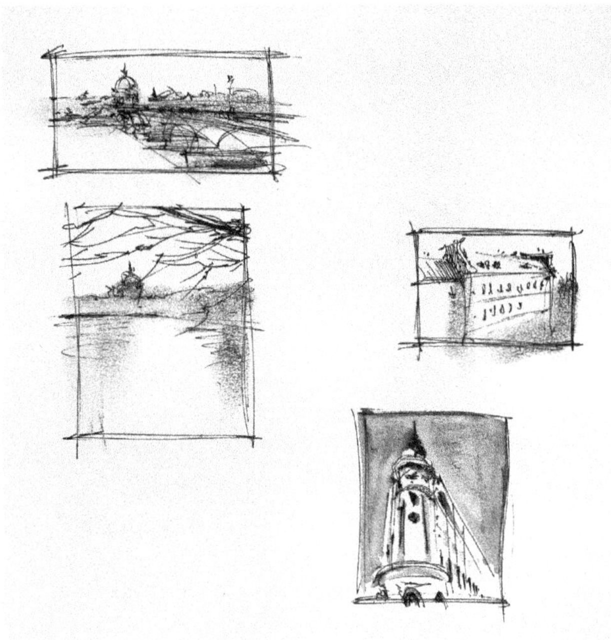

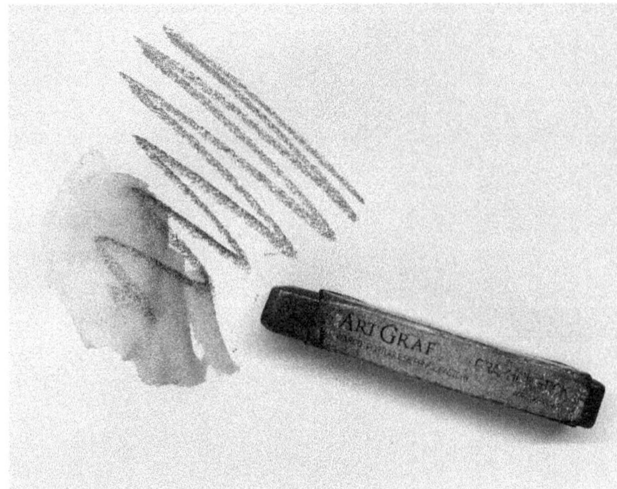

I carry a small sketchbook with cheap paper that I use for creating thumbnails. There's absolutely no pressure when using a book like this, there's nothing precious about it. I can think out loud without worrying about my sketch being pretty. I draw with an inexpensive ink pen, and I keep my pen moving. I'm not measuring precisely. If a line isn't in the correct place, I'll draw another one, until I find the form. The trick is to move quickly.

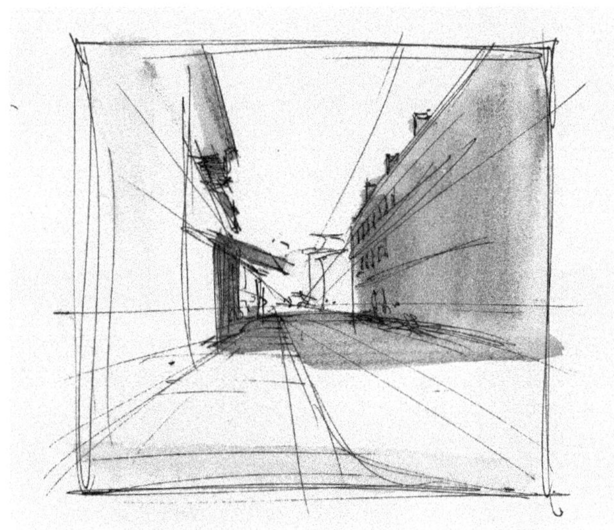

I also use a water-soluble graphite stick to add deep shadows. The combination of ink, graphite, and paper creates three tones. This is enough to show me the overall shapes of what I'm drawing, where the light and shadows are, and basic perspective.

Once I've gotten this far, I like to draw a frame around the sketch. A frame contains the composition, letting me know what I will include and not include. Mission creep is nipped in the bud. This frame also corresponds with my larger page once I begin a bigger piece.

ENGAGE IN A DIALOGUE

Our sketches can be many things. They can be a form of meditation, therapy, exploration, reportage, or a way to record our travels and experience. They are also a beautiful form of communication. We don't always need to think about potential viewers while we're sketching; sometimes it's best not to. But I do believe that sketches are a dialogue. They communicate something to someone, even if that someone is us many years later.

With this in mind, we can use these tools we've gained to communicate our thoughts and feelings with our sketches. If we're not conscious of these ideas, we may unwittingly create something that is confusing or overwhelming. But armed with a little knowledge, we are free to create a dialogue that is engaging.

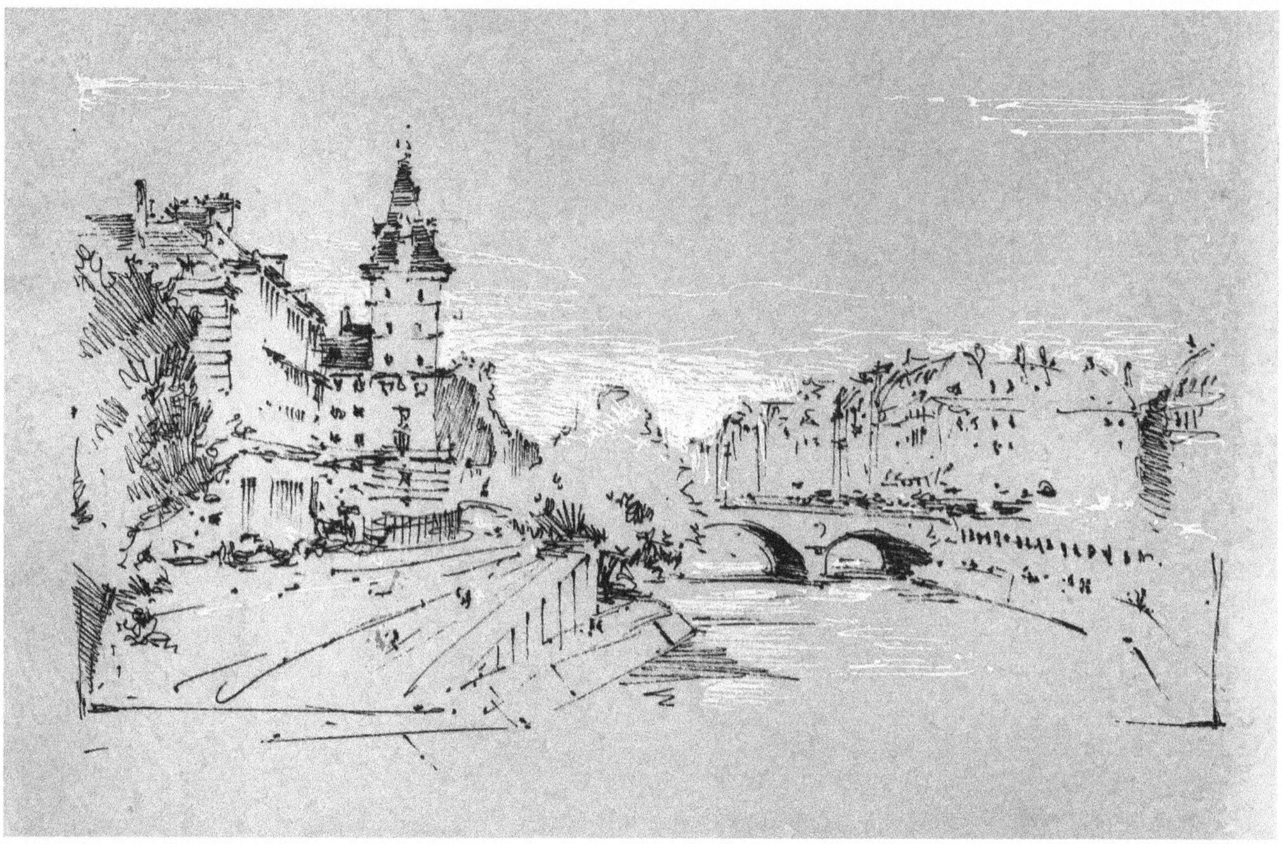

Pont Saint-Michel, Paris. Leaving out unnecessary details and sketching only what's needed to tell the story invites the viewer in as a participant. Ink and white gel pen on tea-stained paper.

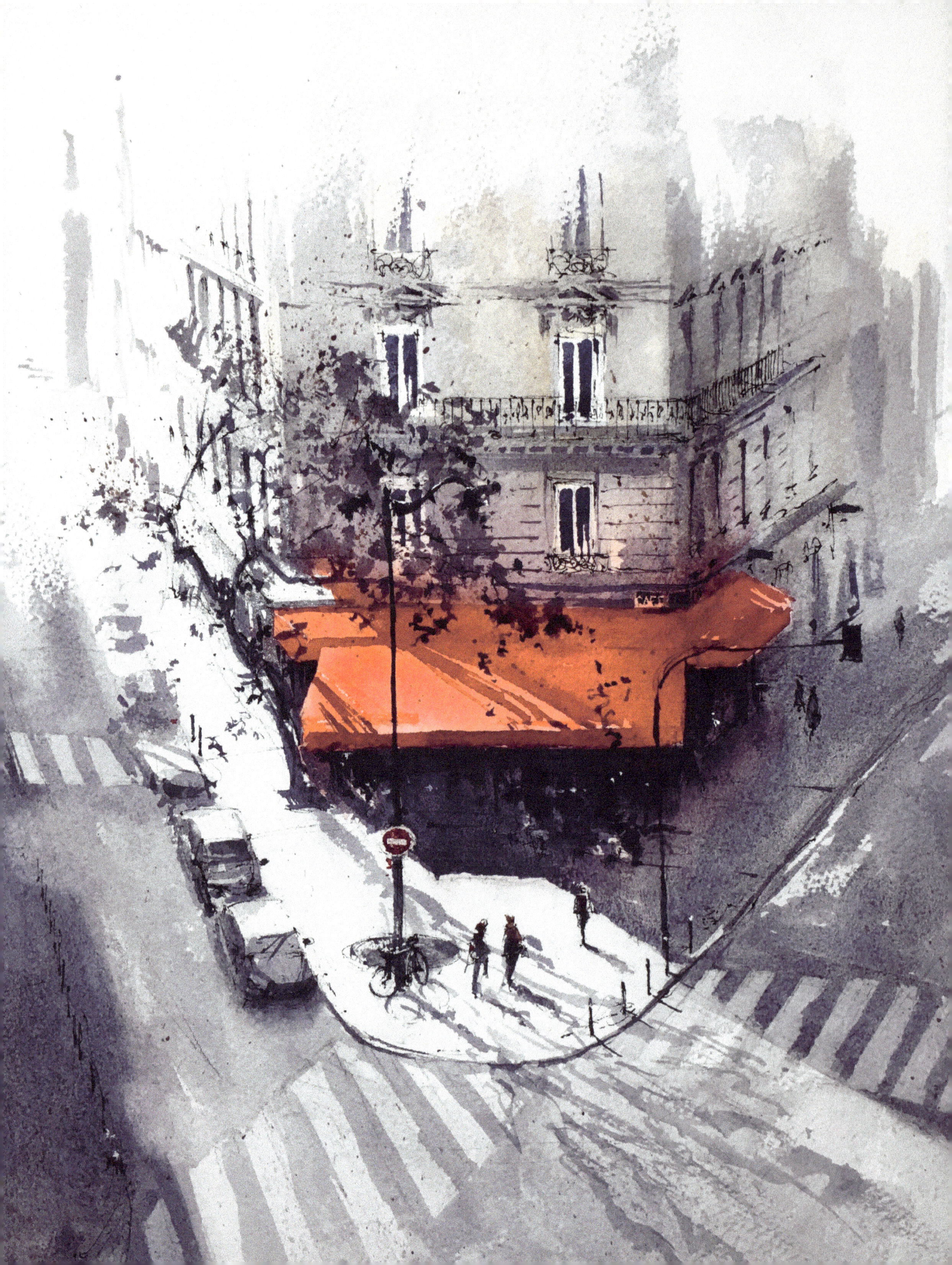

4

PERSPECTIVE

Perspective introduces structure to our artwork. We can bang away blindly on a piano and make a lot of noise, but once we know about chords and melody, we can create music. The same is true for visual art. Splashes of color and unbridled expression can be wonderful things, but with a little knowledge of underlying structure and perspective, our sketches begin to sing.

BASIC BONES

Linear perspective is the skeleton of architectural and interior sketching, and learning the basics is essential. You can bend and even break rules, but you must have a foundation upon which to build.

We all have very similar skeletons. For the most part our bones and skulls are indistinguishable from each other. It's our muscles and flesh, our moods and expressions, our hairstyles and clothing that make us beautifully unique. The same is true with perspective in drawing. The underlying structure, the linear perspective, may be the same, but it's what we put on top that makes our art unique—our pen and brushstrokes, our choice of textures and colors, the way we depict light. All these flavors that are unique to us are where our personality shines.

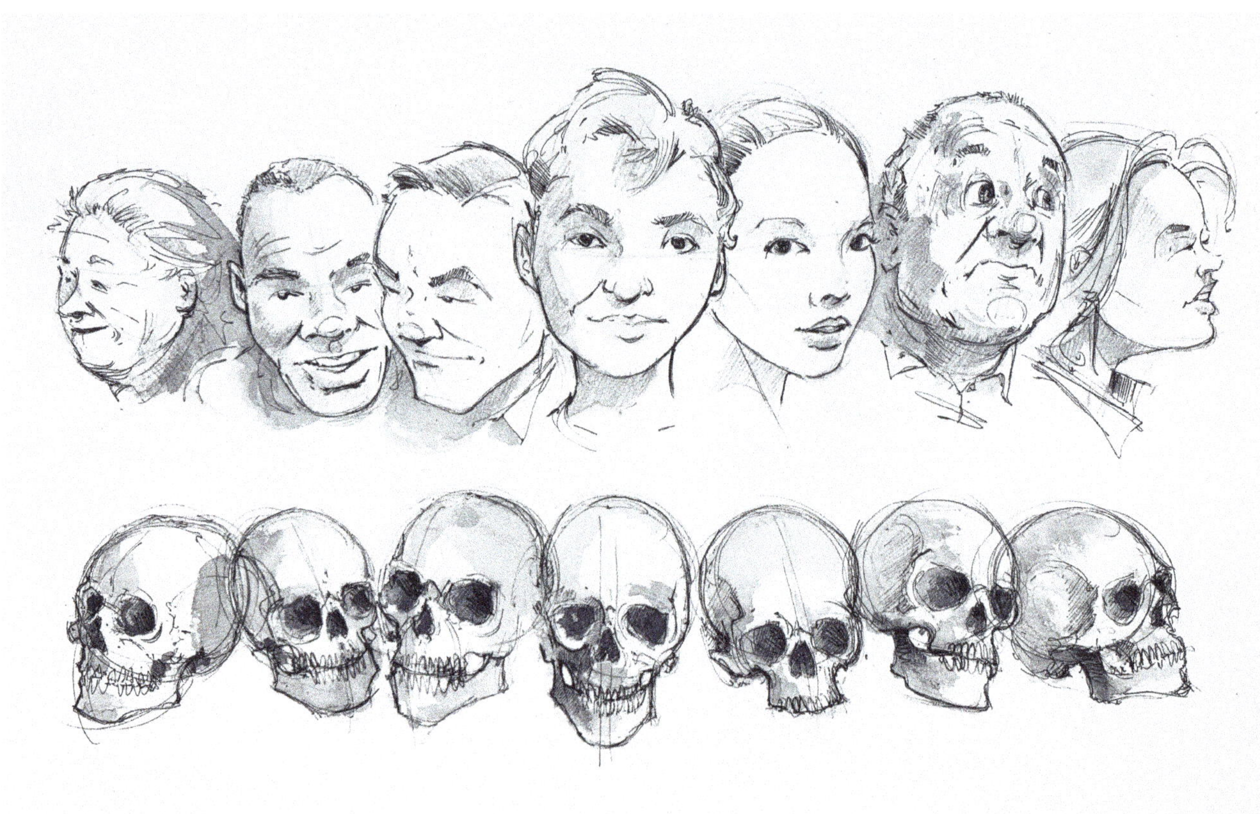

LINEAR PERSPECTIVE

One of the most difficult things to do as an artist is depict a three-dimensional object on a two-dimensional page. It's just not how our brains are wired. Luckily, there are tools we can use to help us. The most powerful tool for depicting depth on the page is linear perspective.

I love the illusion of depth, and I love to create depth on the page. We can use light and shadow to reveal volume. We can use tones and values to depict distance. But if we're doing any sort of interior or architectural sketching, linear perspective is the most effective tool we have for creating depth.

Two different types of perspective are used for sketching: linear and atmospheric. Thanks to the Renaissance artists we have linear perspective, and thanks to Leonardo da Vinci and artists of the Northern European Renaissance we have atmospheric perspective. Linear perspective involves lines, as the name implies, and atmospheric perspective has more to do with tones and gradations of color (more on this in chapter 6, page 84). Both are used to create the illusion of depth.

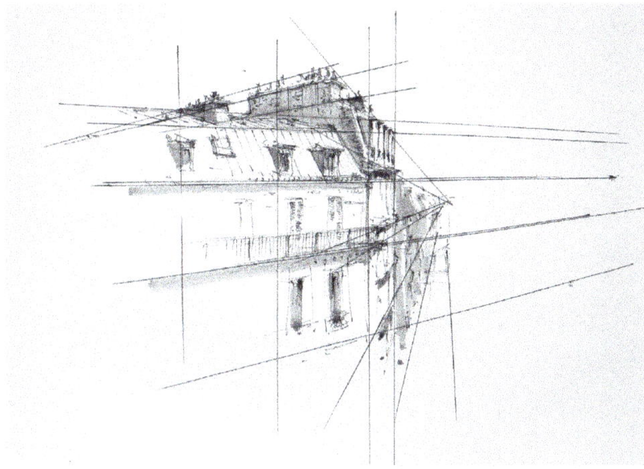

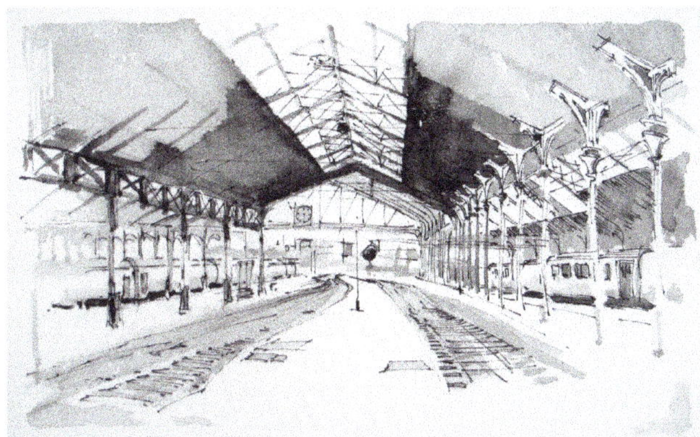

Linear perspective uses converging lines to create depth.

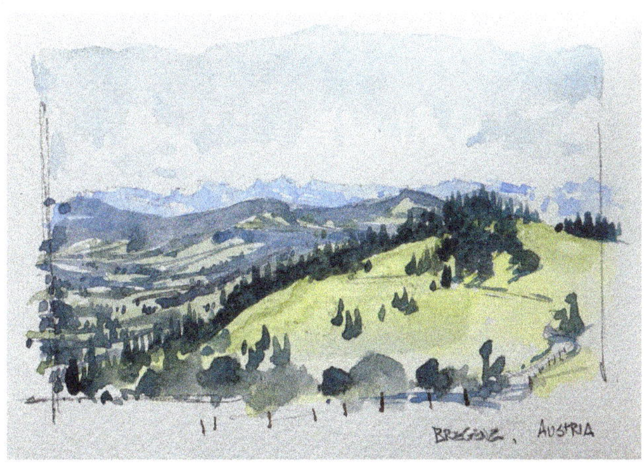

Atmospheric perspective uses color to create depth.

This painting uses linear perspective to create depth on a flat page. Beneath the paint, beneath the ink lines and washes of color, the basic bones of what's going on is perspective. There are foreground, mid-ground, and background elements, which is another way to create depth, but what linear perspective gives us are these converging lines that all lead back to points receding into the distance.

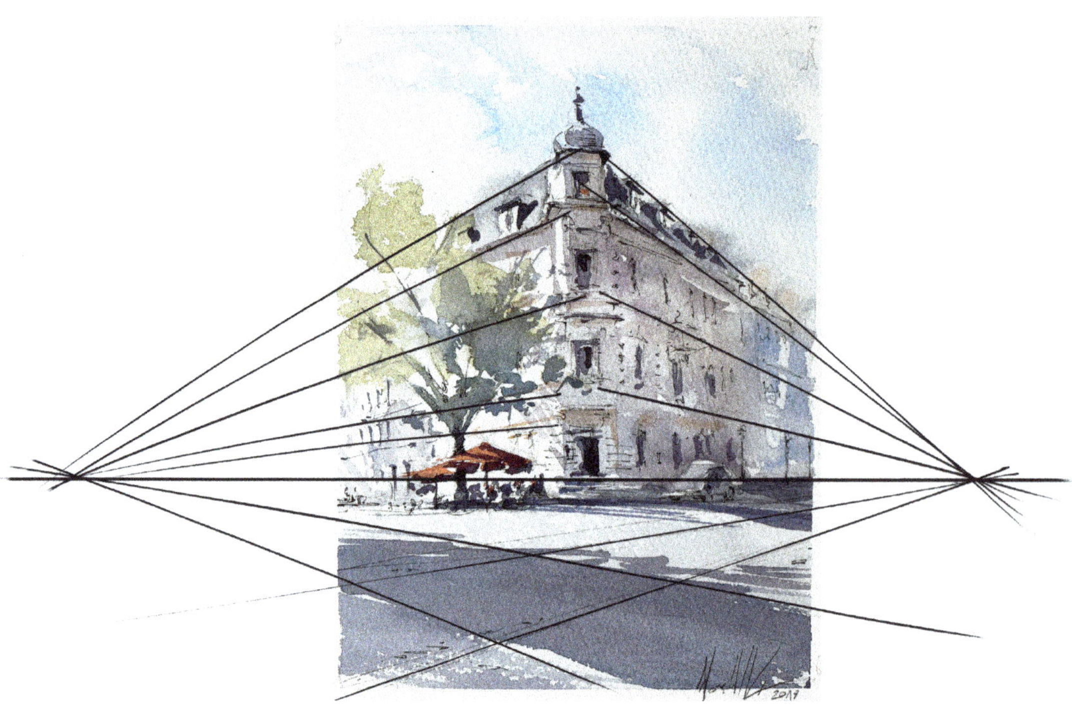

The Horizon Line

The horizon line is a horizontal line that represents your eye line. These terms are interchangeable. The horizon line represents the line on the horizon. When you stand on the beach and look out to sea, where the sky meets the ocean, you'll see a sharp clear line at the horizon. The same is true in any wide-open expanse, such as a desert. In cities, finding the horizon line is a little trickier because buildings obscure the view, but the horizon is still there and some tricks can help us find it.

One-Point Perspective

The point refers to a single point on the horizon line. This is also called a vanishing point because it is where lines will converge and appear to vanish over the horizon.

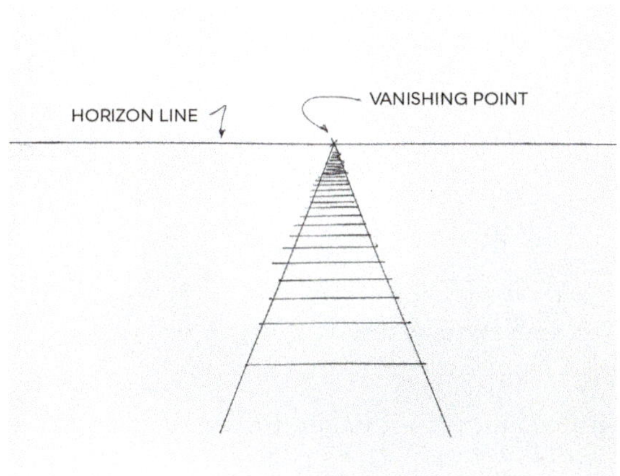

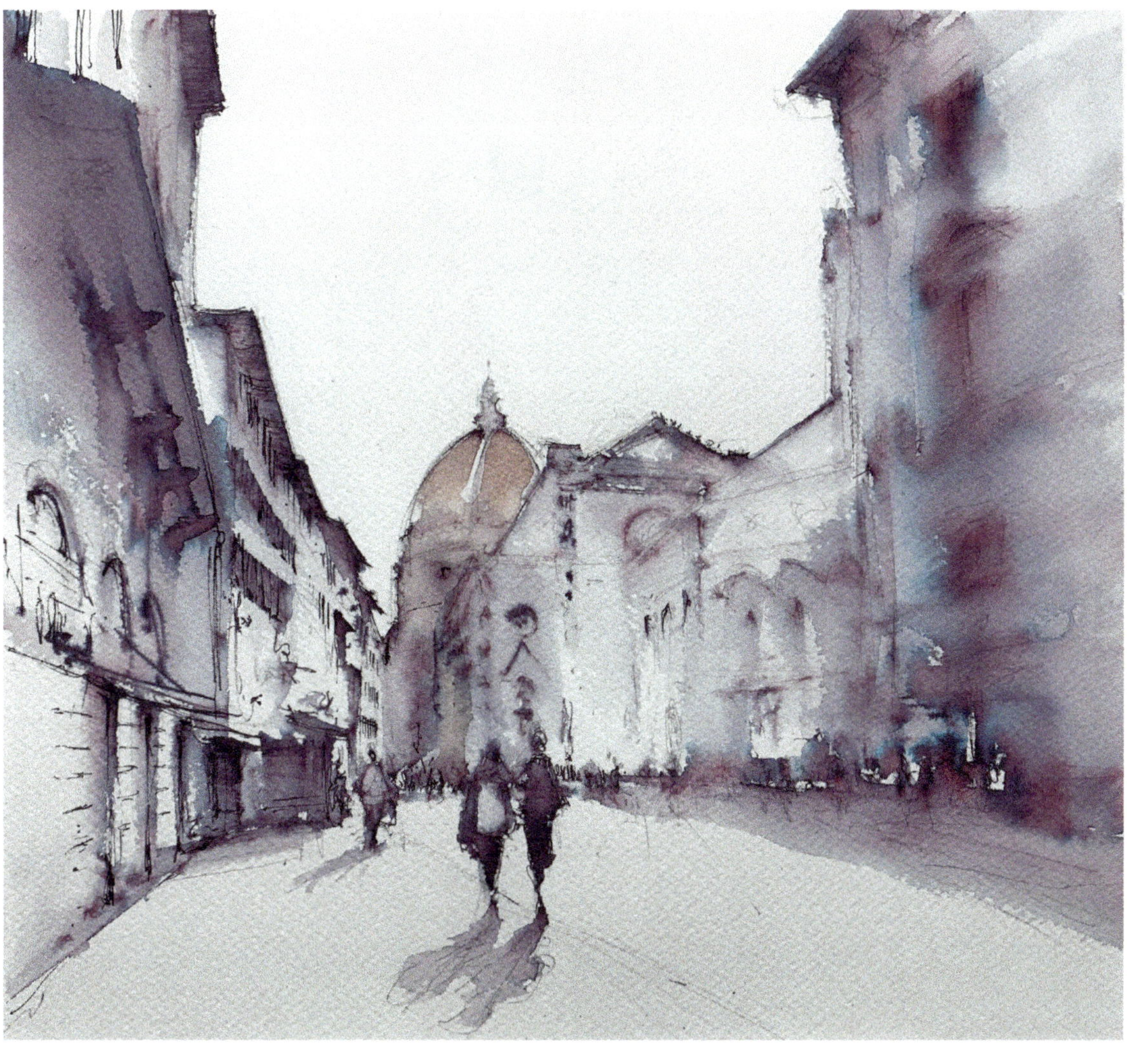

To learn how to draw in perspective it's best to begin with simple lines and shapes.

SKETCHING PROCESS

1 | Draw a horizon line with a vanishing point, and draw a square below that line.

2 | From each corner of the square, trace a straight line back to the vanishing point. We're already starting to introduce some depth into this image.

3 | Draw a second smaller square slightly behind the first one, its corners resting on the lines traced back to the vanishing point. Now we have something that looks like a cube. This shape appears to take up space, and it's drawn in one-point perspective.

4 | Repeat this process by drawing squares, rectangles, and more complex shapes above, below, and on the horizon. With each shape, trace lines from each corner back to the vanishing point.

1

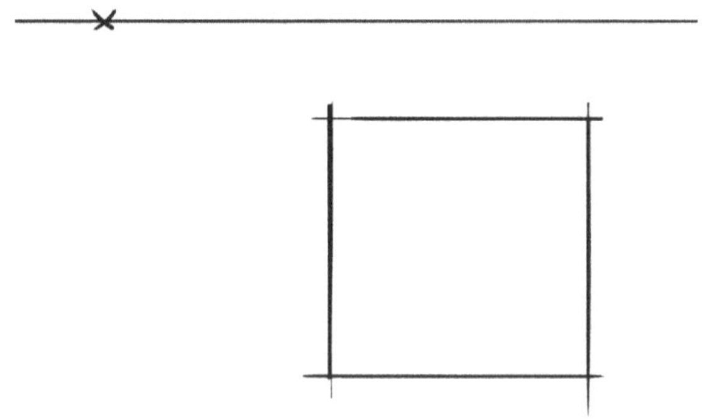

2

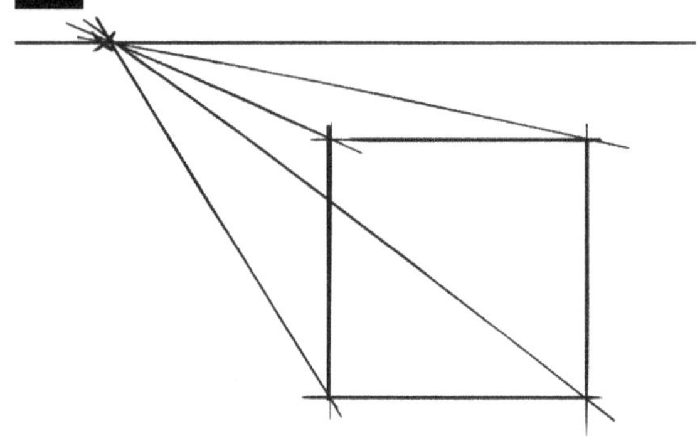

3

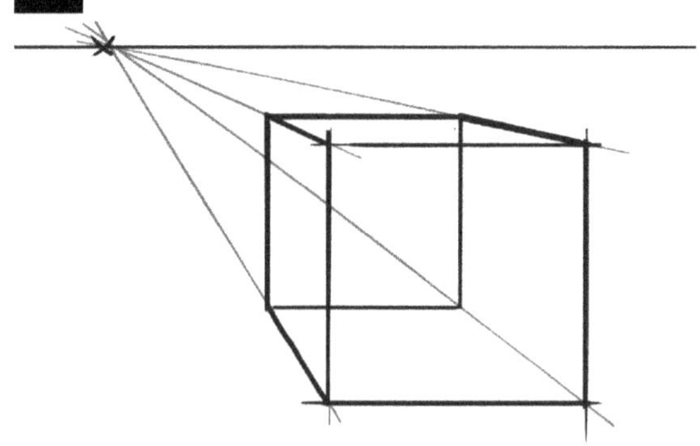

4

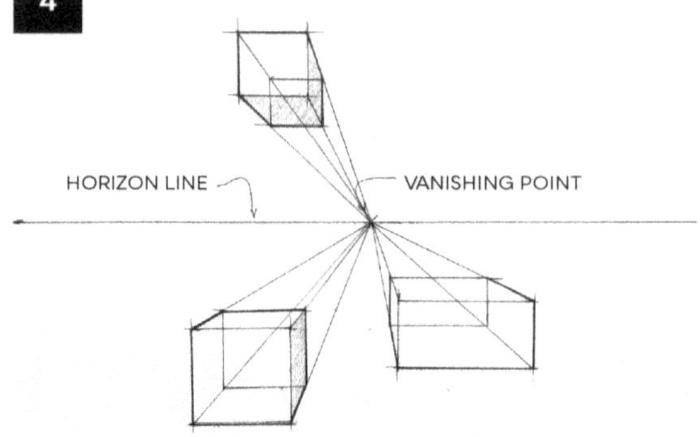

Often the first thing I draw on my page is a horizon line followed quickly by lines emanating out from a single point to create a starburst image.

Once we have these lines as guides, we can introduce vertical and horizontal lines to create the illusion of looking down a street. With this basic structure, what starts to look like a street scene can quickly be sketched in. Details of doors, windows, and people can be added. Populate this scene with as many details as you want.

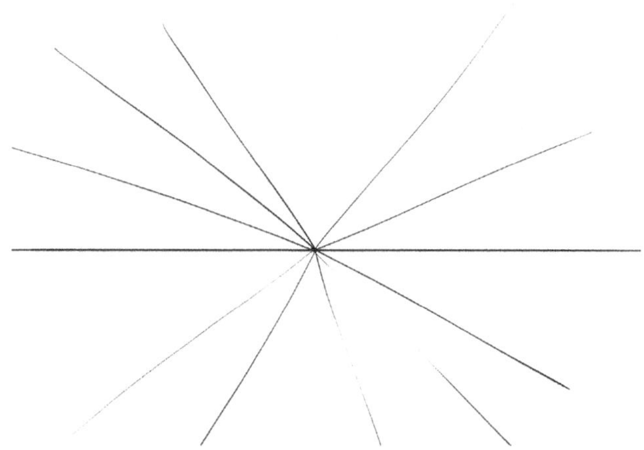

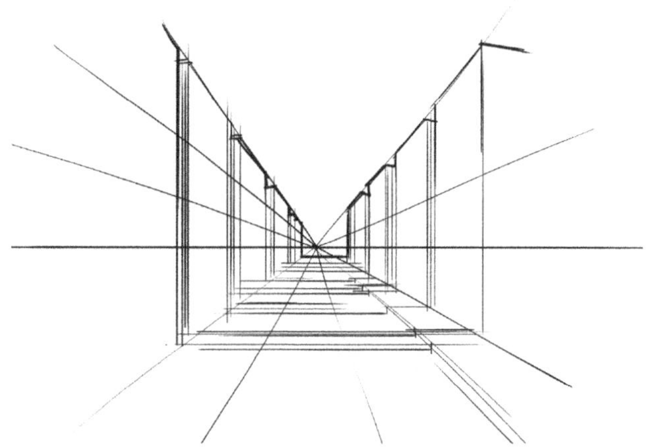

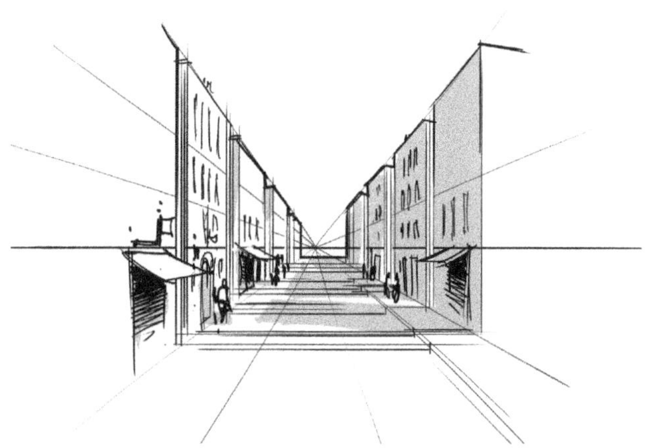

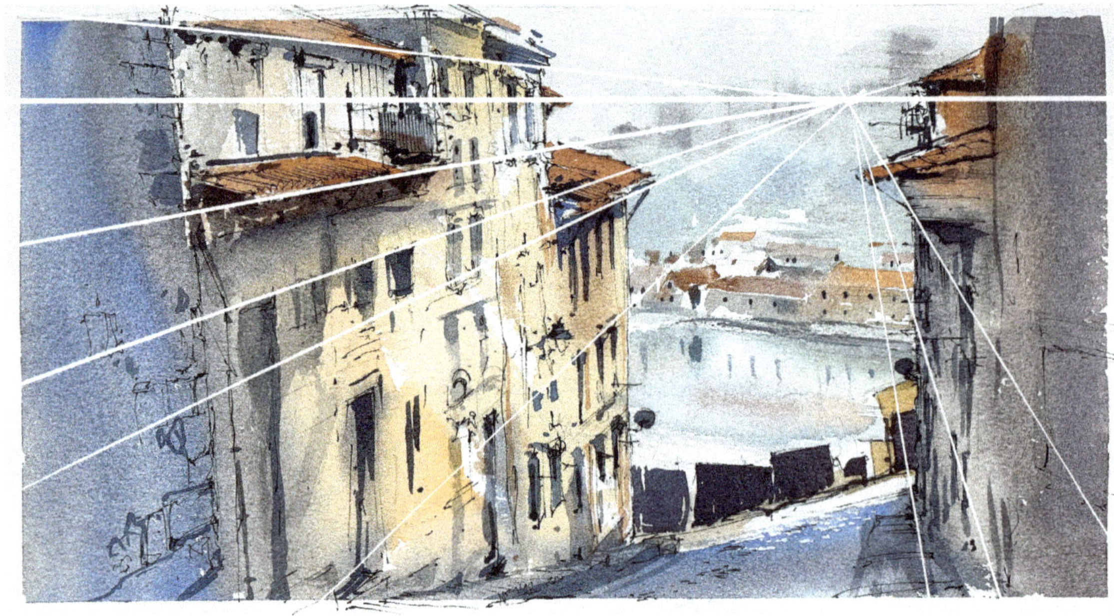

This scene from Porto, Portugal uses one-point perspective. The view is looking down toward a river, so the horizon is high on the page.

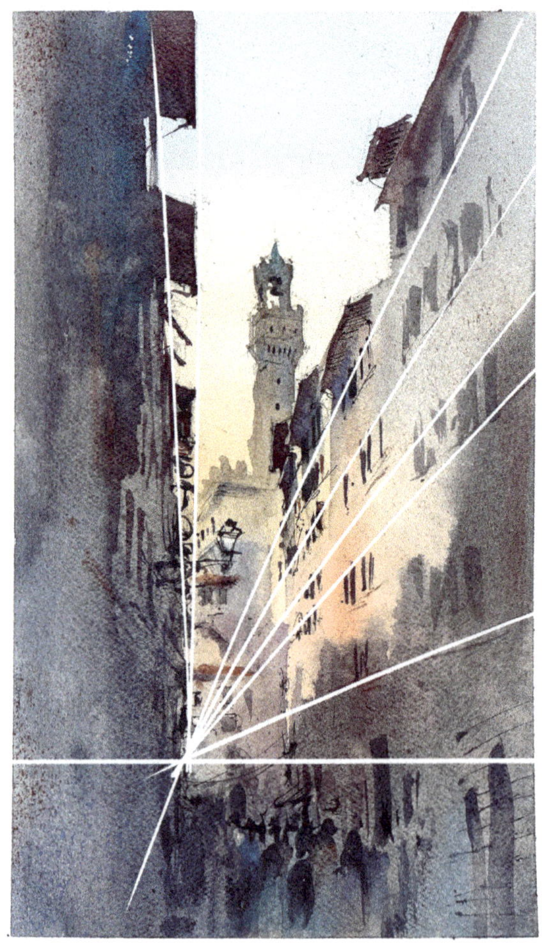

This street in Florence, Italy uses one-point perspective. All rooflines, windows, and balconies point to a single point near the end of the street.

A Singular View

One-point perspective is a great tool when your view is looking down a long street. In Paris, this method is perfect for the grand avenues. It works wonders in New York City, San Francisco, Chicago—any city laid out on a grid. Whenever you can look a long way down a street, you can rely on one-point perspective. One-point perspective can also be used to sketch aisles at the grocery store or rows of bookcases at the library.

Two-Point Perspective

Two-point perspective is much more fun—it's a more dynamic way to depict shapes realistically.

SKETCHING PROCESS

1 | Once again, start with a horizon line. Instead of putting a single point on the horizon, place two points, one on the left and one on the right. Draw a single vertical line that represents the edge of a cube.

2 | From the top and the bottom of this line, trace straight lines back to both vanishing points.

3 | Make two more vertical lines parallel to the initial line.

1

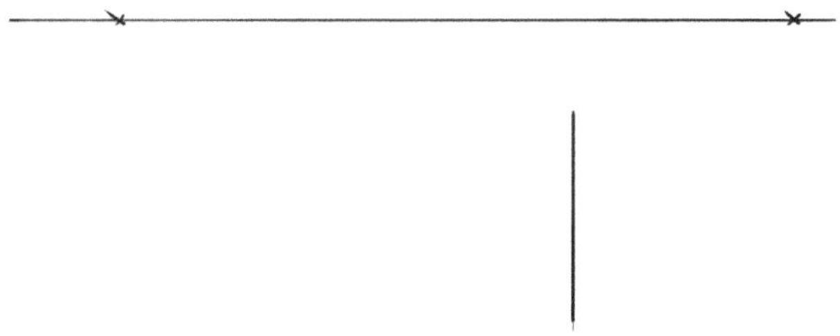

2

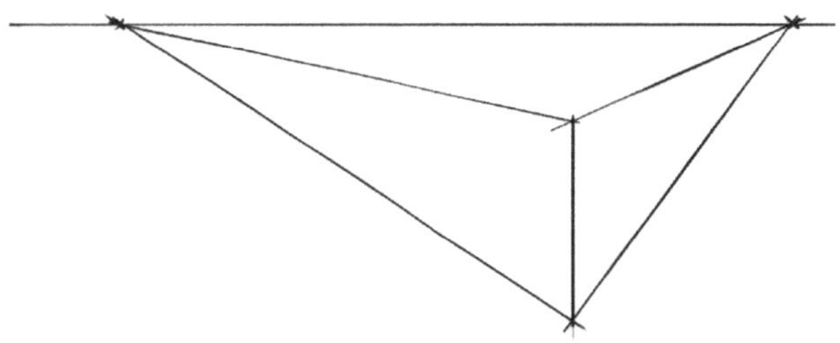

3

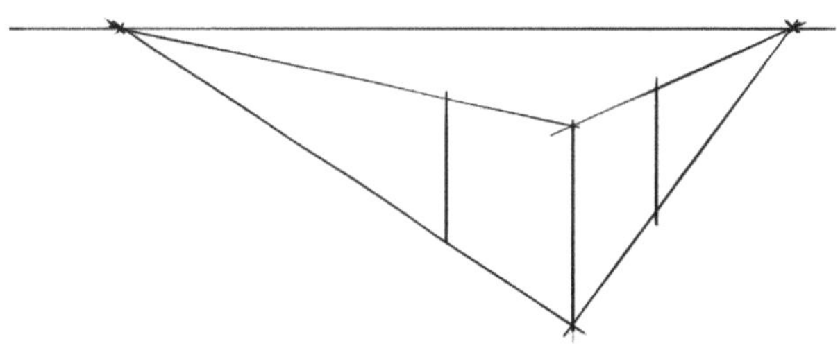

4 | Draw lines from the top and bottom of these new lines back to the vanishing points.

5 | Add some shade to depict volume.

Now we have cube shapes that have some dimensionality. They're also drawn in perfect perspective, because we've traced all our lines back to our vanishing points.

The basic shape of this building (below) is a cube seen in two-point perspective. All the rooflines, window lines, dormers, and cornices form lines that converge on one of two vanishing points.

4

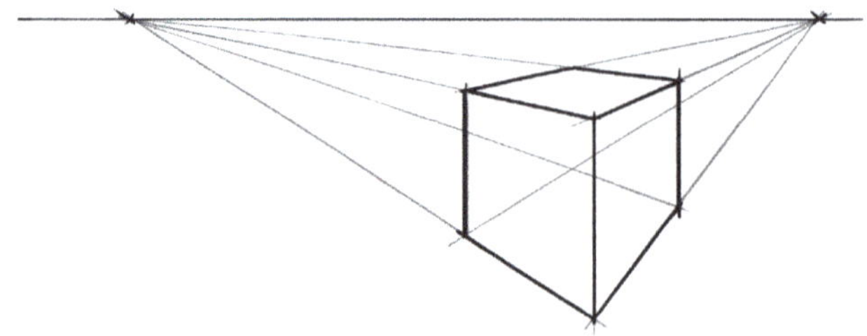

5

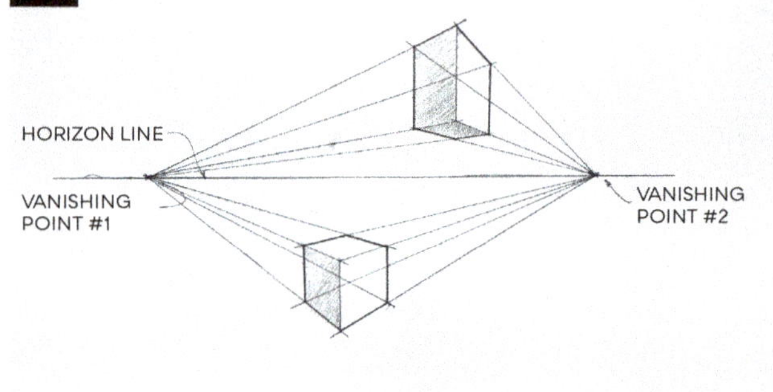

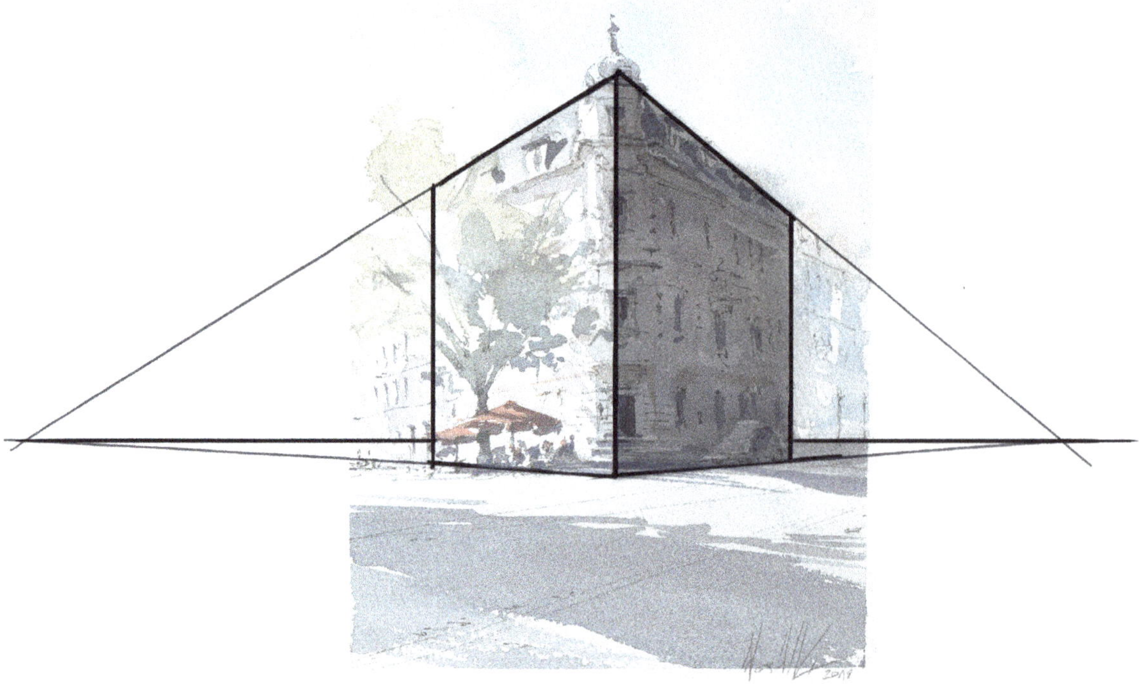

Three-Point Perspective

We can get far in our sketches with one- and two-point perspective, but adding a third point gets us closer to how our eyes actually perceive the world.

The third perspective point doesn't sit on the horizon line with its brothers. This refers to a point either high overhead or low down, somewhere near the center of the Earth. Three-point perspective comes into play if we're drawing tall trees in a forest, or cathedral columns reaching high above. These objects converge on a point high overhead.

When drawing buildings, outdoor scenes, or interiors, three-point perspective is useful for depicting tall shapes that recede away from us. When standing at street level looking up at a building, the top floors will be farther away from us than the ground floors. It may not be enough to draw in two-point perspective. We may need to employ this third point to convey that sense of height.

This third point can be hard to plot, as it will most likely be off the top of your page. In fact, this point will be at the zenith, directly overhead, or the nadir, directly underfoot.

For the purposes of sketching, rather than reach for an astronomical compass, it may be enough to be aware of this concept and aim for a point even if you can't see exactly where it should be.

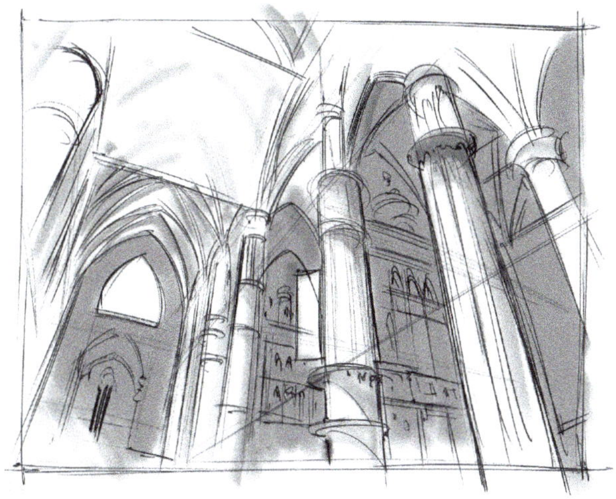

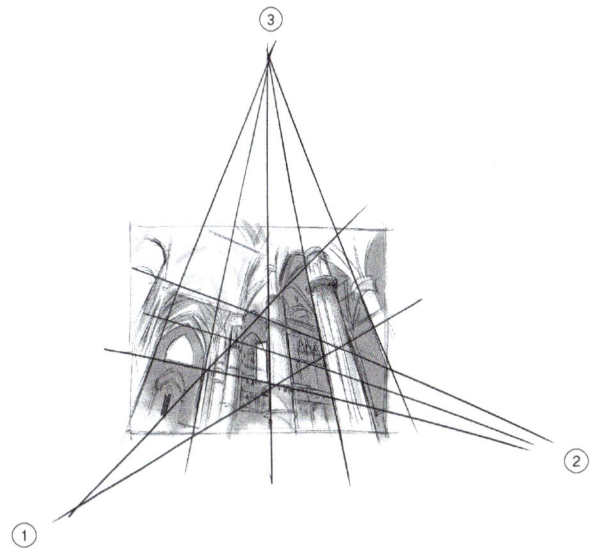

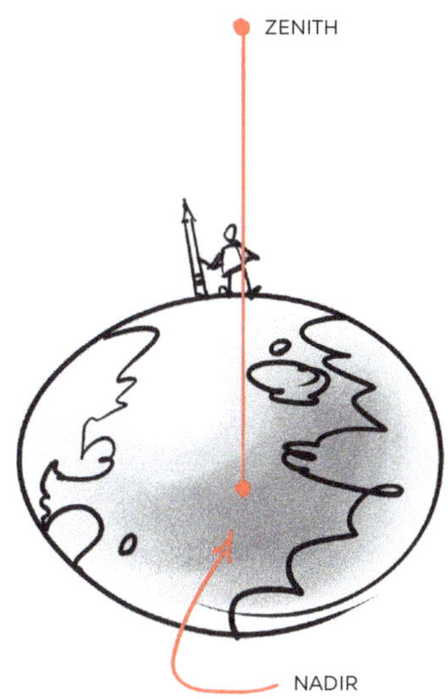

Perspective on a Curved Street

This is a sketch I did on a winter day in Milan, Italy. The warm colors and shabby details of these buildings are what drew me to this scene. I love the way the light softens all the colors as they recede into the distance.

At first, this scene appears to employ one-point perspective. I'm looking down a single street, and all the buildings recede toward a point somewhere in the background.

But because this street curves to the left, each building is aiming at its own unique vanishing point. They all share the same horizon line, but for each building there will be a unique vanishing point on the horizon.

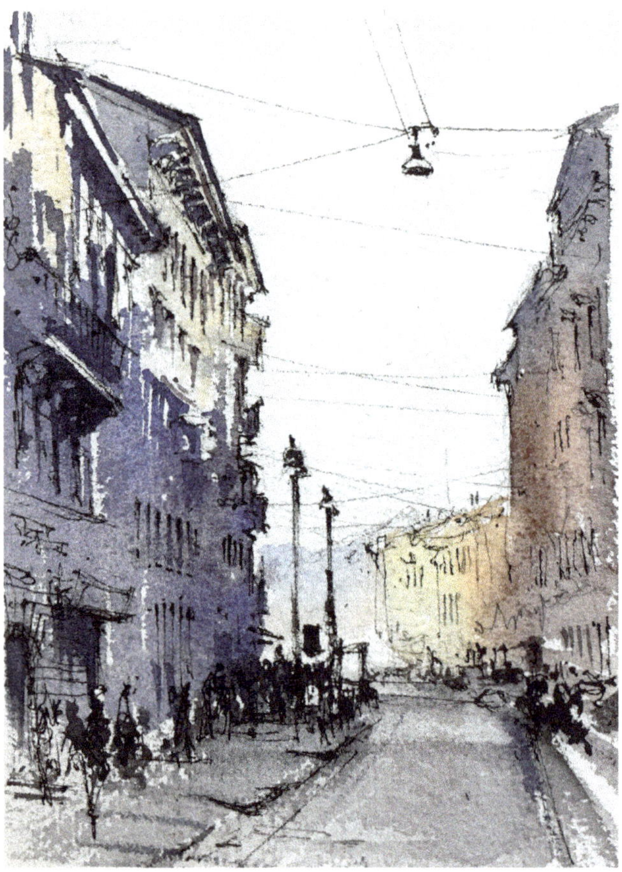

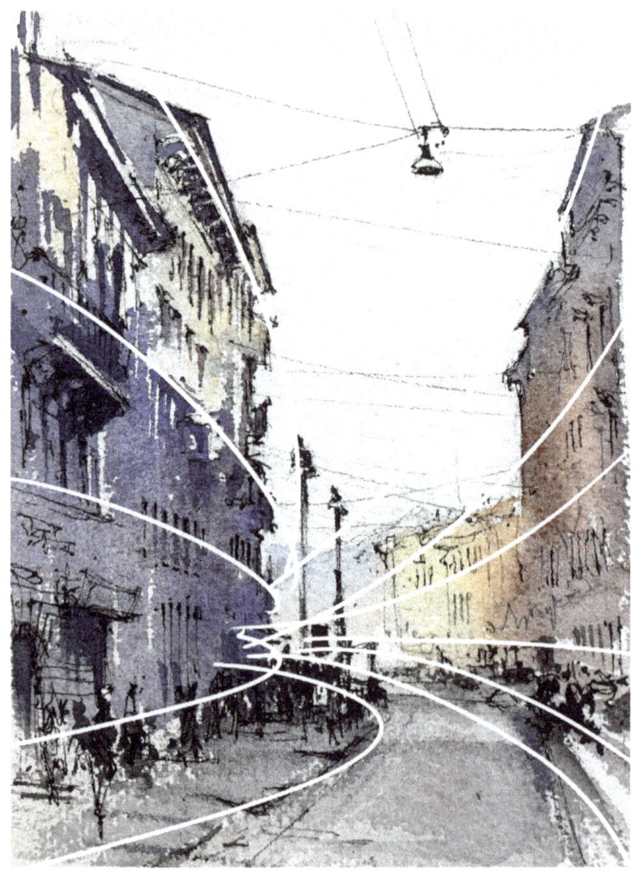

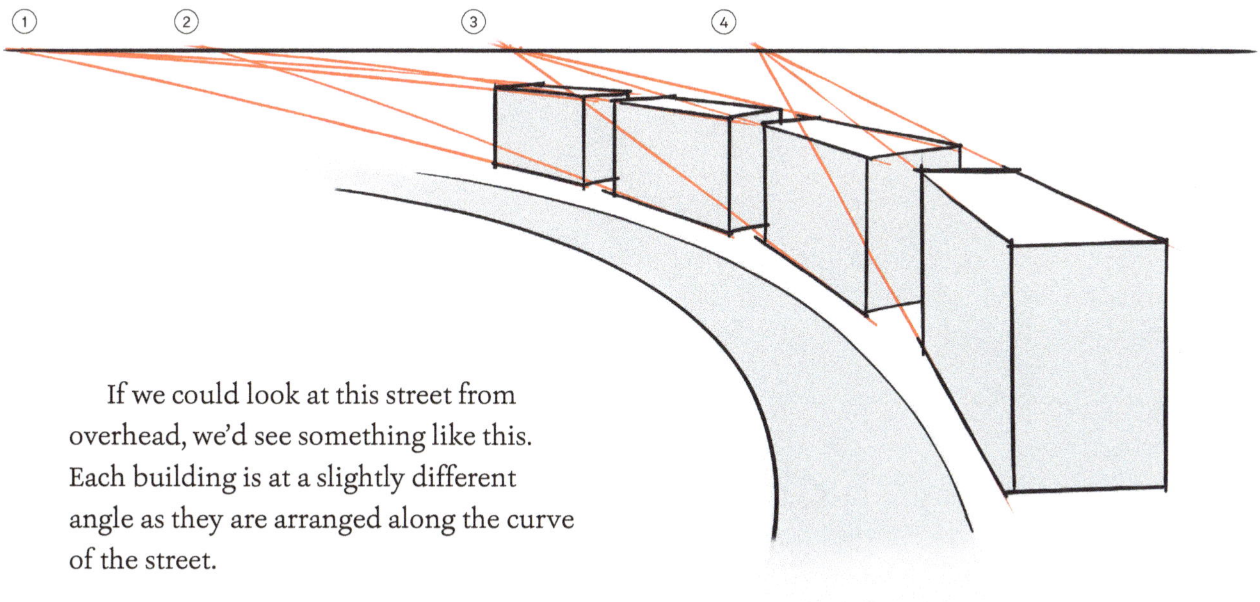

If we could look at this street from overhead, we'd see something like this. Each building is at a slightly different angle as they are arranged along the curve of the street.

CREATING A FRAMEWORK

Some artists have a real resistance to learning the rules of perspective. They feel it will restrict their art, and make things too stiff and mechanical. But perspective is the bones of all architectural drawing. It gives structure and proper form to everything that comes next. Rather than stifle our creative expression, perspective provides a solid framework upon which our sketches take flight.

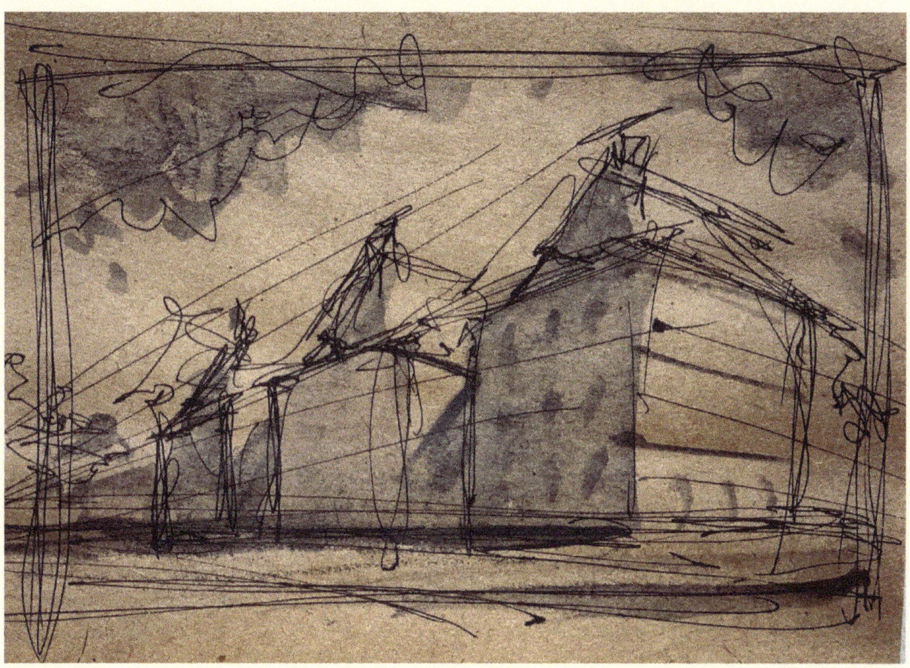

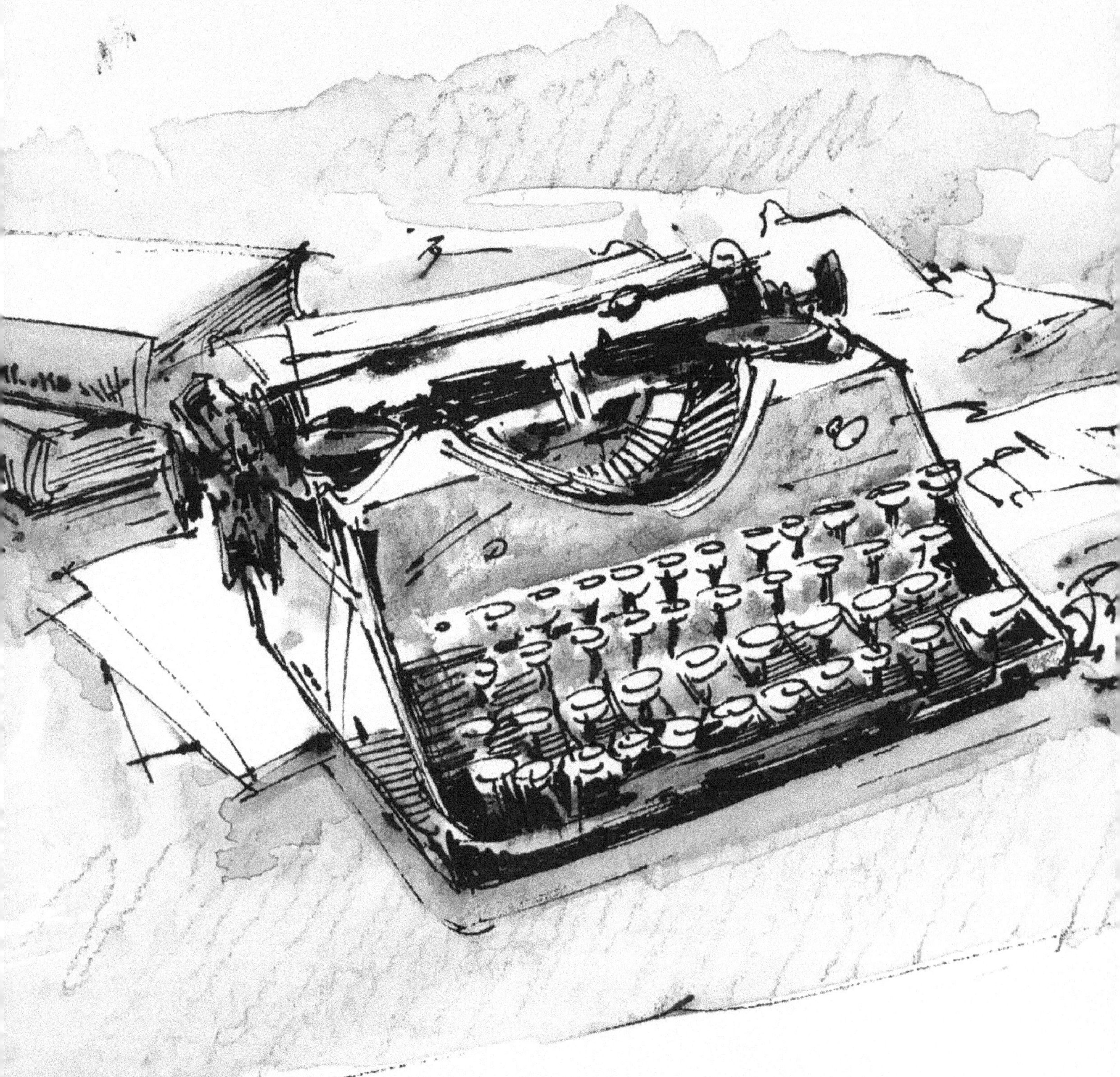

5

STILL LIFE

If mixing pigments and making color swatches is akin to practicing your scales on a musical instrument, sketching and painting a still life are like playing a beautiful little sonata. It may not be a full-blown symphony, but making your way around a collection of beautifully arranged objects can open hidden doors on your journey as an artist.

A POEM MADE VISIBLE

I was always slightly allergic to still lifes. They seemed boring. I couldn't see a story there. In French, the term is *nature morte*–dead nature. I just didn't see the point.

After seeing a few still lifes that I genuinely adore, I'm slowly changing my ways. To see the still life paintings of Henri Fantin-Latour or Olga Abramova is to see concise poetry. These artists exhibit rhythm and harmony, an economy of tone and contrast.

> ***"As music is the poetry of sound, so is painting the poetry of sight."***
>
> —JAMES MCNEILL WHISTLER

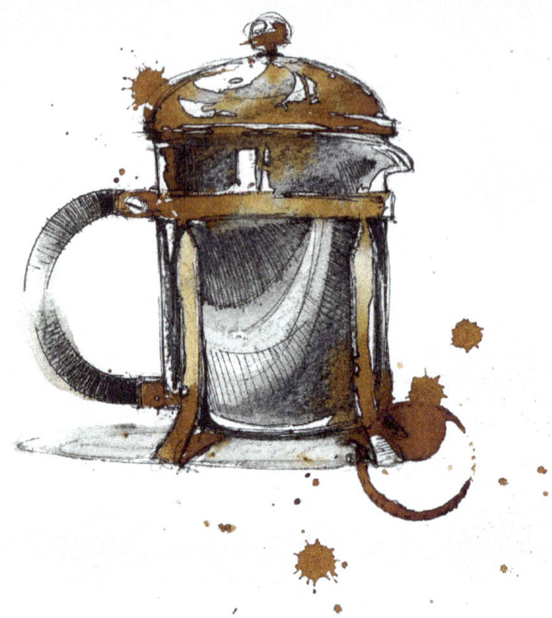

Not every still life has to be a bowl of fruit. My French press coffee pot, ink and graphite.

A NEW WAY TO SEE OBJECTS

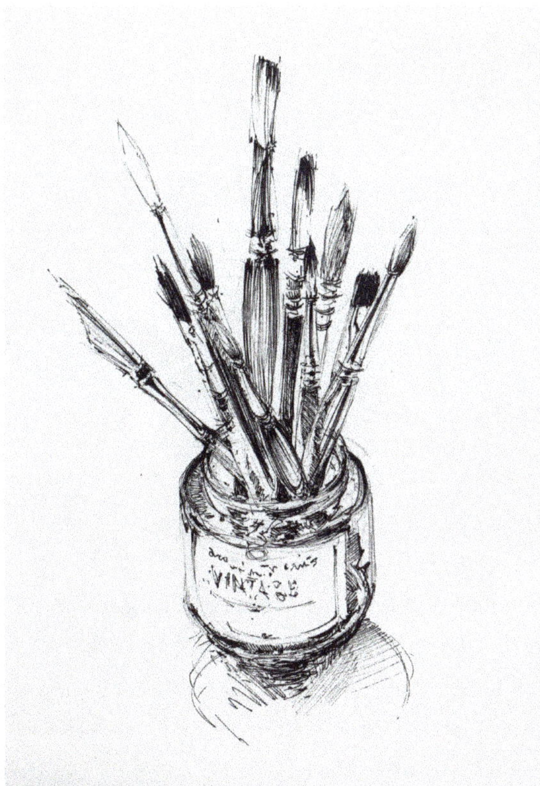

This is a jar of some of my favorite brushes. It's a simple group of objects, but it holds meaning for me, and this is key for depicting still life. You must feel what these objects have to say. Truly see them. These brushes form a little family. Each one is an actor waiting in the wings, and here they're all huddled together ready to perform. "Pick me! Pick me!" they seem to say.

Sketching Process

1 | Begin with a quick pencil sketch to find the overall form.

2 | Move to an ink pen, keeping your lines loose. You want to depict energy and movement, even in a still composition.

3 | The glass jar has a squat solidity to it, holding everyone in place, but also reflecting and refracting light.

> ***"Attention without feeling, I began to learn, is only a report."***
>
> —MARY OLIVER

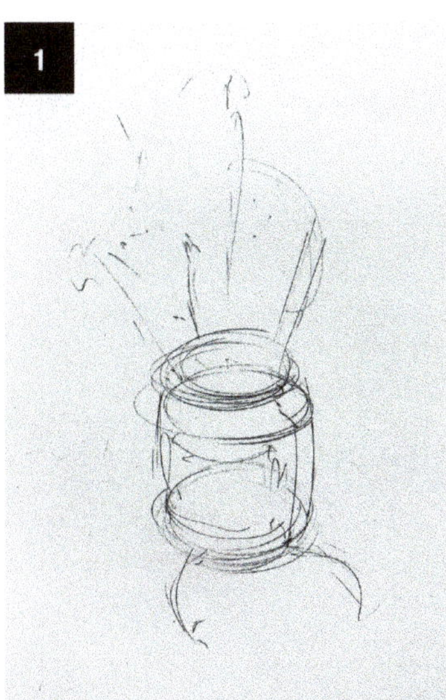

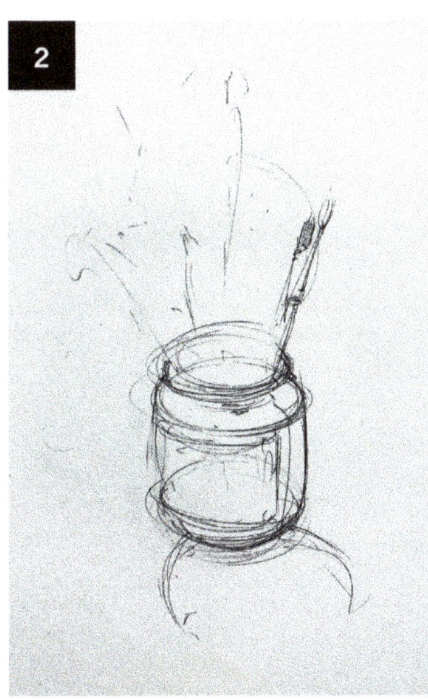

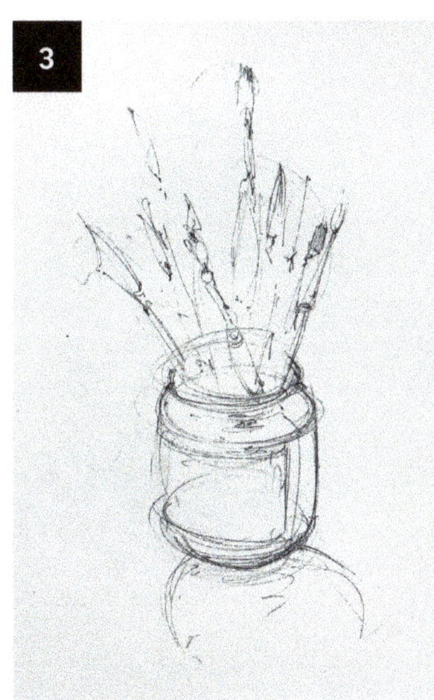

RENDERING LIGHT

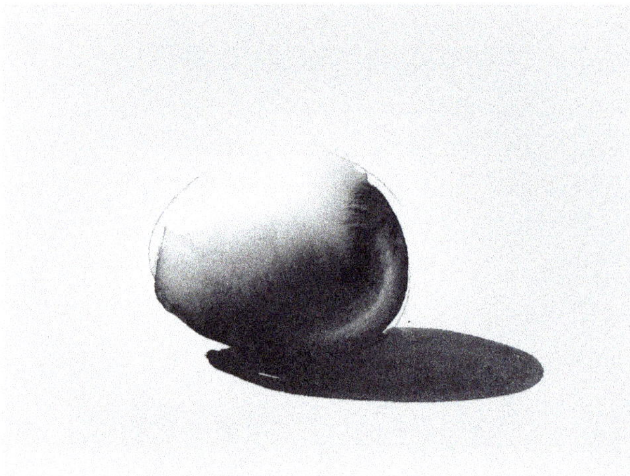

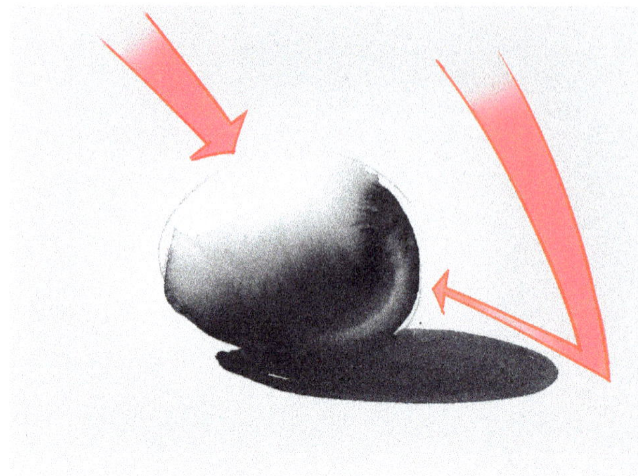

Still life is one of the best ways I know to study how light reflects and refracts on different objects. This can teach us volumes about the color and quality of shadows.

When light shines on an object, it creates highlights, shade, dark shadows, and a range of mid-tones. But light also bounces! Light reflects off other surfaces, bouncing back, and illuminating shadows in interesting ways.

Reflected light is such a beautiful phenomenon that to see it captured in a sketch is a joy to behold. To render this effect, we must see that the darkest part of a shadow isn't the far side of this ball, furthest from the light source. The darkest part is about two-thirds of the way around the ball. Light bounces off the ground, reflecting into the deep shadow, creating a slight highlight.

ADDING COLOR

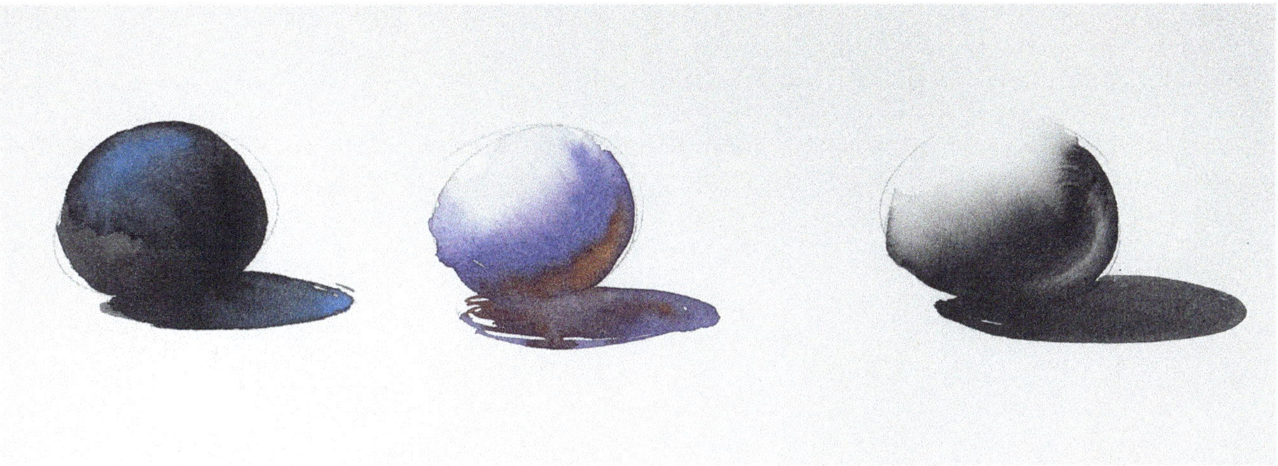

When color is added, the effect gets more interesting. An object may be a certain color, but reflected light is often a different color. Light bouncing off a warm orange surface will reflect a warm orange light, even if it's reflecting onto a cool blue object. Pushing warm colors into cool shadows is a wonderful technique to practice.

Sketching a still life offers the perfect opportunity to observe the effects of light reflecting, bouncing, and coloring objects. When these objects are glass, light bends and refracts, creating unexpected highlights within deep shadows.

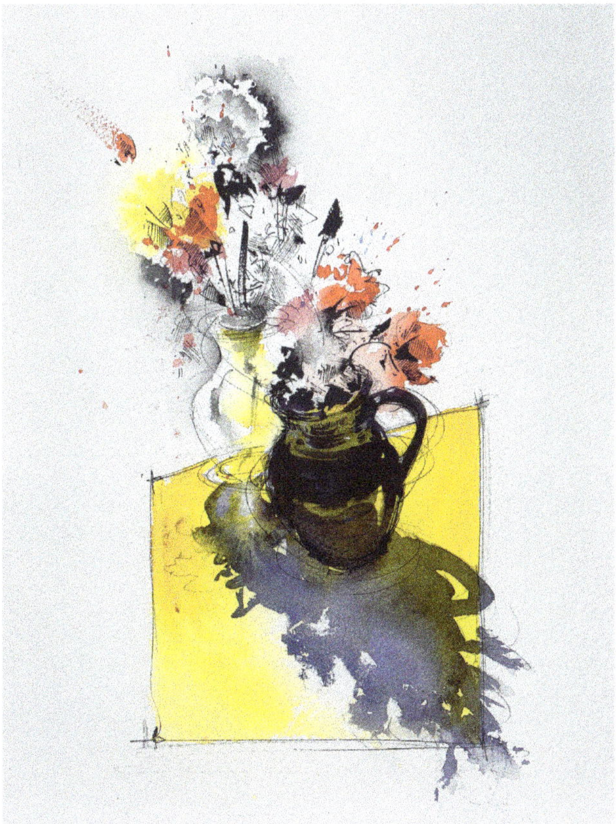

This sketch of two flower vases offers countless possibilities to capture light and shadow. The objects are ceramic and glass on a bright yellow table, so there are different reflective textures and colors. To contrast with the yellow table, I painted the shadows a cool lavender.

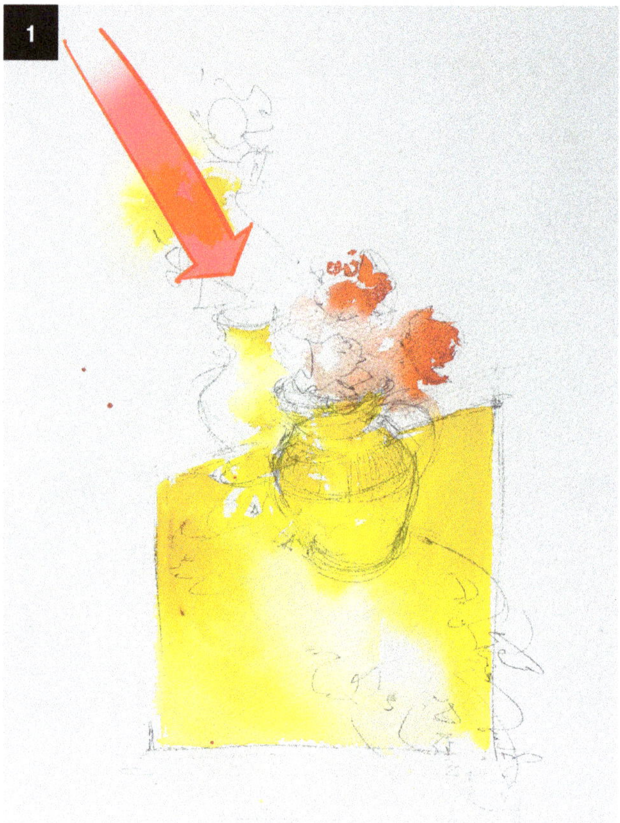

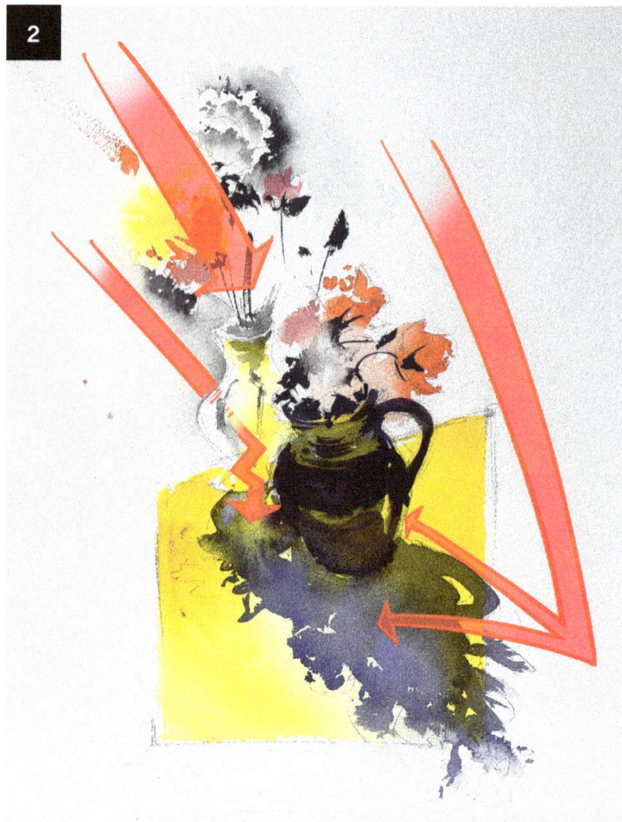

Sketching and Painting Process

1 | After lightly sketching the vases and flowers, I painted a wash of yellow for the table. Light is coming from the upper left, behind the objects. This creates a highlight on the yellow table, so I left this slightly lighter.

2 | Adding the lavender shadow is a chance to vary the density of this color, creating the illusion of light reflecting into and lightening the shadow. Sunlight also bounces onto the darkest parts of the ceramic vase, creating yellow highlights in an otherwise dark brown object. And finally, light refracts through the glass vase on the left. This light shines through the glass, creating a patch of light on the table in the shadow.

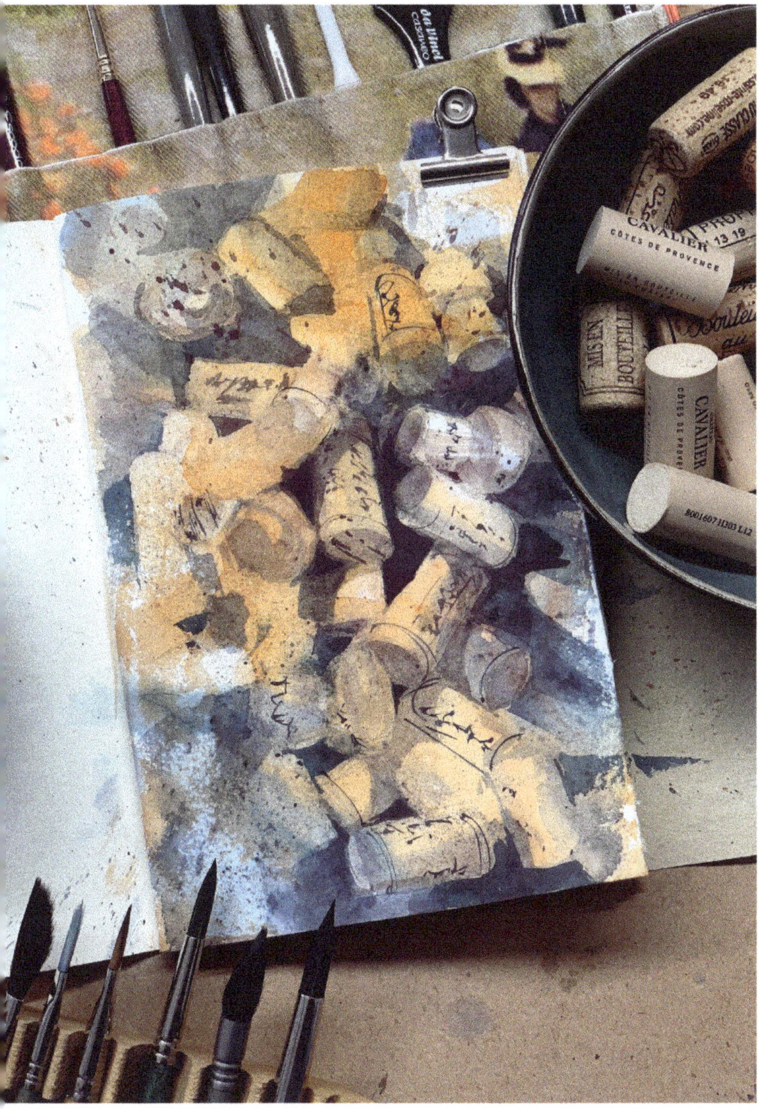

Sketching this bowl of wine corks provided a wonderful opportunity to play with warm and cool colors to create depth.

PAINTING AS TRANSLATION

When we sketch and paint, our goal should not be merely depicting a scene accurately. Rather, we're translating a feeling and a moment in time. If you've ever read word-for-word literal transcriptions of poetry from another language, you know how lifeless it can be. But in the hands of a great writer, someone who translates the emotions into the poetry of another language, they can sing. Don't worry so much about capturing accurate colors—be more free with your choices to get at the feeling of your subject.

Translate the emotions you feel into the paint on your page. Once you think of painting as translation, your images will soar.

> ***"A picture is first of all a product of the imagination of the artist; it must never be a copy."***
>
> —EDGAR DEGAS

STRUCTURE

I primarily draw and paint architecture, but ideas about structure apply to landscape, still life, and figure drawing as well.

We may be drawing on two-dimensional paper, but we can't forget that we are drawing three-dimensional objects, so it's best to think in terms of volume. Sketching the outline of something can be a nice exercise, but a more useful way to approach drawing is by depicting the structure and volume of objects, just as a sculptor would.

To do this we must think in terms of three-dimensional shapes. Rather than seeing a circle, square, or triangle, see a sphere, cube, and pyramid or wedge. These are the shapes we see around us every day that make up our environments. To give life to our sketches, thinking about these shapes this way is a great start.

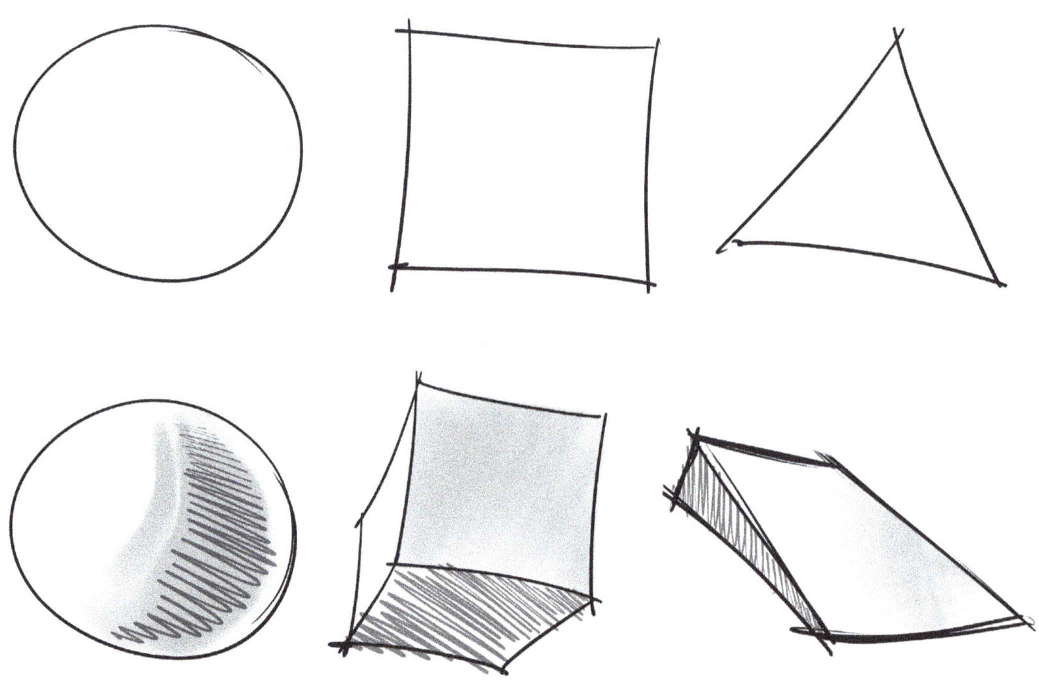

NEGATIVE SPACE

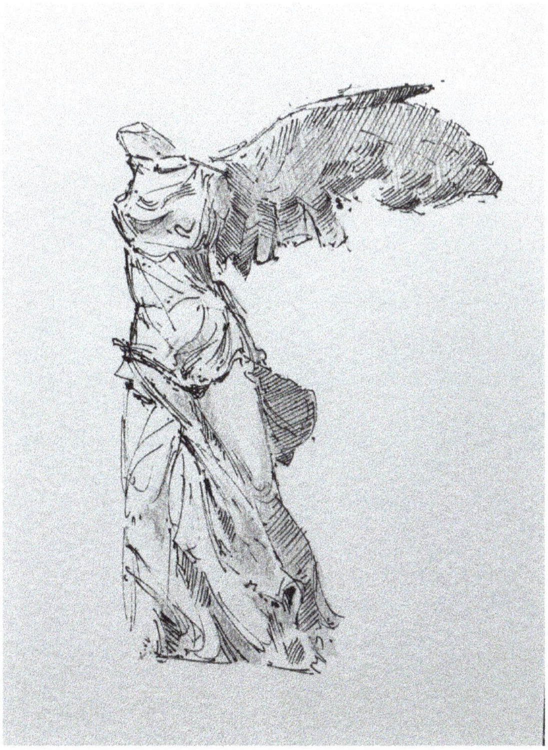

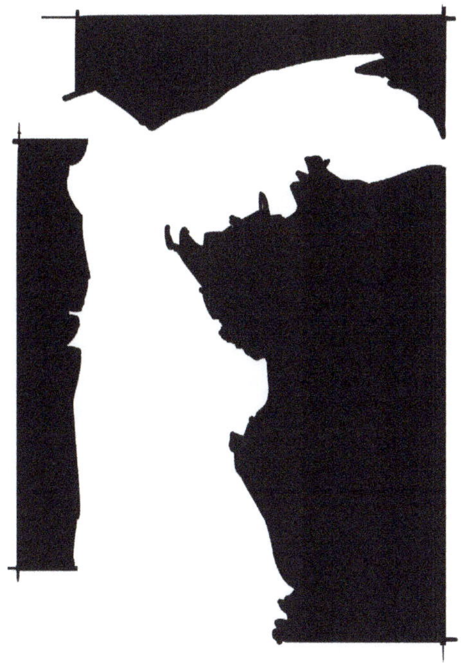

When you're first getting your head around an object to sketch, a useful tool is thinking about the negative space.

Negative space is everything your object isn't.

It's helpful to think about the shape of negative space as a tool to define your main subject. When sketching the roofline of a building, the negative space is the sky. When sketching a bridge, the negative space is the shape that fills in the arches.

Once you've drawn a certain object, and if it doesn't look quite right, shift your focus and check the shapes of the negative space. Learning how to see the negative space around your subject can become a powerful tool to help align the proportions of a sketch.

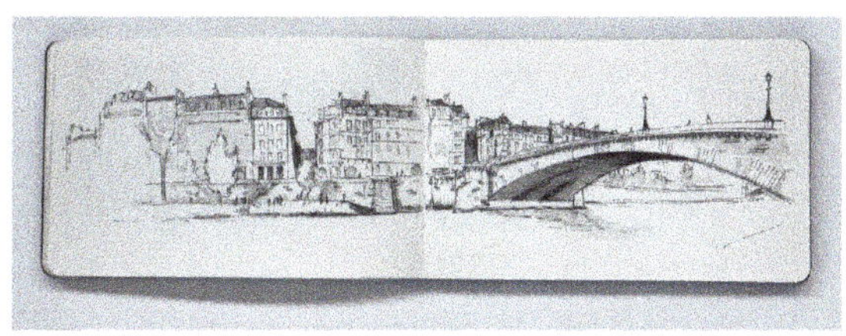

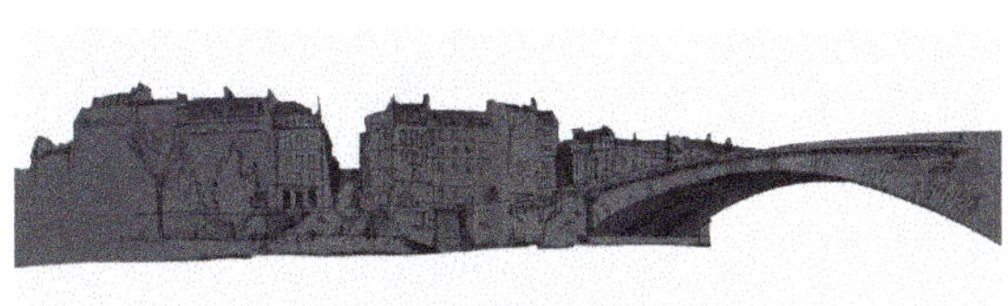

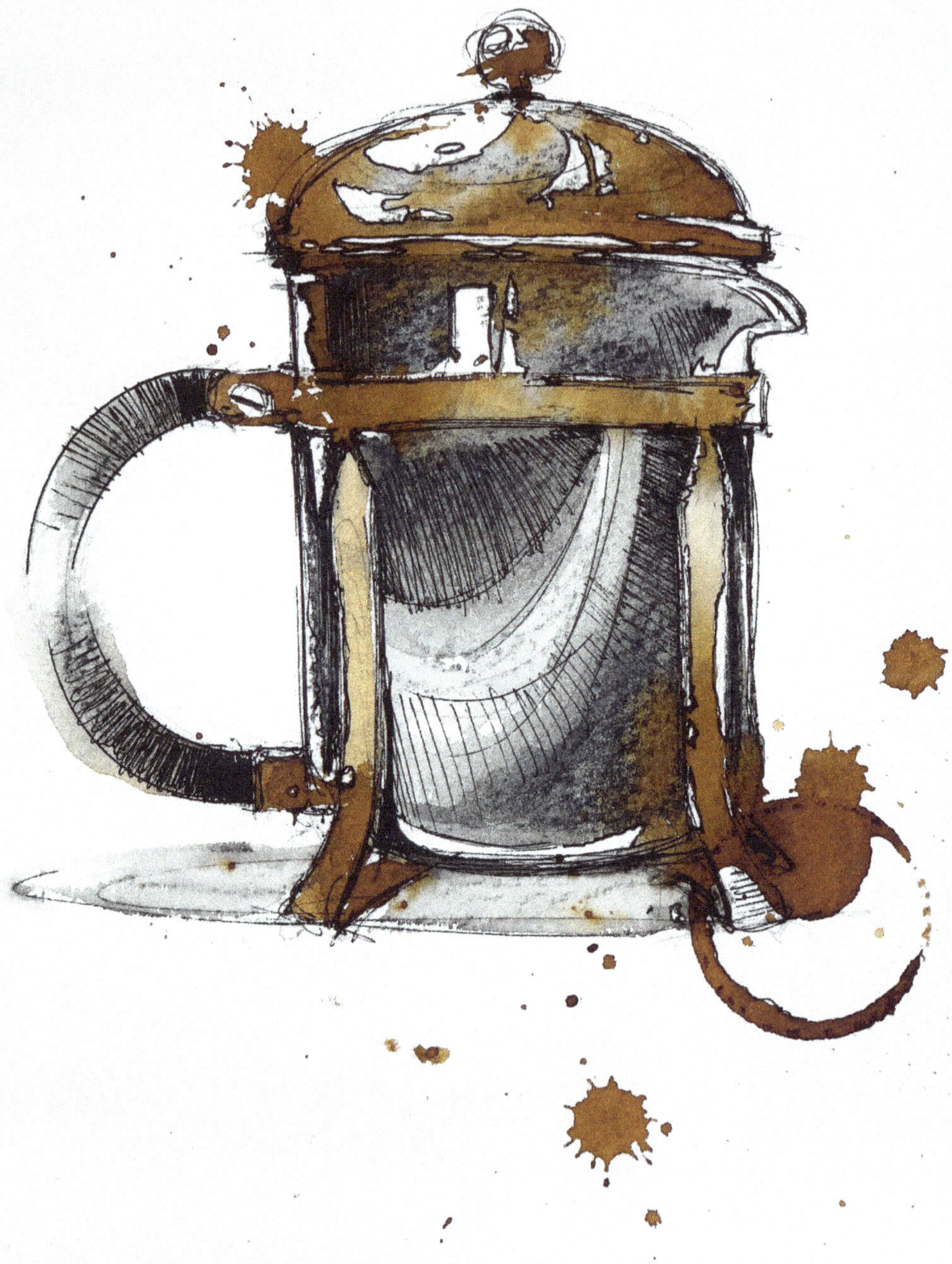

Not every still life has to be a bowl of fruit. My French press coffee pot, ink and graphite.

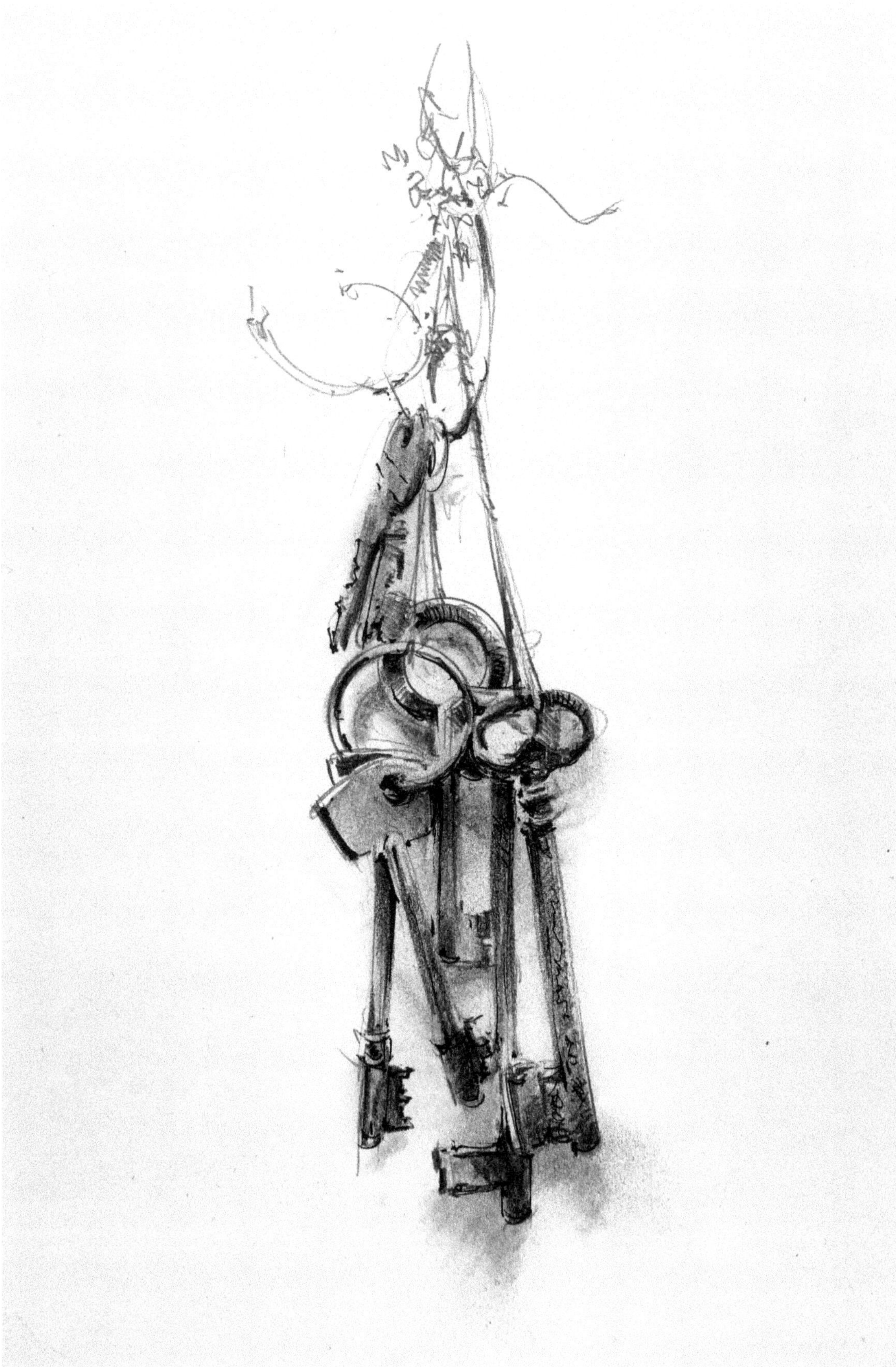

Old keys provide plenty of opportunities to play with light, shadow, and texture. Pencil and ink on paper.

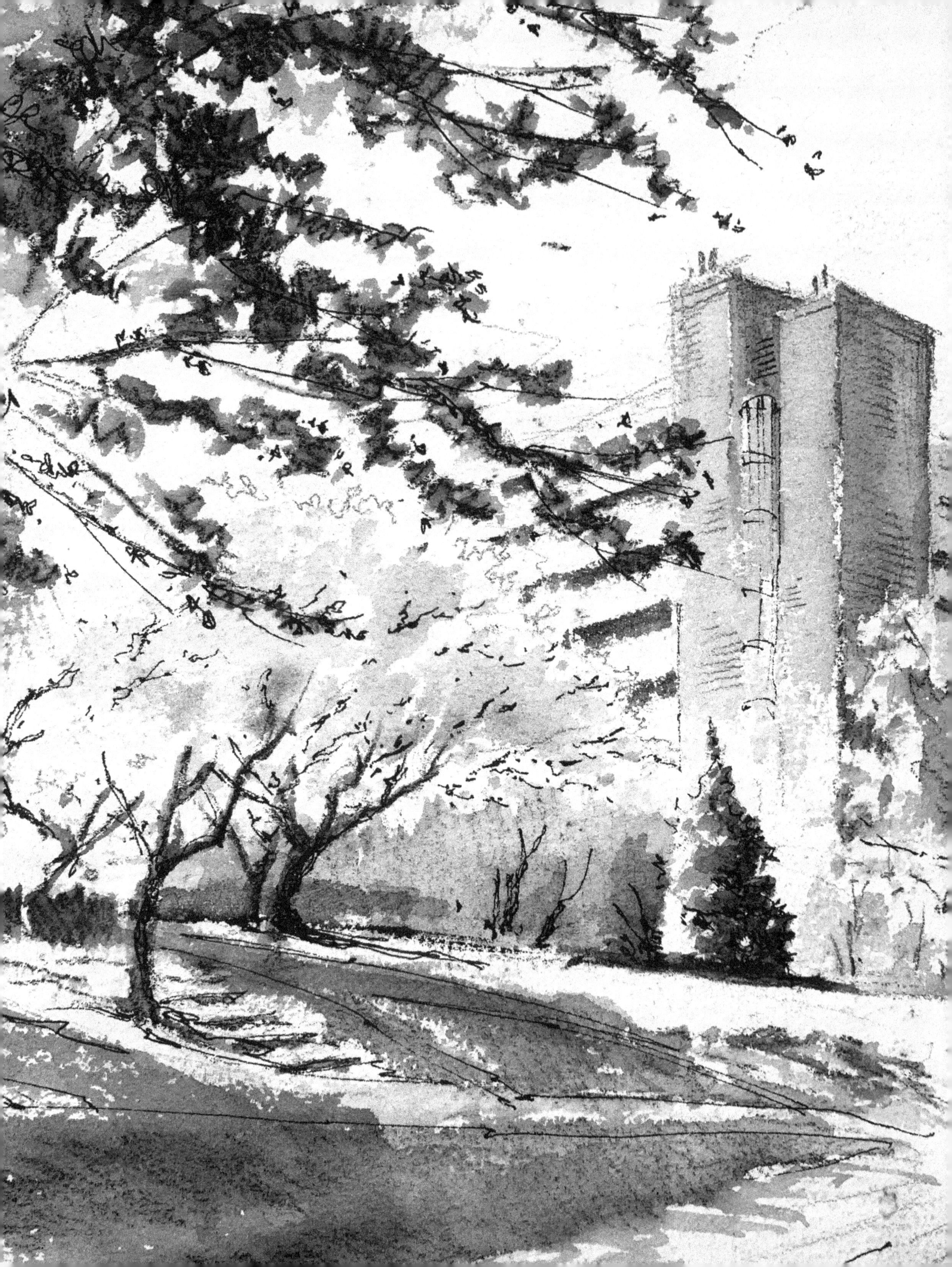

6

LANDSCAPES

Landscapes are entire worlds into which we can get blissfully lost. When a view takes your breath away, it's with pencil and pen, brush and paint, that we can catch the elusive and translate it onto the page. Creating a landscape is to see to infinity in a sketchbook, to stop time, and capture distance with a pen.

LANDSCAPE COMPOSITION

When sketching landscapes, composition is of utmost importance. We may not have a piece of architecture with linear perspective to draw our eye in, and there might not be an obvious center of focus. This makes the idea of composition even more important. Use composition like any other tool to bring clarity to your sketch and to ensure the story being told is what you intend.

It's helpful to do quick thumbnail sketches. Adjust your sketch to make a more pleasing composition.

Landscape composition uses all the same tools as other types of sketching. The idea is to create a center of focus with the rule of thirds, and contrasts of light and dark (read more about this in chapter 3, page 47). Create balance with large white clouds over a dark landscape or use natural elements such as waterfalls for strong vertical lines that contrast wonderfully with horizontal pools and rocks. Natural landscapes also give us particular lines that guide the viewer's eye into and around a piece. Roads and rivers are natural guides that invite us to follow their path.

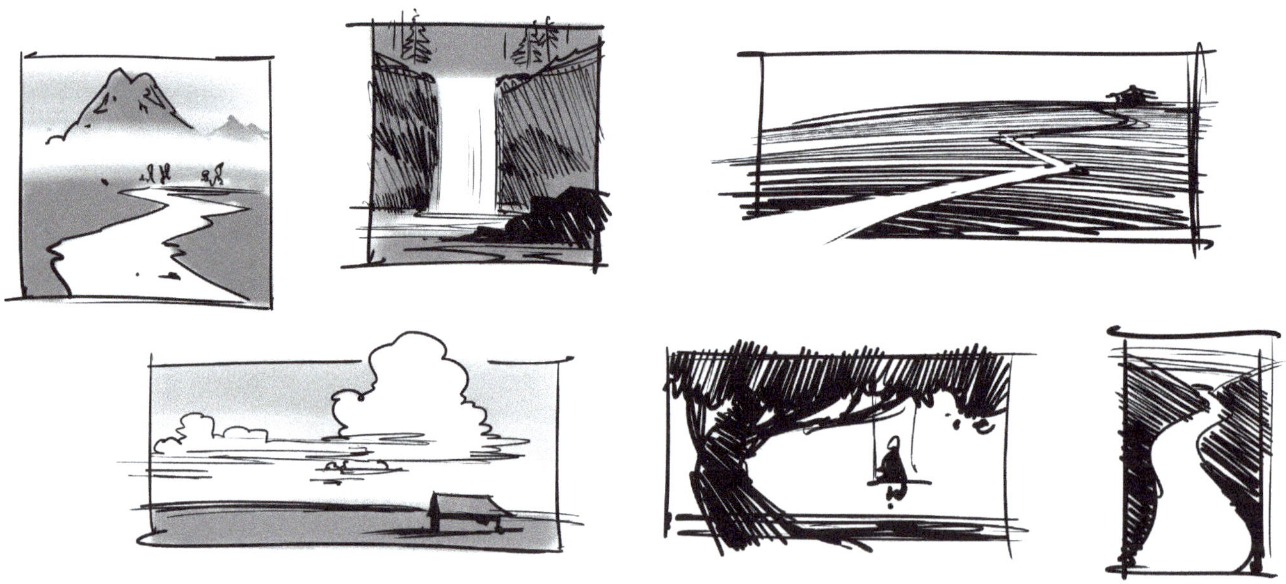

SKETCHING LANDSCAPES AND LINE WEIGHT

Line weight refers to how thick or thin any given line is. When sketching with only pencil or pen, we can vary our line weight to create depth. Foreground objects tend to have a heavier line weight, while objects in the distance will have a lighter line weight.

Use a few different fine liner pens with varying widths to change your line. Fountain pens are also the perfect tool for this, especially those with flexible nibs. These pens are designed for calligraphy and creating letters with a huge variety of thick and thin lines. While sketching with these pens, it's easy to vary the line width.

Even in incredibly detailed and complex drawings, if there is a variety of line weight, the viewer has no trouble reading the image. Conversely, when there is no difference in line weight throughout an image, we read a jumbled mess. If your sketches feel heavy, this might be why.

I often sketch foreground objects in pen and use pencil for objects in the distance. The pencil naturally has a lighter weight. With just two tools, pen and pencil, I can achieve basic atmospheric perspective.

Along with line weight, the amount of detail we include or exclude acts as a form of atmospheric perspective. Objects closer to us tend to be more detailed, while those farther away are less defined.

These techniques are a way to bring an image into focus and create a center of focus. Along with ideas discussed in chapter 3 (page 47), we can combine what we know about perspective and details to enhance our center of focus. Images should contain a variety of levels of detail.

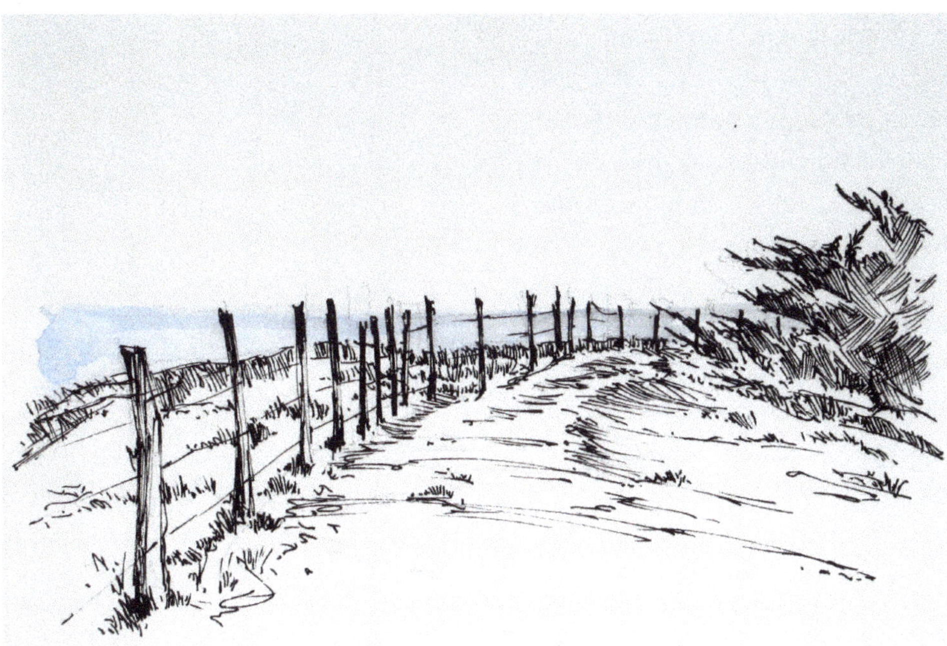

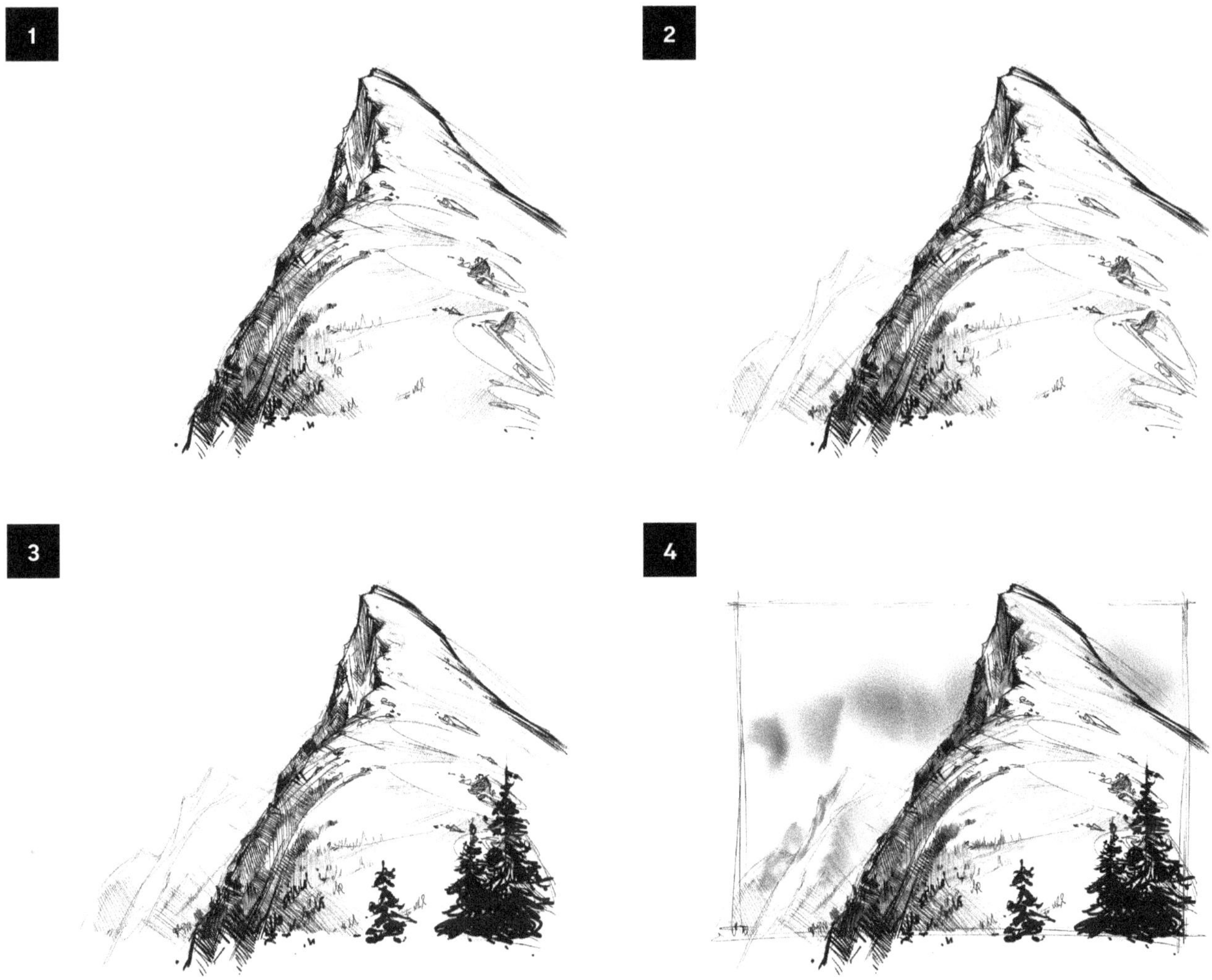

Sketching Process

SKETCHING A MOUNTAIN SCENE

1 | Sketch the mountain in the foreground with ink, making it more prominent.

2 | Sketch the background mountains with pencil. Pencil naturally has a lighter line weight than ink, so these mountains appear to recede into the distance.

3 | Use an even heavier line to sketch foreground trees, creating even more depth. These elements are closest to us, so they appear more saturated and defined.

4 | Final shading with a soft pencil brings everything together.

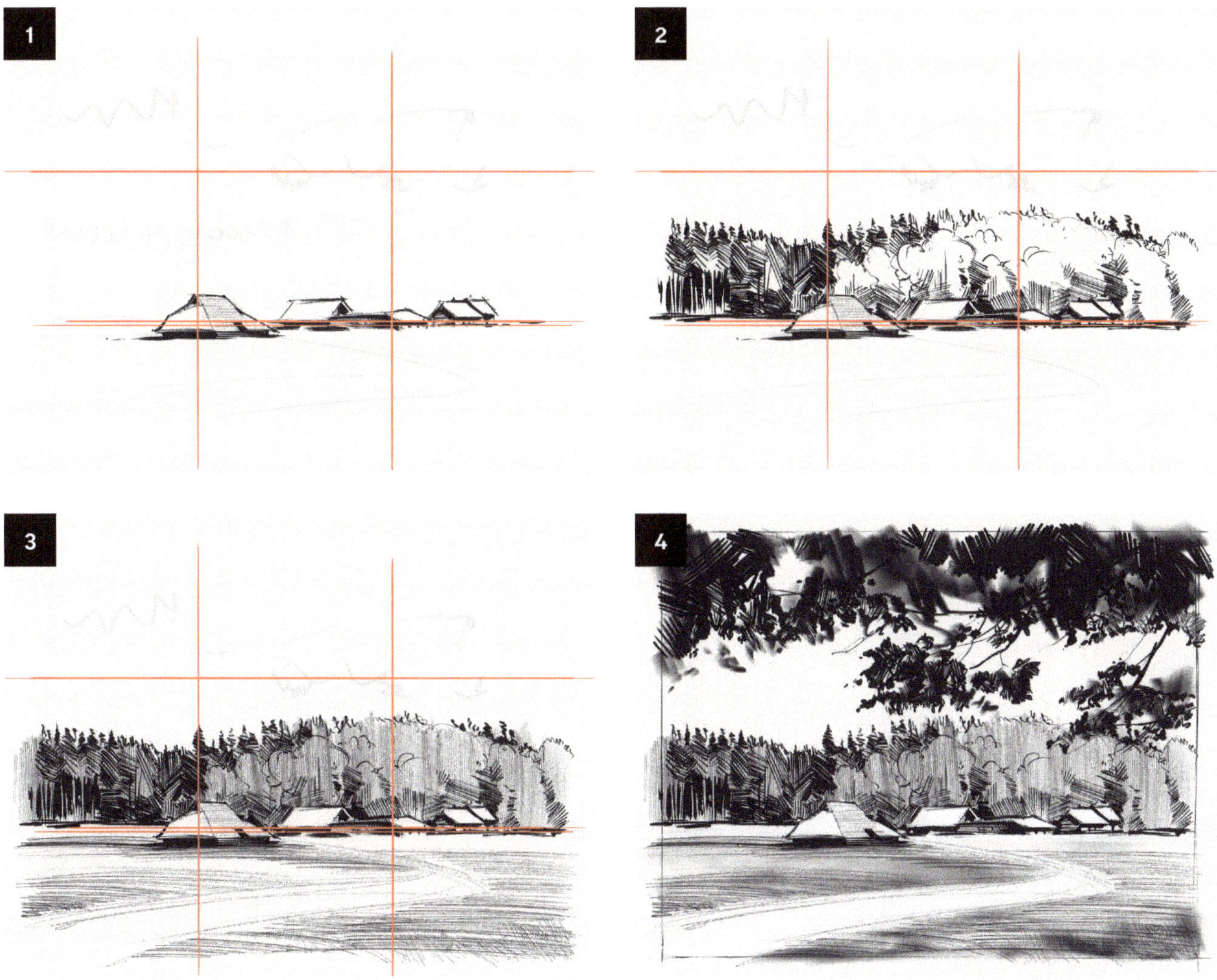

Sketching Process

SKETCHING A RURAL SCENE

For this sketch of a rural scene in Latvia, I used the rule of thirds to initially compose the drawing. This scene is made up of roughly three horizontal bands: the lower third is an open field, the middle third is a farm and background forest, and the upper third is the sky and a layer of foreground branches.

1 | I wanted the farmhouse to be the center of focus, so I placed that in the lower left section.

2 | Fill the middle third in with a dark curtain of background forest.

3 | To enhance the contrast and keep the farmhouse as the center of focus, darken everything around these buildings. This separates the farm from its background and keeps it from getting lost in the trees.

4 | Next, add foreground branches in the upper third of the image. These act as a proscenium arch would in a theater, framing the image.

Shading is added to pull everything into focus. Darkening the foreground branches has the effect of reducing their detail. This forces the focus back to the farmhouse, which now is the lightest part of the composition.

ATMOSPHERIC PERSPECTIVE

Creating landscapes is a wonderful opportunity to use washes and glazes of color to depict atmospheric perspective.

Along with linear perspective, atmospheric perspective is a powerful tool for depicting depth. As objects move farther away from us, their colors become muted and tip slightly blue. We can see this clearly in rows of mountains receding into the distance. We can use this concept in our landscape paintings.

Watercolor likes to be laid down with lightest colors and washes first and darker areas at the end. Because of its transparent nature, darker values will cover lighter ones. When we look at a landscape scene, the lightest tones and values are usually those furthest away from us. So, when sketching and painting with watercolor, start with what is furthest away and work toward the foreground.

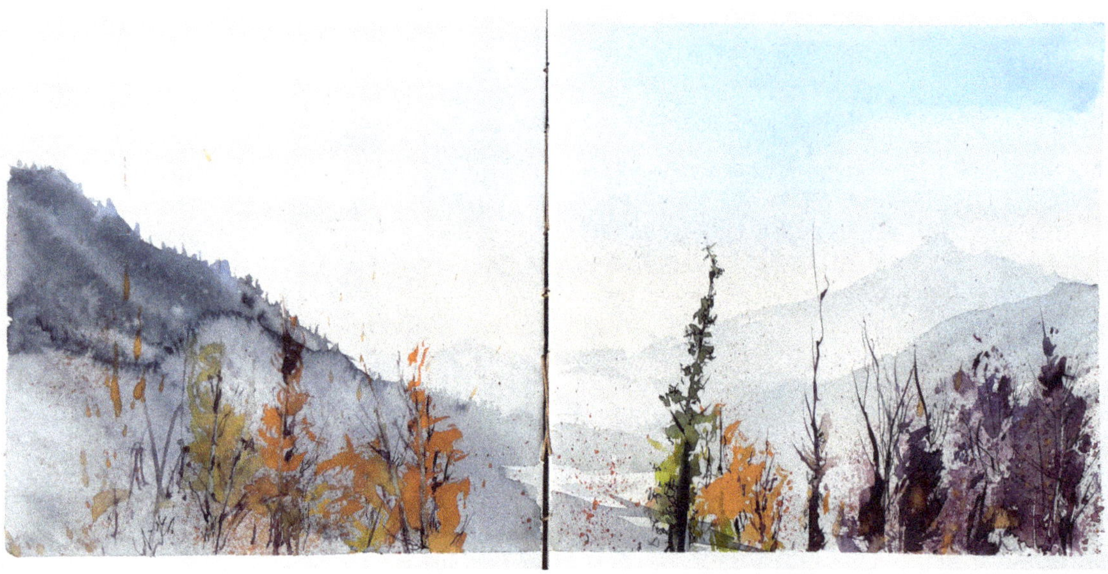

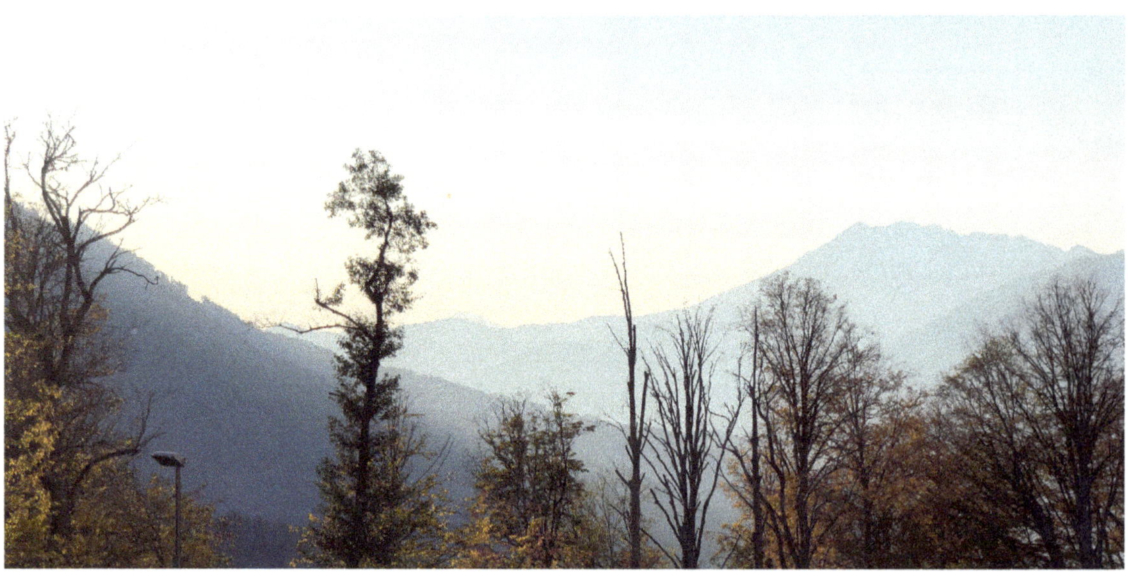

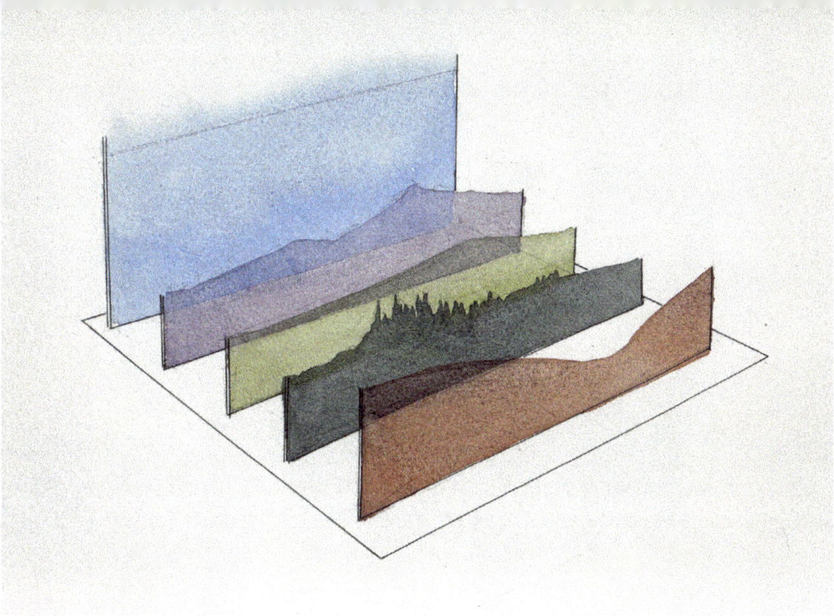

When painting landscapes think in terms of layers. Work from background to foreground, light to dark, and from cool colors to warm colors.

We can approach a scene like this with a limited palette of five colors: blue, purple, light green, dark green, and brown. These colors can change according to what we want to depict, but the idea is to move from cool to warm tones as we paint from background to foreground.

Using cool and warm colors will create a sense of depth, but by adjusting the texture of our colors, the illusion becomes more complete. Cool background colors that have softer edges will appear slightly out of focus. The warm colors of foreground elements will have hard edges.

To soften the edges of a color, use a wet-on-wet technique (read more about this in chapter 9, page 125). By soaking your paper and then letting it dry somewhat, the softness of the edges can be fine-tuned. Use this technique for distant mountains. As we move to foreground elements, our colors get warmer, and by painting on dry paper we can create hard-edged subjects.

By combining color temperature and edge definition we have everything we need to create convincing atmospheric perspective.

Working from cool background colors to warm foreground colors creates an illusion of depth. The depth is further enhanced by softening the edges of background colors.

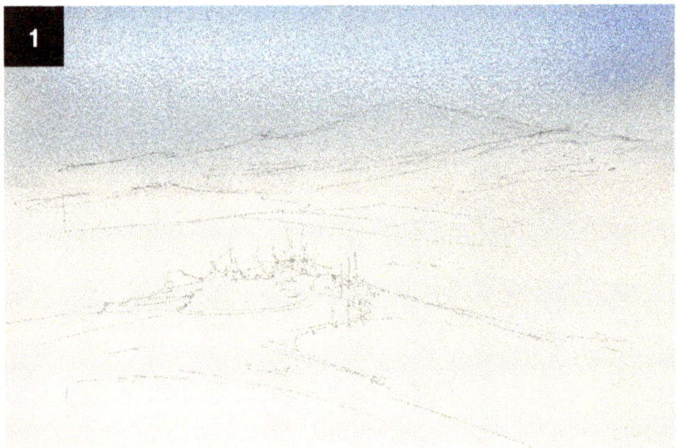

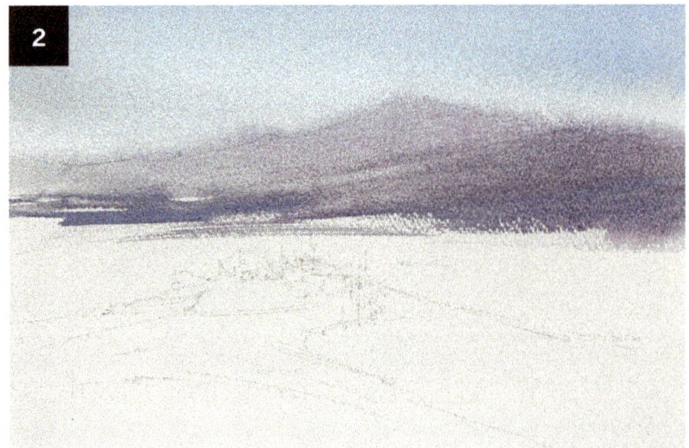

Sketching and Painting Process

1 | Sketch the scene lightly in pencil, blocking out hills, trees, and other major portions of the landscape. The lightest part of a composition is usually the sky, so we'll begin with that. Paint is applied on wet paper to create a soft blend of color.

2 | Once the blue of the sky is dry, wet the paper again and apply faint washes of light purple for distant mountains. Painting onto wet paper softens the edges of these mountains and makes them appear even farther away. As we work our way from distant background to foreground, the next layer will be a slightly darker blue for midrange mountains.

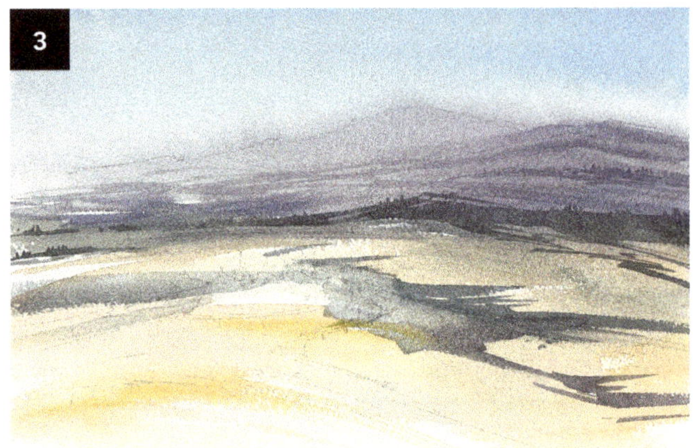

3 | As we are moving down the paper from top to bottom, try to imagine this scene coming to life as it moves closer to us in space. Now we can warm up our colors, adding pale greens and some raw sienna.

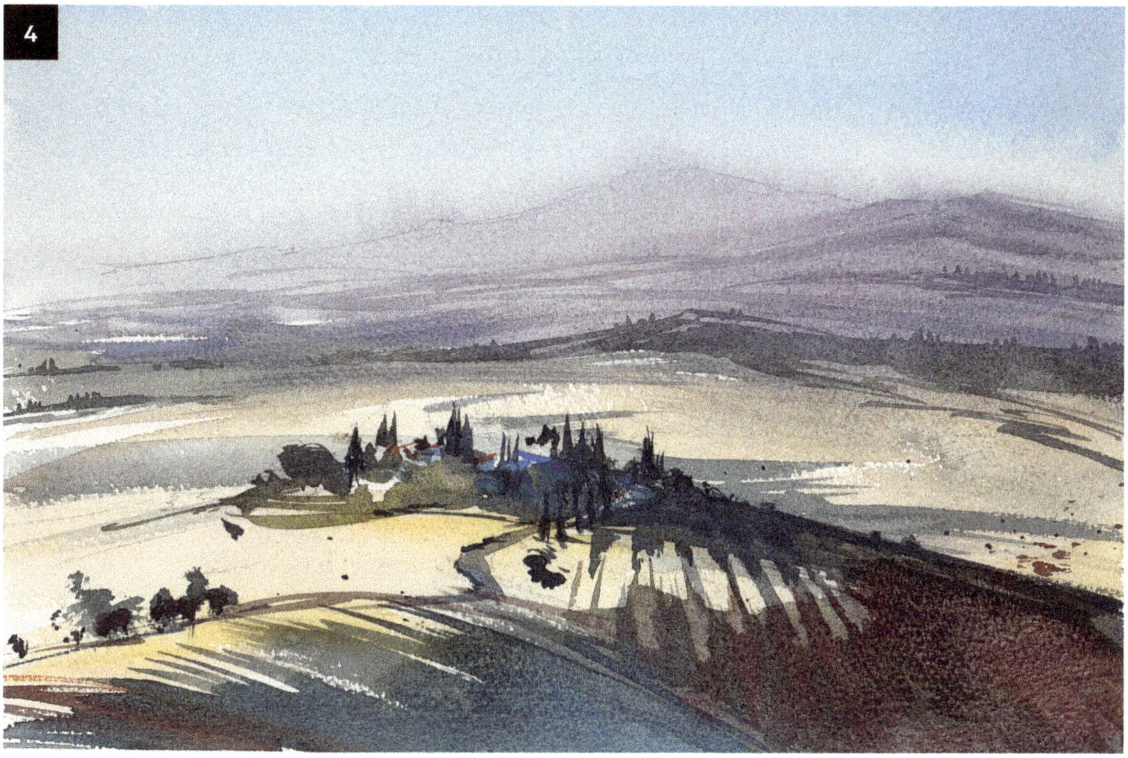

4 | We're almost to the foreground, so it's time to add saturated greens and browns. Until this point, details have been fairly loose. Now trees and other objects start coming into focus.

For final touches, add the darkest pigments. This is where our most saturated colors will be: dark greens, grays, and blacks for details such as trees and buildings.

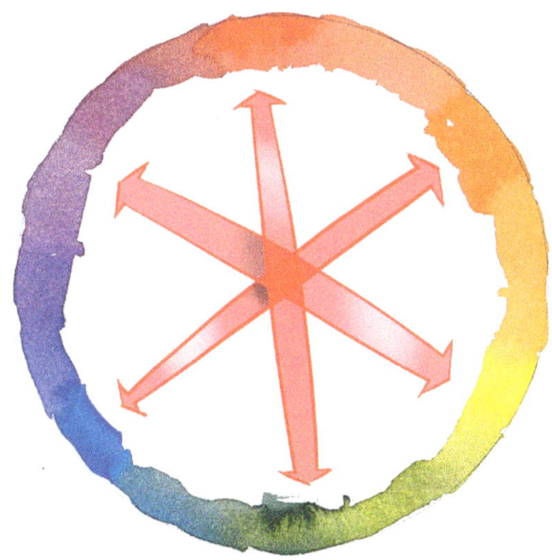

Creating Depth with Complementary Colors

Using complementary colors is another powerful tool to create depth and contrast on our page.

Complementary colors are colors on opposite sides of the color wheel from each other: red and green, purple and yellow, orange and blue. By placing one color in the background, and its opposite, or complement, in the foreground, depth is created. These colors work wonderfully together, but they also keep each other at arm's length. That arm's length creates the illusion of depth on the page.

CREATING DEPTH AND CONTRAST

One way to think about sketching landscapes is like layers of curtains in a theater. Stage sets often need to convey great depth but are restricted by the confines of a small stage. We're doing the same thing here. The page of our sketchbook may be small, but we need to concentrate this vast expanse of landscape into this small space. We must push the colors in ways that help tell this story.

The use of complementary colors is another powerful tool to create depth and contrast on our page. Purple mountains and bright yellow foreground fields (1) naturally create the illusion of depth in a simple and effective way.

I used the same technique in this painted sketch (2) done in the hills above Fabriano, Italy. Morning clouds filled the valley, so the distant mountains were barely visible. This row of foreground trees became the perfect complement to a misty background. The illusion of depth is created with the contrast of dark trees in sharp focus, versus the soft, muted colors of the valley.

1

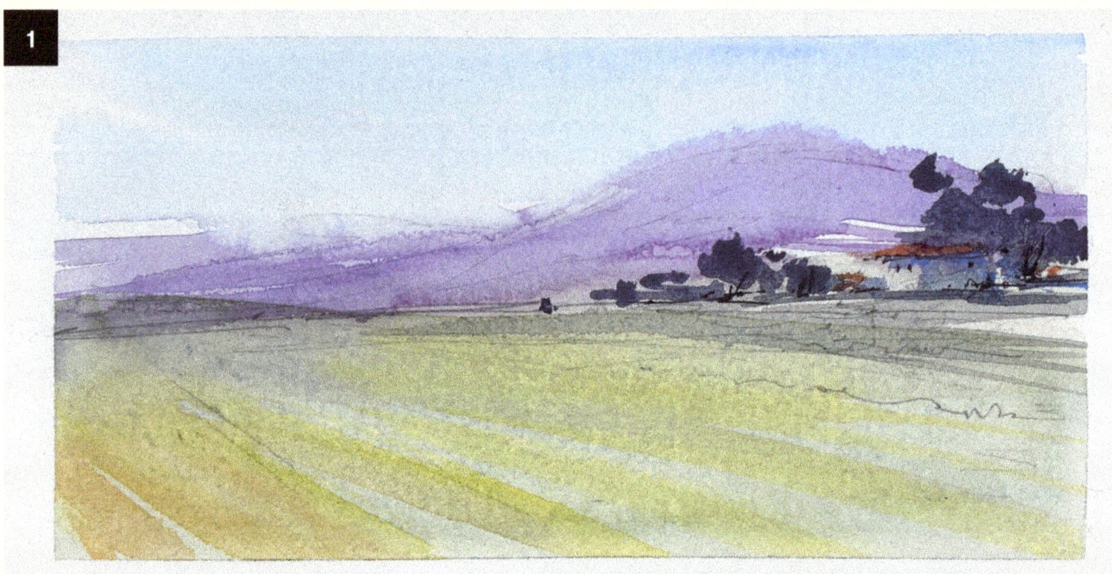

2

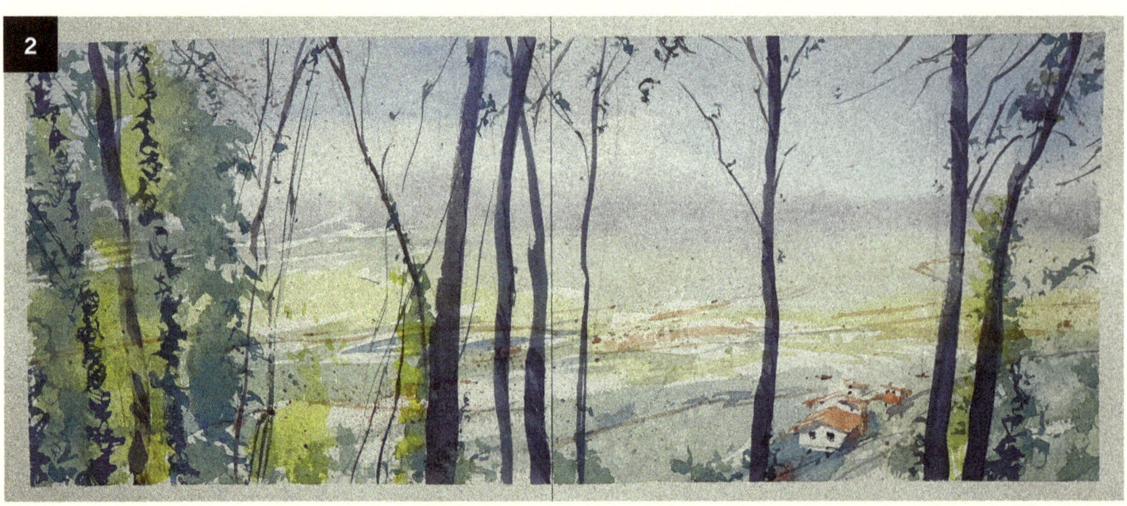

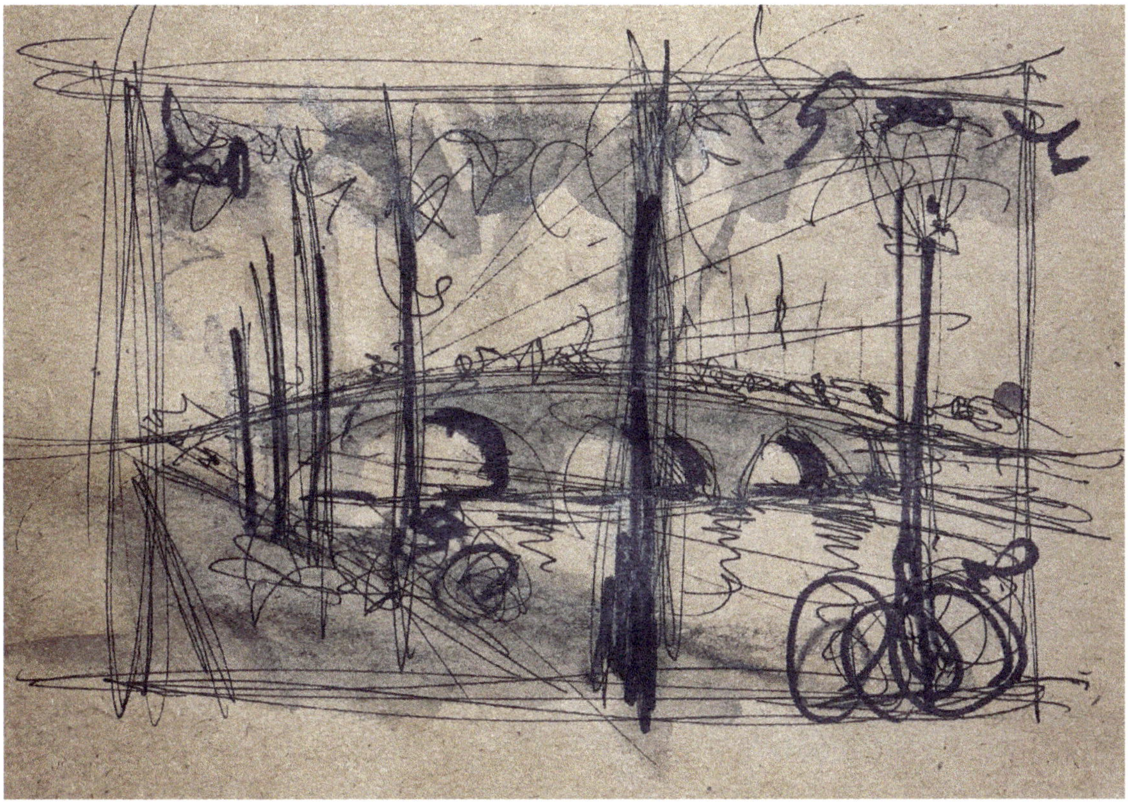

Creating Depth with Layers

Another way to create depth in a landscape is sketching and painting with layers. Objects placed in the foreground, mid-ground, and background instantly create the illusion of depth. In this thumbnail sketch, I worked out layers using just a few values–darkest for the closest objects, medium gray for the middle distance, and the paper color for objects furthest away. This is atmospheric perspective in its simplest form.

The Beauty of Atmospheric Perspective

When painting with watercolor, depicting atmospheric perspective is a beautiful way to create depth and a sense of distance. Many artists have only this one tool with them when they paint. Their linear perspective might be inaccurate, their sense of proportion might be off, but if they can depict a hazy receding distance, the viewer can't help but sigh at the beauty.

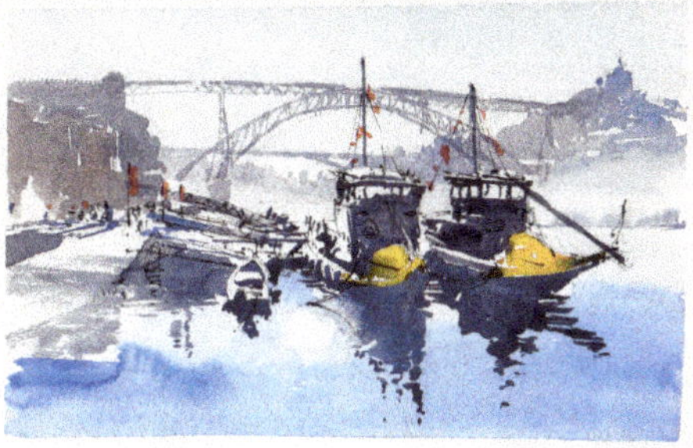

DRAW VERBS, NOT NOUNS

The hardest thing is getting what's in front of you onto the page. But what's in front of you? Do you want to depict a scene accurately? There are many ways to define accurate. Does this mean an accurate depiction of the colors, the light, the activity, or the mood? And how do you depict a mood? How best to depict joy, or heat, or wind? A trick I learned while storyboarding is to draw verbs, not nouns. Draw "crash" or "throw" or "punch."

And while there's a different language to landscapes, sometimes stepping away from the dogma of nouns—building, tree, reflection—can be freeing. Sometimes I want to depict a rhythm, or the flow of a certain piece of architecture. I'm not thinking about nouns like arch, bridge, or rooftop. I'm looking at the relationship of these shapes, the bulk of a building, how a roofline *weighs* on a wall, and how a tree *leans*.

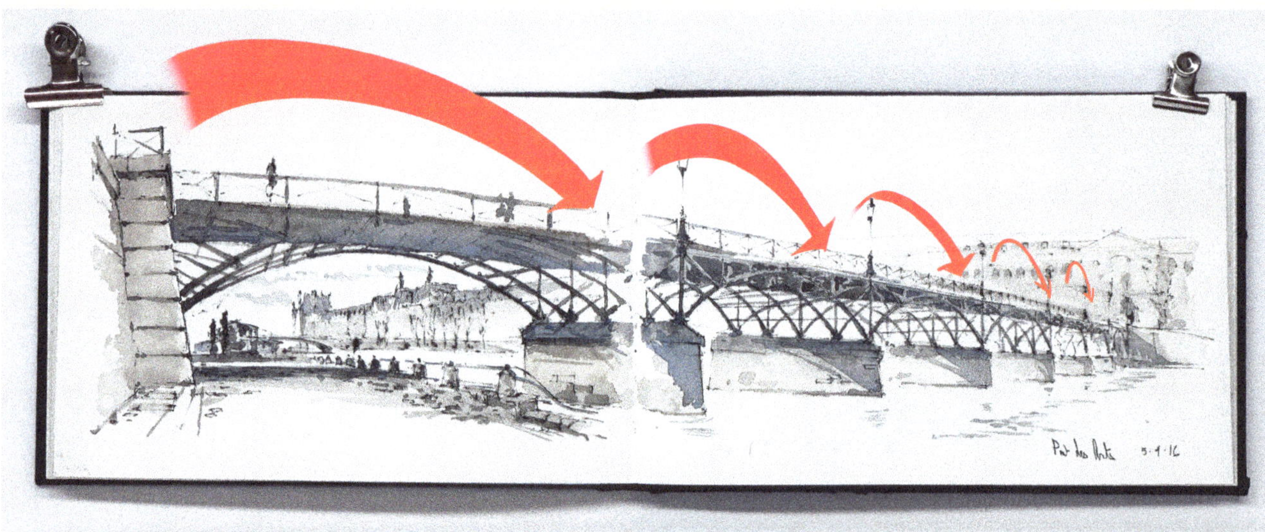

This bridge skips across the river like a stone skipping across a pond.

KNOWING WHEN TO STOP

Knowing when a sketch or painting is done can be one of the most elusive skills to learn. This usually comes about with years of practice and, unfortunately, by ruining many paintings. There's a line you cross, and once crossed, you immediately know you've gone too far. But to approach this invisible finish line and stop just short of it is a tricky skill to master.

When I know I'm getting close to finishing a piece, I listen for a quiet voice in my head that begins to whisper, "you're almost done." This voice never shouts, but it is insistent. It will just quietly say, "stop." It's easy to miss this voice. It's also easy to ignore. But when you carry on and paint those extra brush-strokes that are a bridge too far, that voice says, "See? I told you. Maybe you'll listen next time." And there will always be a next time. The next sketch, the next painting, tomorrow or next week. This voice is one to listen for. It's elusive and hard to recognize, but once you know what you're listening for, you'll be able to hear it, and it will become familiar. Get to know this voice. For each of you it will be different. This whisper can be your best friend.

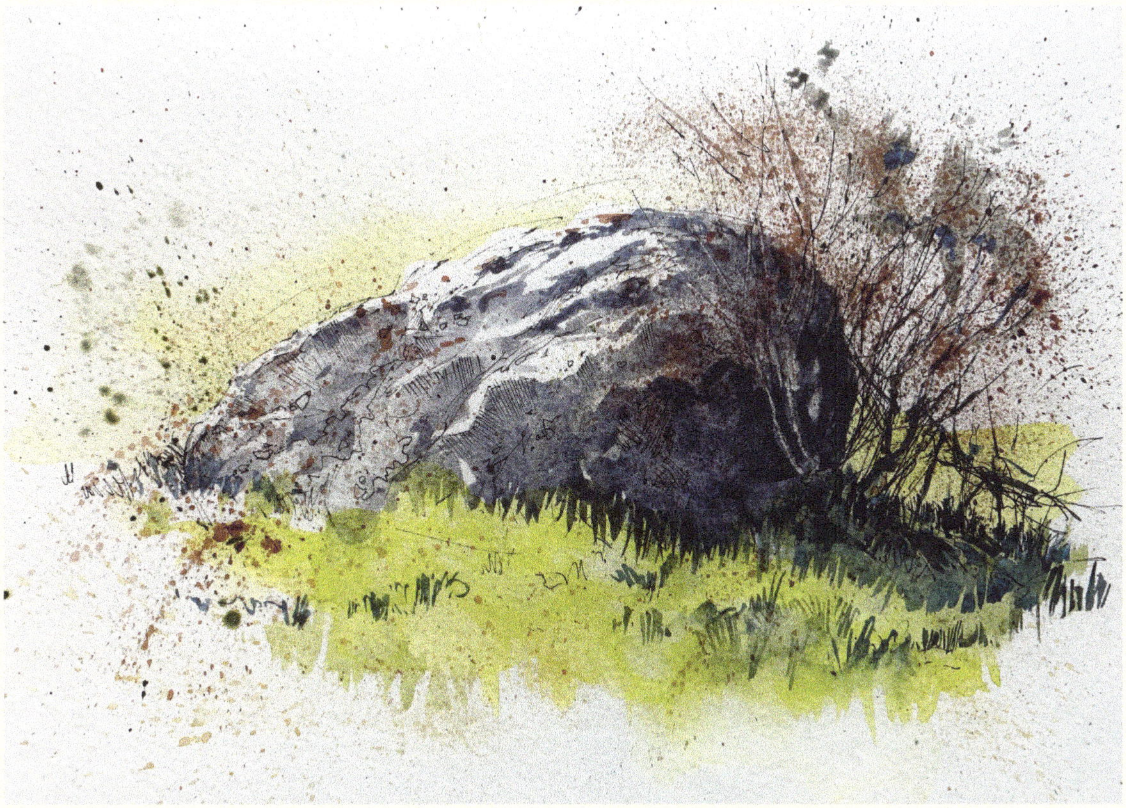

Springtime sunshine in Northern California. It can be tempting to get caught up in details and textures and just keep going, but we must listen for the voice telling us the painting is done. More details can always be added, but they're harder to take away. So set your sketch aside and come back to it later. Sometimes the perspective of time can tell us that our piece is done.

7

ARCHITECTURE

I love sketching and painting architecture. When I moved to Paris, I fell in love with the way light defines the shape and forms of the old-world buildings. Every detail suddenly became a handhold for sunlight or a refuge for shadows. Dormer windows, balconies, rooflines—all of these intricate details give personality to a building.

AN OVERVIEW OF BASIC FORMS

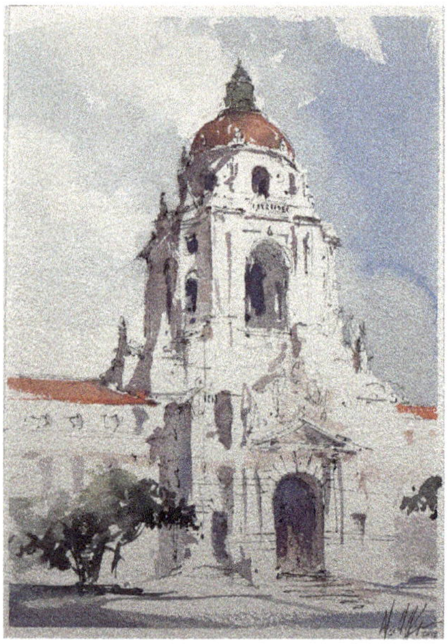

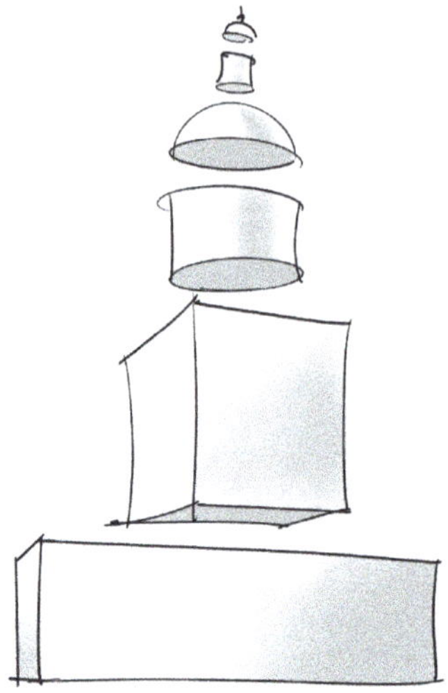

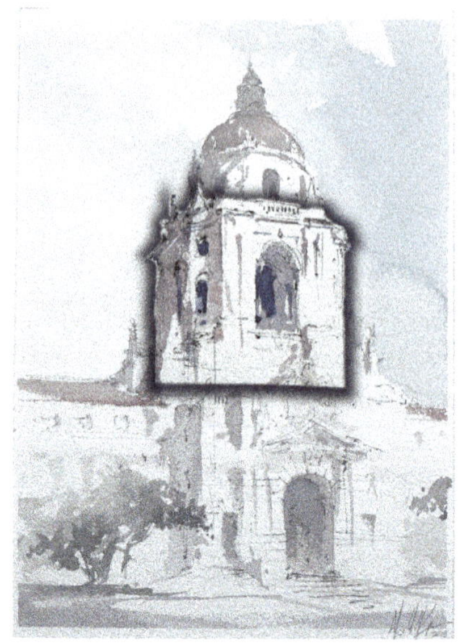

Most of the architecture we see around us is made up of cubes, cylinders, and triangular wedges. Beneath all the details that are so fun to sketch, we must learn to see these basic shapes.

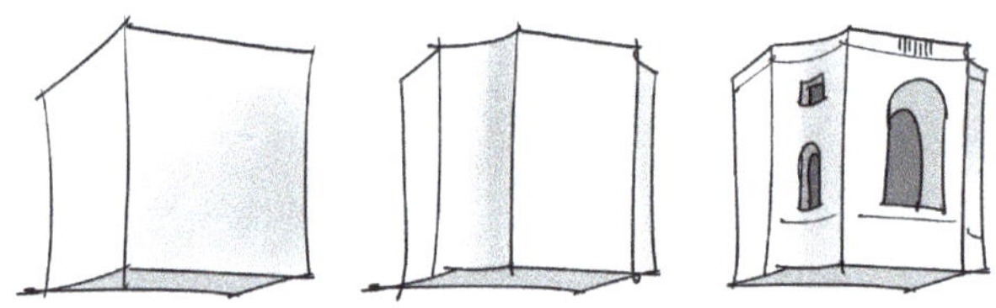

Large Shapes First

When sketching architecture, it's important to sketch in the large shapes first. With practice you'll strip away details and see the basic form at the heart of a building. Most buildings are cubes of varying size. It's important to learn how to draw in perspective so we can render these cubes and boxes in their proper proportions.

This building reminds me of a wedding cake with its stacks of layers. It seems complex at first, but once dissected, it breaks into manageable chunks:

- The building has a flat rectangular base.
- In the center of this base is a box.
- On top of that is a cylinder.
- And finally, a dome.
- On top of the dome is another cylinder, and a tiny dome.

Once we see these basic shapes, we can add smaller details, carve shapes into them, and punch out archways.

The small box below the larger dome is filled with Corinthian columns, cornices, and archways. These details can be intimidating, but our process of breaking it down into shapes is the same. This box has curved notches carved out of each corner. The central archway is placed in the center of one face. The columns are stuck on the outside of this shape.

We can continue sketching the building in this fashion, becoming more precise in our details.

ROOFS

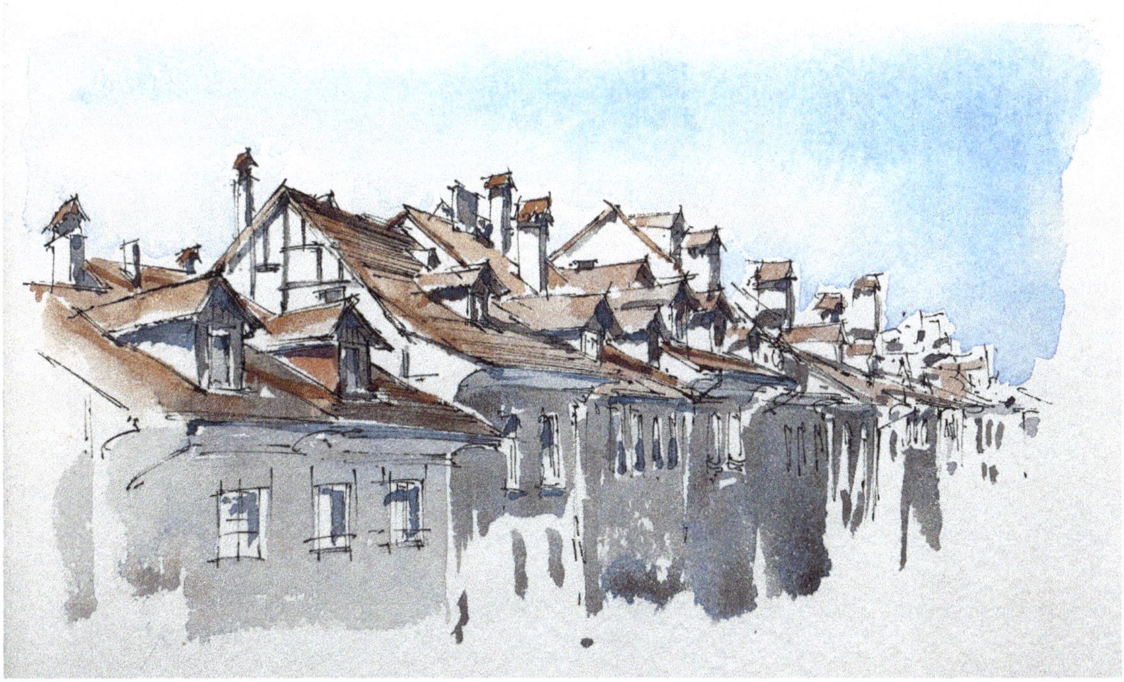

Drawing roofs is perhaps the trickiest part of sketching architecture. Roofs have unusual angles that point to different vanishing points. There are dormer windows, chimneys, and skylights—countless details that can be fascinating, but can also trip us up.

Sketching Process

Just like with the main body of a building, we want to concentrate on the large shapes first.

1 | Some rooftops are shaped like a trapezoid. Draw a basic rectangular cube with a trapezoid-shaped roof.

2 | Add chimneys. These chimneys follow the same perspective lines as the building itself, with the roof leaning back. These roofs aim at their own vanishing points.

1

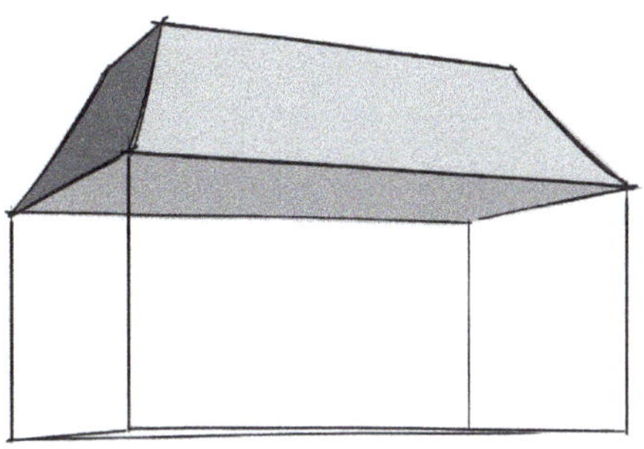

2

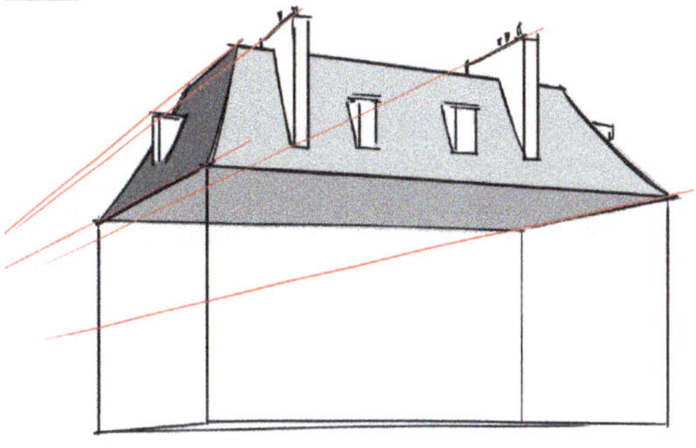

ARCHITECTURE

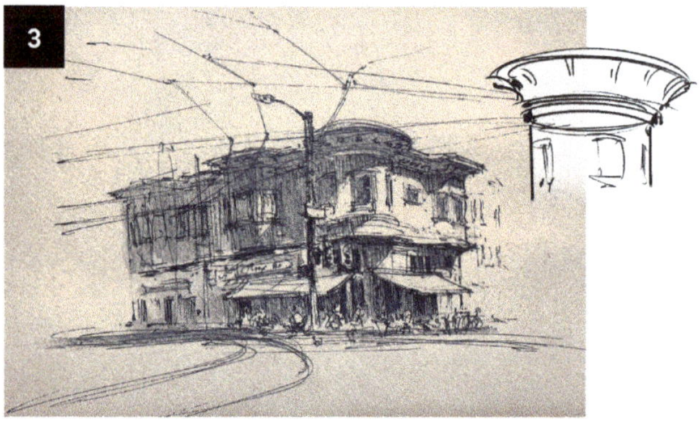

3 | It's important to draw roofs to scale. Drawing roofs too large is a common mistake. Very few buildings are wearing a ten-gallon cowboy hat. Most are sporting a fedora or stylish cap that complements the overall appearance. The wide-brimmed roof of this San Francisco building looks like a stylish futuristic hat.

ACTION FIGURES

It's helpful to think in terms of action when sketching roofs. What is the roof doing? Is it weighing down the building? Slouching like a lazy cat? Standing tall and inquisitive? Thinking of what the roof may be doing helps infuse energy and personality into your sketch. Each line you draw takes on this action. It's a personal choice as to how cartoonish to make a sketch, but even drawing realistically, thinking in terms of action verbs can be a secret ingredient to add life.

A Crown of Personality

If buildings are characters, roofs are often a fancy hat, a piece of flourish perched on top, adding uniqueness. Roofs are the architectural equivalent of hats at a royal wedding.

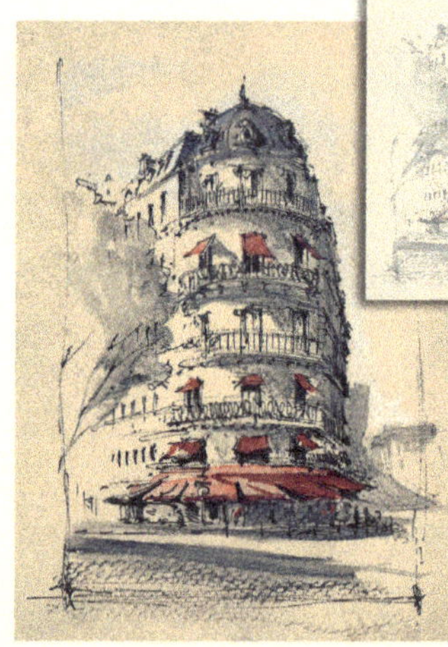

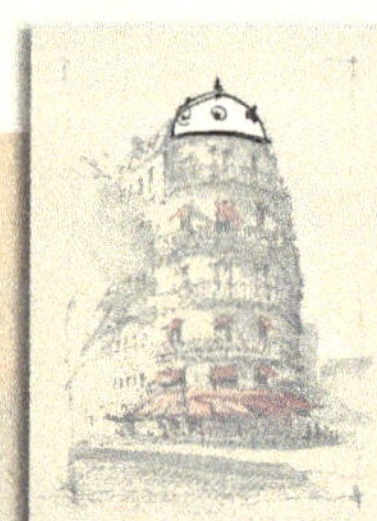

The domed roof on this building looks like a small beanie. Notice how small it is in relation to the rest of the building.

DOORWAYS AND ARCHES

Doorways and arches help ground a building and connect it to the life on the street. Usually these are inset into the face of a building and follow the same rules of perspective as the rest of the shapes.

Doorways are entries into a space. They can contain deep shadows and hints of another world inside. These will often be the darkest part of your sketch.

1 | Doorways follow the same rules of perspective as the buildings they are a part of. Their basic shape may be rectangular, but they also have volume and depth, so they should be drawn using two-point perspective.

2 | Doorways are built for humans, so they can't be smaller than a person. Doorways and entrances connect buildings with people, and it's this connection that is crucial when it comes to scale. Make sure your doorways are the correct scale relative to life on the street. Doorways can also be grand and imposing, like the entrance to a cathedral, but again, it's the connection to figures in your sketch that tells a story of harmony.

1

2

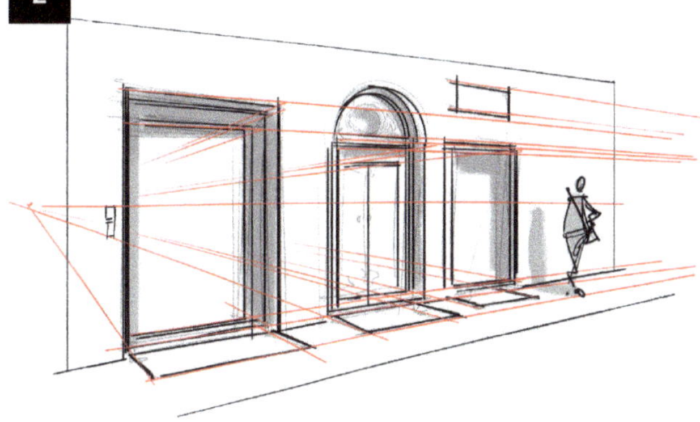

WINDOWS

I'm much more interested in what's going on at street level and the intricacies of rooflines than I am with the middle floors of a building. In most of my sketches, it's the café that is the star of the show. The middle floors are a supporting character. But if supporting characters don't do their job, our whole production can grind to a halt.

Window placement on a building is much more important than what those windows look like (see details in chapter 2, page 40). Windows need to be good little soldiers, standing in line and maintaining their place. Any variation on the exact shape or outline of individual windows is less important. Not all members of a marching band are the same height, but if someone is out of step you will see it in an instant.

Sketching Process

1 | Draw rows of windows on a building, making sure they are aligned. Their placement is more important than their individual details.

2 | Sketch in the windows. Windows can be indicated with very few details, as long as they align with each other.

3 | Windows often have frames, ledges, and balustrades that protrude from the face of a building, while the windows themselves are inset into the facade. It's interesting to know some of the complex geometry, but we're not making technical blueprints, we're sketching. And our sketches are telling a story.

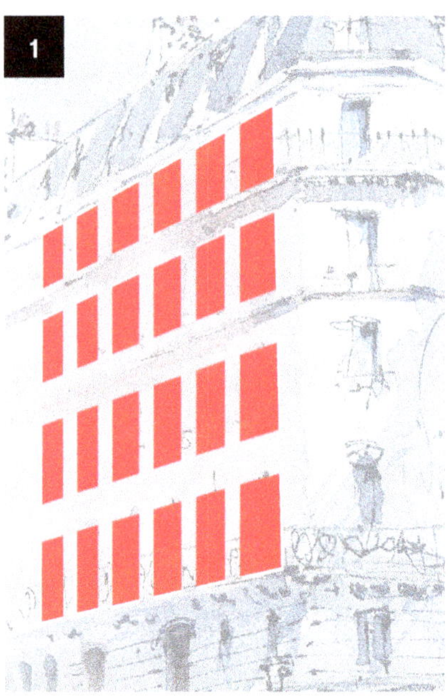

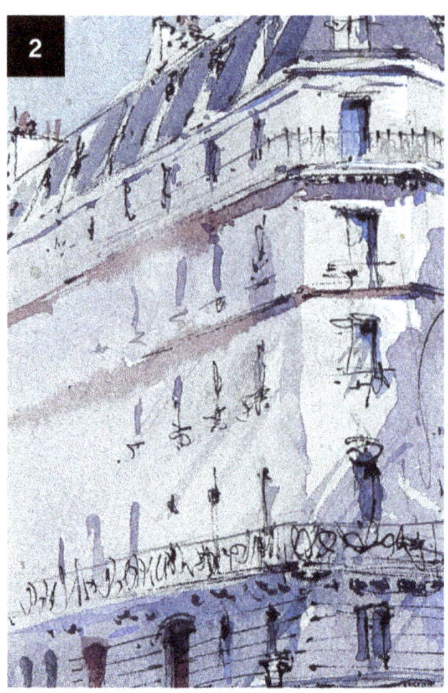

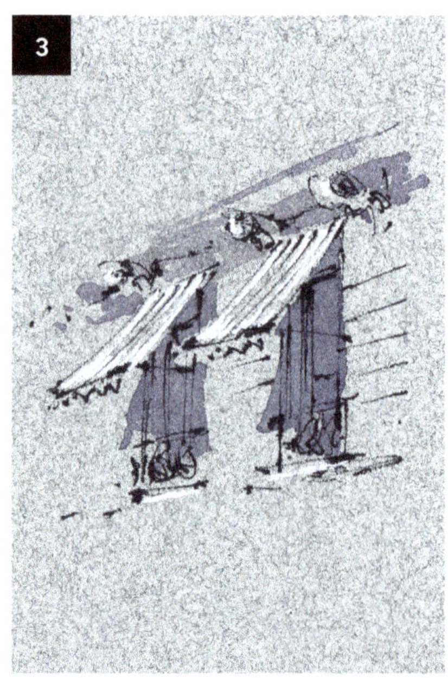

BALCONIES

Like their cousins the windows, balconies need to follow the rules when it comes to perspective. Where they are and how they are aligned on a building is more important than any details you place on them.

Parisian buildings have rather strict rules when it comes to balconies. Thanks to French official Baron Haussmann in the 1860s, almost every building in Paris is six stories tall, with balconies on the second and fifth floors. Within this somewhat rigid framework, there is quite a bit of variety. And it's in this variety where we can have fun.

For the purposes of sketching, I like to think of all the details associated with balconies as squiggles and noodley bits. This gets me away from any dogmatic architectural definitions.

Of course, every city has its own unique architecture and visual language. But by and large, balconies follow the rules. Allow them their flair when it comes to banister railings and supports, but the balconies themselves need to stay in line.

Sketching and Painting Process

1 | Hold a dagger brush vertically to create calligraphic patterns that represent banister railings.

2 | Banister railings are a place to show some flair. With a few wiggles and squiggles, they come to life. Details are less important than a repeating pattern that reads as a banister.

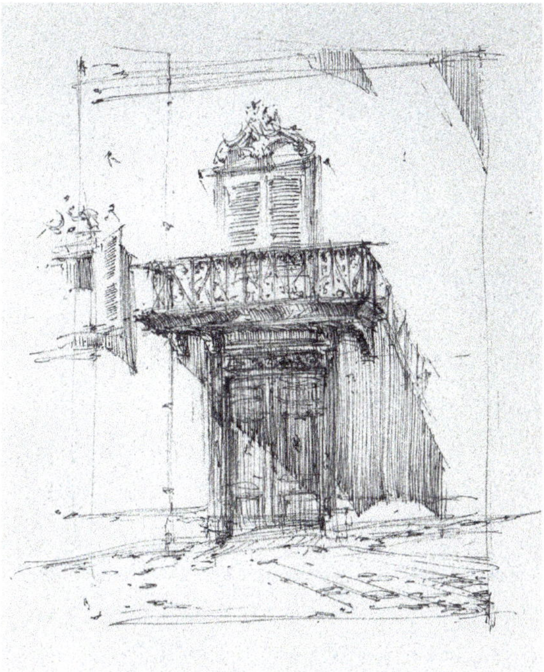

Balconies are often defined by their shadows. Volume is revealed and depth depicted by the strength of the shadow.

1

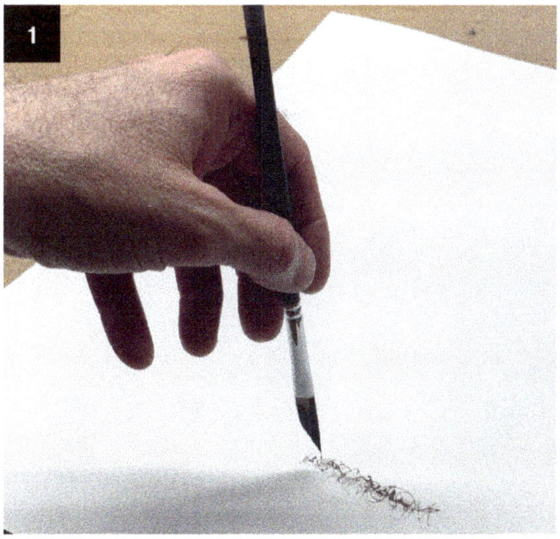

2

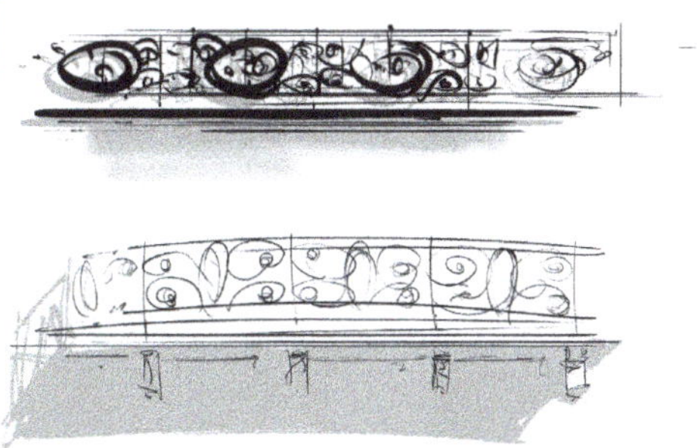

AWNINGS

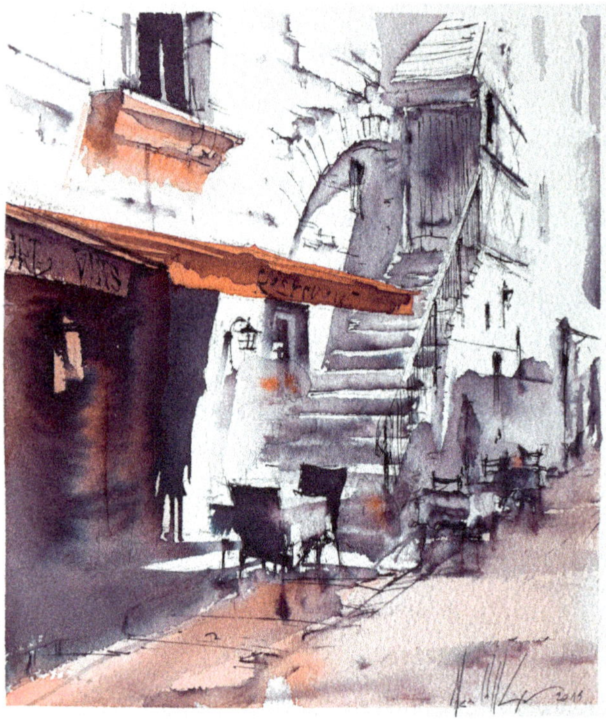

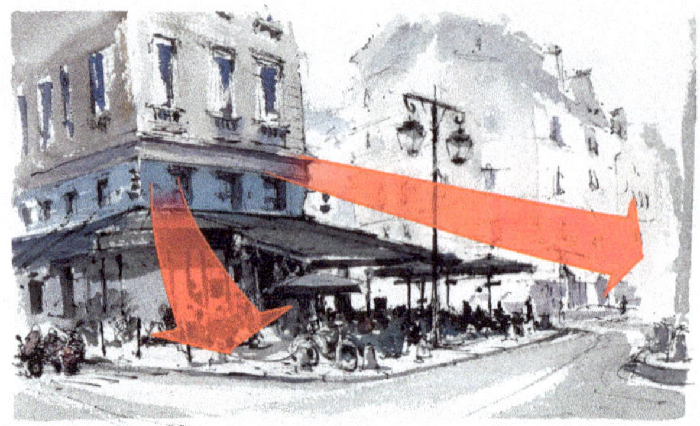

Awnings jut out from buildings with vibrant energy.

Café awnings are a joy to paint. They always remind me of skirts and dresses, that extra flair where buildings show off. They're often the brightest part of a painting, and they follow their own rules. Awnings, umbrellas, and signs are the pops of color, the flashy details, the life and energy of a sketch. This is where we can have some fun.

Most elements of architecture are made up of squares and circles. With volume, squares become cubes and tower blocks, circles become cylinders, columns, and domes. Awnings and umbrellas, on the other hand, are made up of that most energetic of shapes, the triangle. While buildings move at a stately four-step march, awnings jump and jive to a different beat. The juxtaposition of these different rhythms is always exciting.

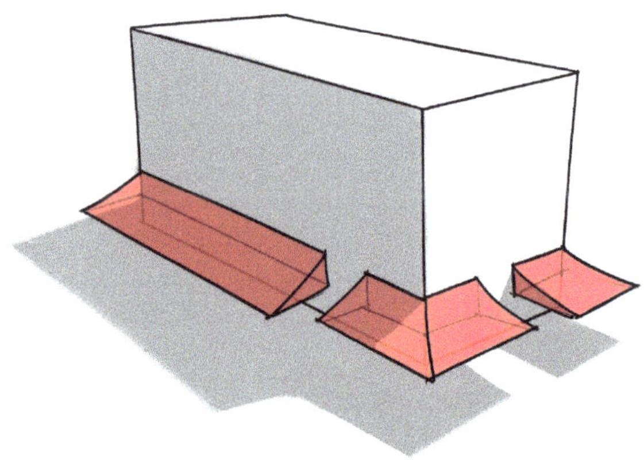

Awnings also wrap around buildings, following the rules of perspective, forming dynamic triangles and wedges.

Awnings stretch around corners and jut out into the street. They flash their colors and shade cozy tables and intimate encounters. An awning in your sketch will demand attention and draw the eye. This will automatically be where you'll find the highest contrasts of light and dark, and colors.

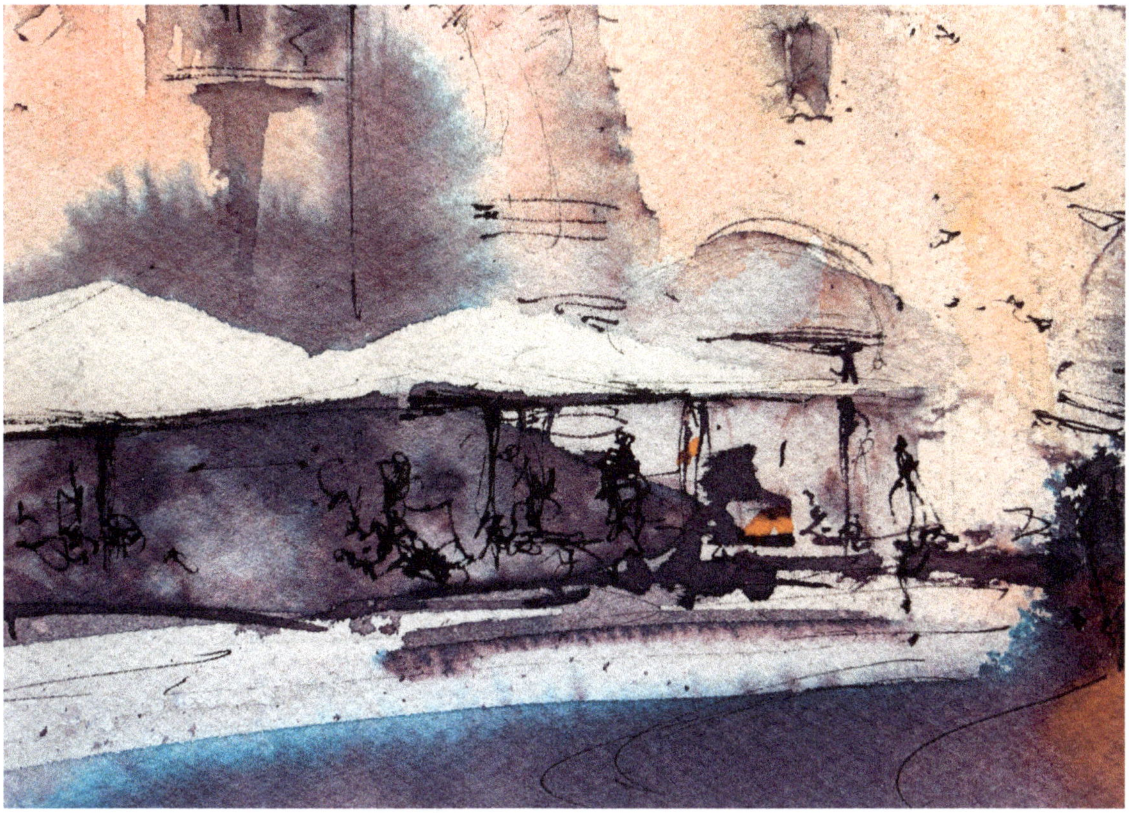

Umbrellas covering an outside terrace are a wonderful opportunity for contrast. In this image, I darkened everything around the umbrella, leaving triangles of light. Adding silhouettes of figures under an umbrella, no matter how abstract, creates a sense of activity and focus.

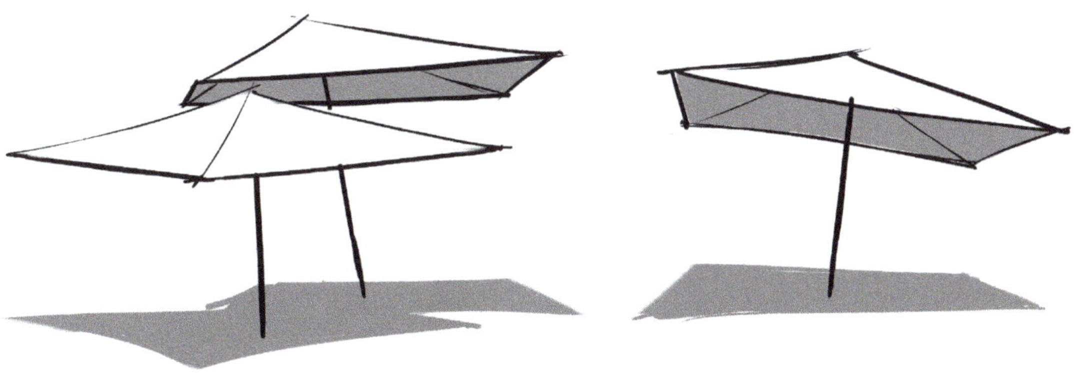

Square and round umbrellas dance to their own tune. Adjust their perspectives and angles to give them more personality.

SIGNS

Street signs, lampposts, and store signage are the details that add accent and staccato to our sketches. It's helpful to develop a shorthand with these details. The idea is to convey the energy that these objects express. I'm less concerned with an accurate representation of every letter of a sign than something that conveys the true meaning.

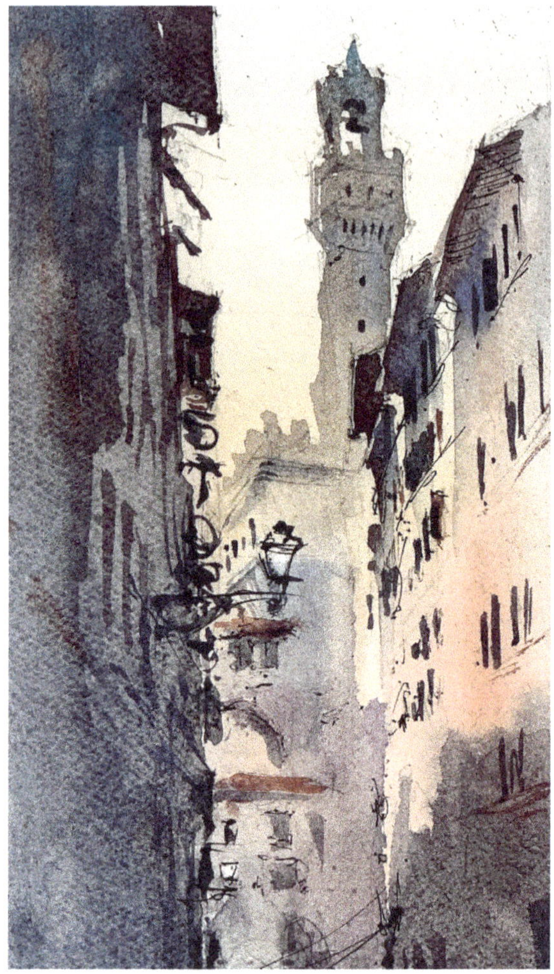

Spell Check

Rather than taking the risk of spelling signage words wrong in a sketch, I prefer using a white gel pen or darker ink and adding an indiscernible squiggle.

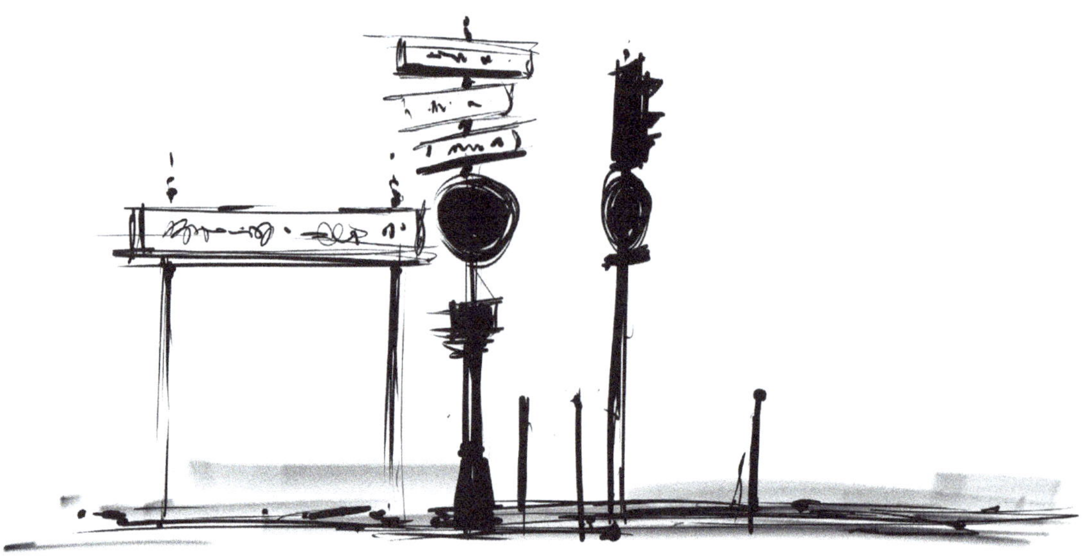

ARCHITECTURE AS CHARACTER

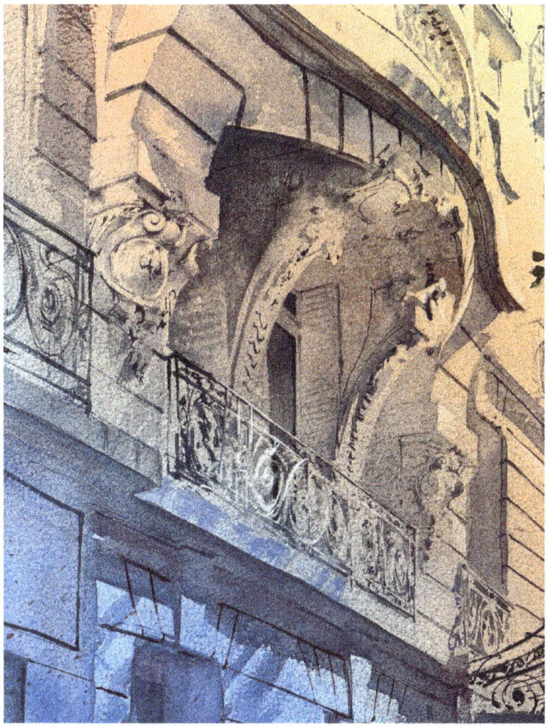

Sketching and painting architecture is like discovering a brilliant cast of characters.

Because I'm always thinking in terms of story, I look for buildings with a story to tell. Whether it's a tranquil café, a busy intersection, or an intricately detailed cathedral, there's always a story being told. These buildings become individual characters in a city. It helps me to see architecture as character. Maybe a particular structure resembles an exhausted old man, or a proud soldier, or an elegant movie star.

These buildings have personality, which manifests itself in what the building is doing. These aren't inanimate piles of brick and stone; they're active.

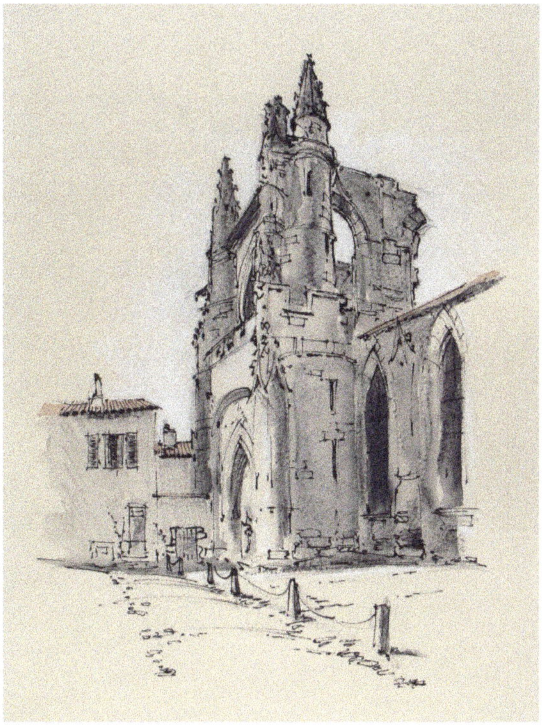

This partially ruined church on the island of Île de Ré, France, feels like an ancient soul. It's a once proud man, now worn down by a long life of struggle. He quietly clings to dignity as life moves on.

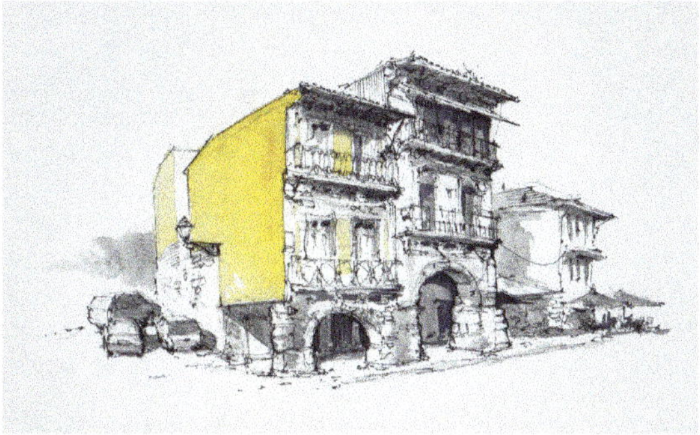

These houses in Porto, Portugal are three aging brothers. They've had laughs and loves and misadventures together. Beneath their shabby exterior, there's a twinkle in their eyes.

Sketching Process

1 | Choose some buildings to draw, and find the verb or action associated with each structure. Rather than painting a tall tower, paint it stretching to touch the sky. Or, paint a bridge reaching its way across the river.

These black and white thumbnail sketches reduce images down to their essential shapes. With details and color removed, it's easier to imagine an action being performed by otherwise inanimate objects.

2 | Make up stories about the structures you're sketching. This action will infuse itself into your sketch, and each line, each brush stroke, will have the energy of the story you're telling.

> ***"The artist does not draw what he sees, but what he must make others see."***
>
> —EDGAR DEGAS

1

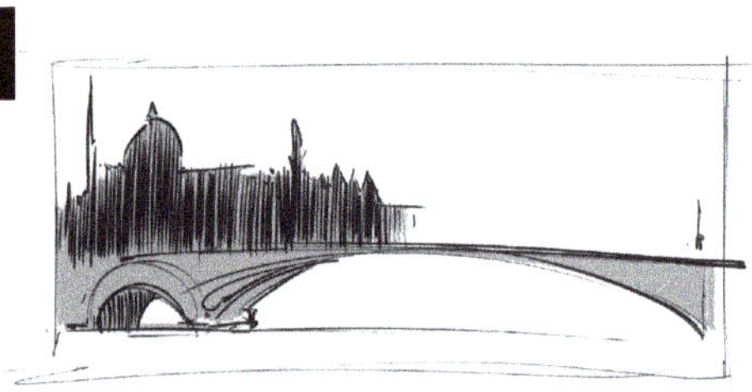

2

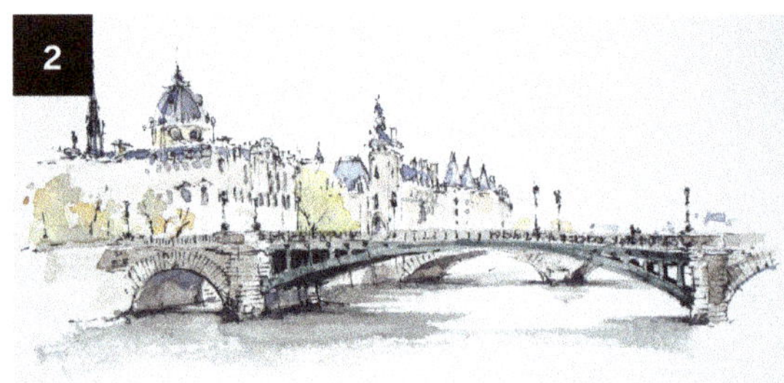

1

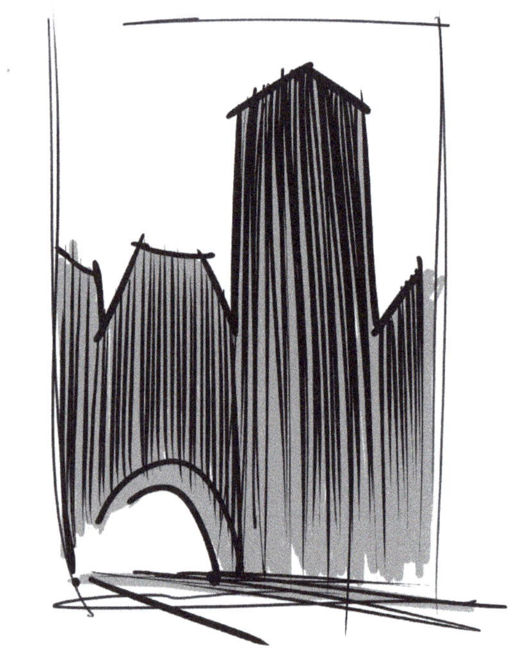

2

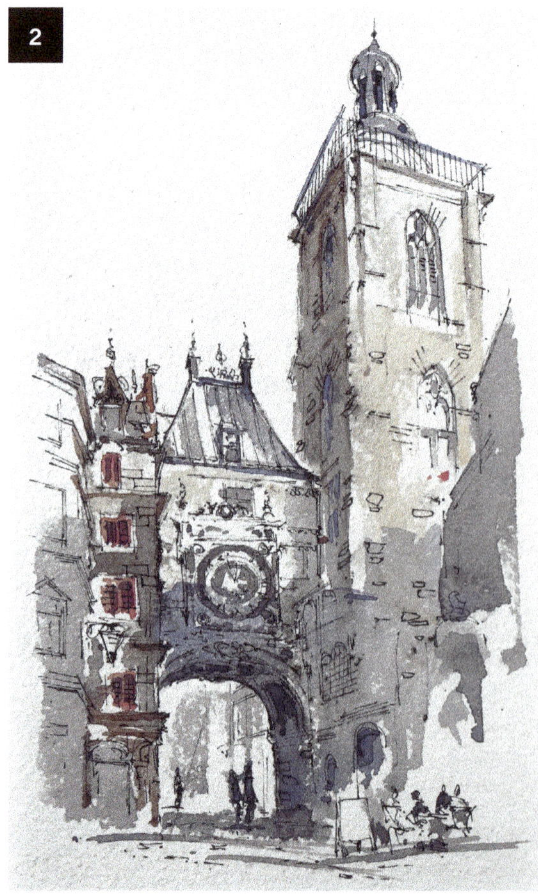

A LOVELY GESTURE

I stumbled into this technique of sketching buildings as characters while drawing a church in a piazza in Venice, Italy.

I was having trouble capturing the combination of square and round towers, bulging transept, differing angles of rooflines—there was just too much variety of architecture filling up this small square, too many differing forms vying for attention, and too large an angle of view filling up my page. When I stopped and thought about what this church was doing as a character, it all became clear.

This church was bounding into the piazza. It was rolling and bouncing, and it had motion and action and direction. Suddenly my sketch became easy. As long as I portrayed the gesture of this structure, I couldn't go wrong.

Gesture is a concept usually applied to figure drawing, and refers to drawing a figure simply, with just one or two lines. For me, gesture is equally important when sketching architecture.

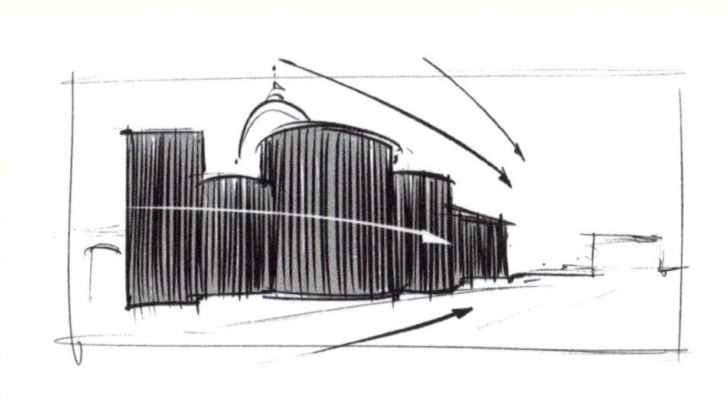

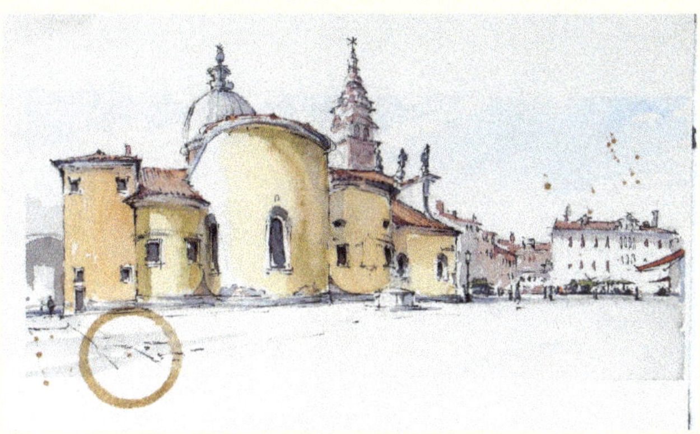

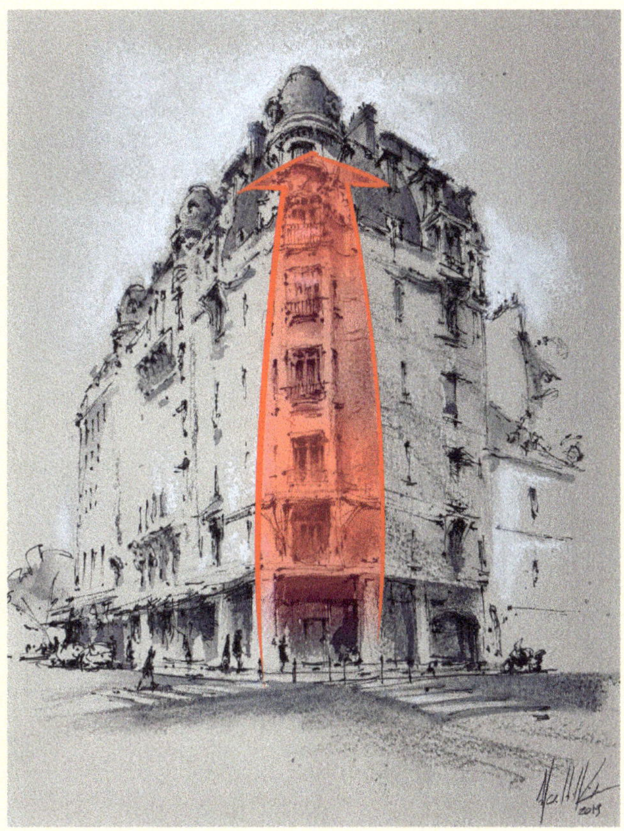

This building seems to reach for the sky. Its gesture is one of stretching upward.

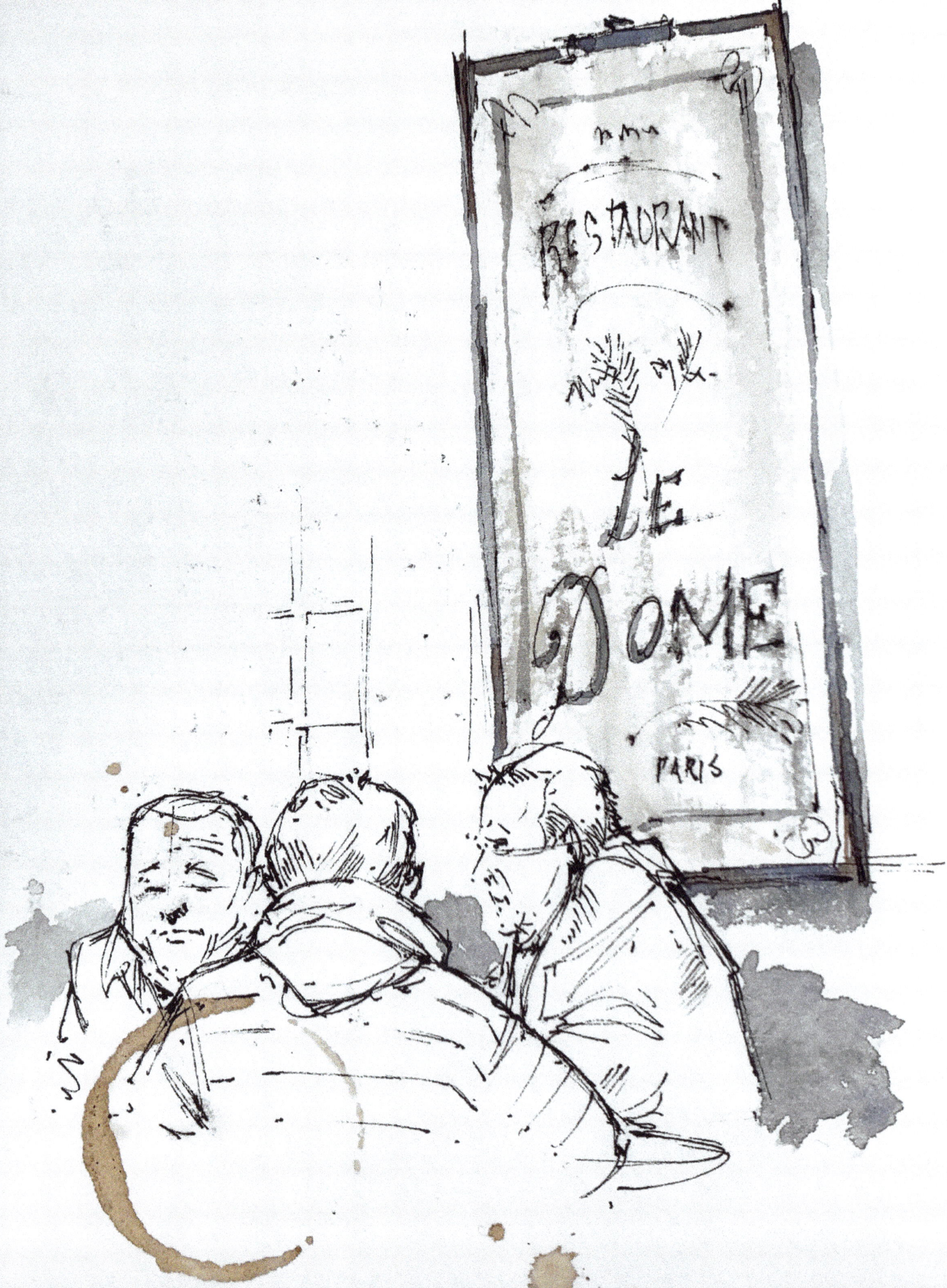
RESTAURANT
LE
DOME
PARIS

8

FIGURES

Sketching figures teaches us speed and how to capture the bare essentials of form and gesture. I sketch people in train stations, cafés, in the park, anywhere I can sit and people watch. The challenge is to capture a gesture quickly. People don't tend to stand still waiting for us to finish our drawings. We must be quick with our pen.

THE BASIC FIGURE

Sketching figures teaches us how to capture the bare essentials of form and gesture.

Sketching Process

A gesture is capturing a figure in its simplest form, with one or two lines.

1 | Start with an oval shape for the head, then one S-shaped line for the spine.

2 | Shoulders and hips are represented by horizontal lines that are usually tilted in opposite directions. People rarely stand evenly balanced on both feet; they usually favor one leg. With one leg straight and the other bent, this forces the hips to tilt.

3 | The shoulders then tilt in the opposite direction.

4 | Fill out features to complete the figure.

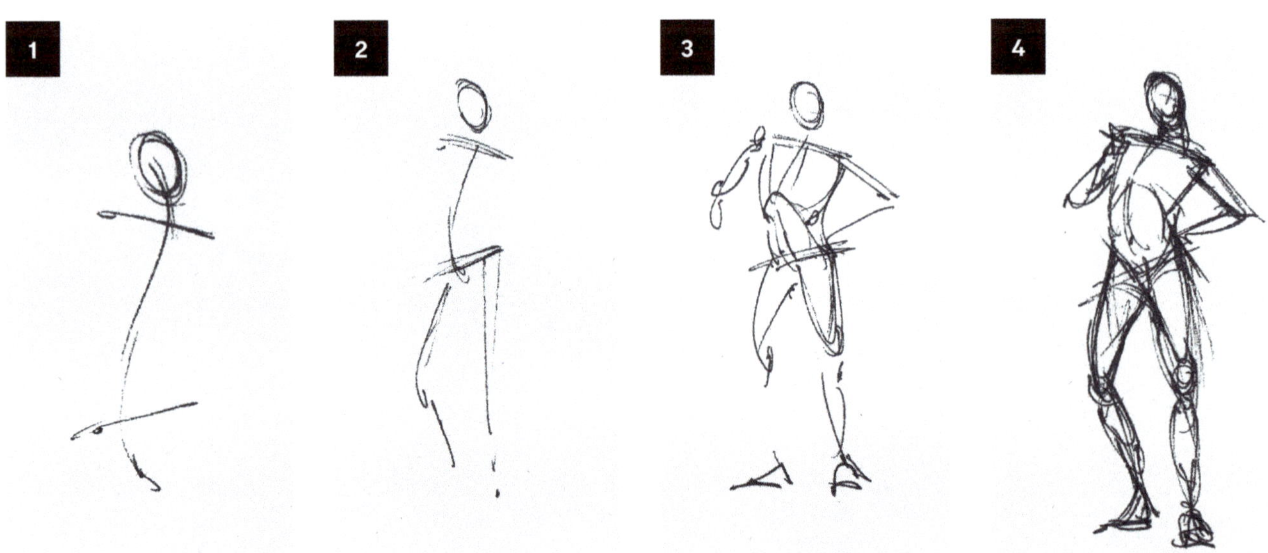

ADDING VOLUME

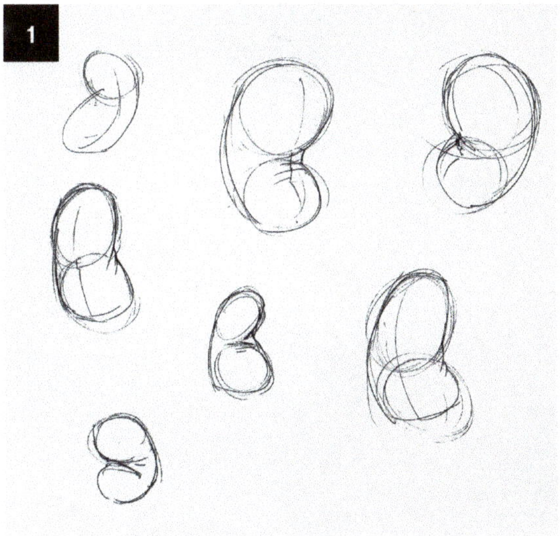

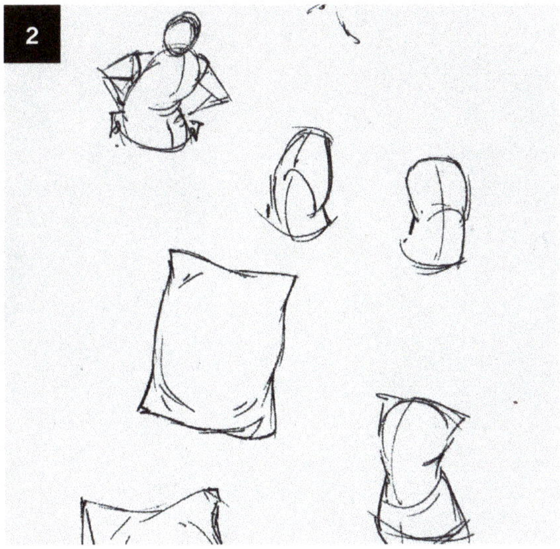

Sketching Process

1 | A great way to draw volume is to practice drawing what is knows as the bean. We want our figures to have volume and mass to them, rather than be two-dimensional stick figures.

2 | Imagine a squishy jellybean or pillow and draw it in as many forms as you can.

3 | Add shoulders and hips to the jellybean or pillow shapes.

4 | Draw three-dimensional tubes and shapes, rather than just an outline.

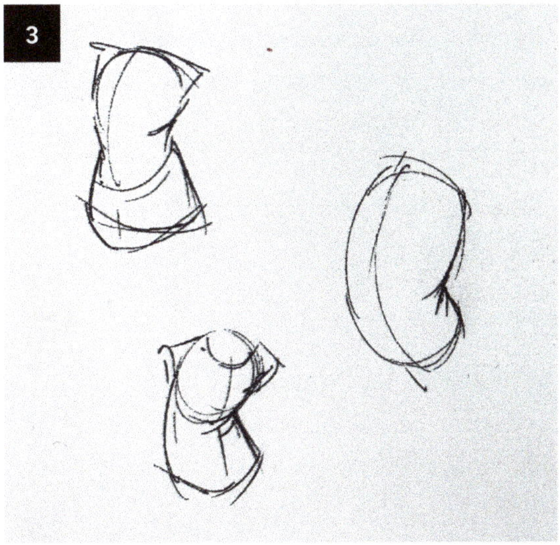

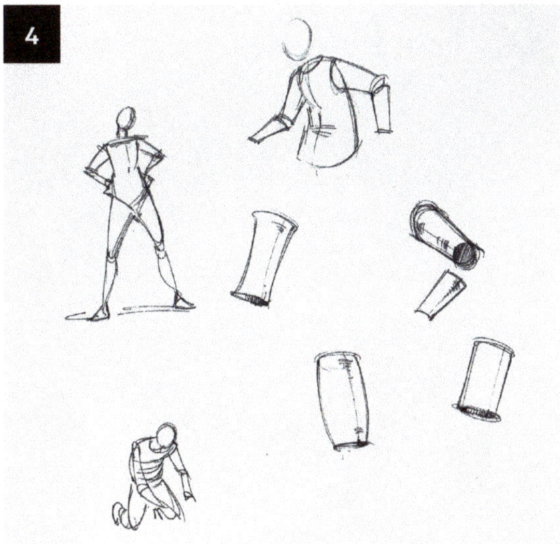

4

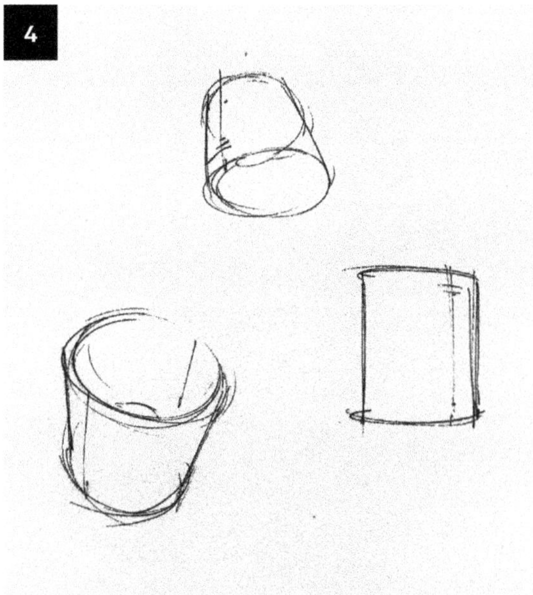

5

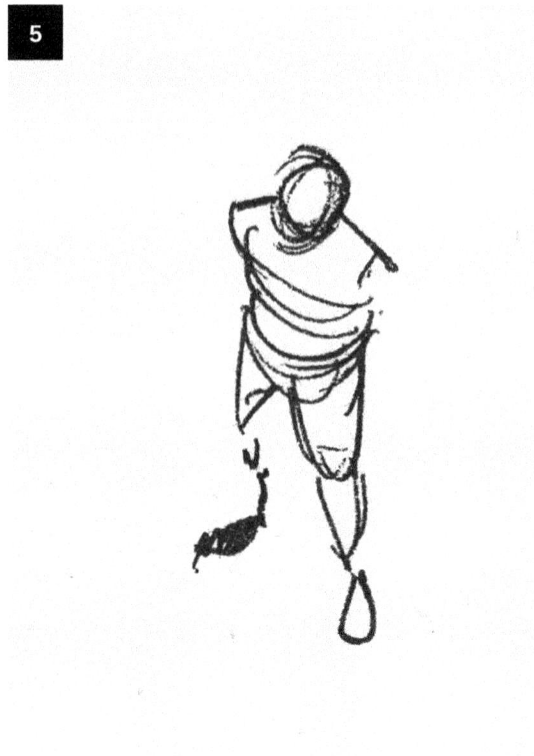

4 | When viewing people from a high angle, the same rules of volume apply, but now the head sits lower over the shoulders. The "bean" of the torso is more compact. Practice by drawing a can or drinking glass from different perspectives.

5 | Apply this to drawing a torso, then draw the rest of the body, keeping volume in mind.

6 | Imagine a light source is coming from a specific direction and add shadows for even more dimension.

6

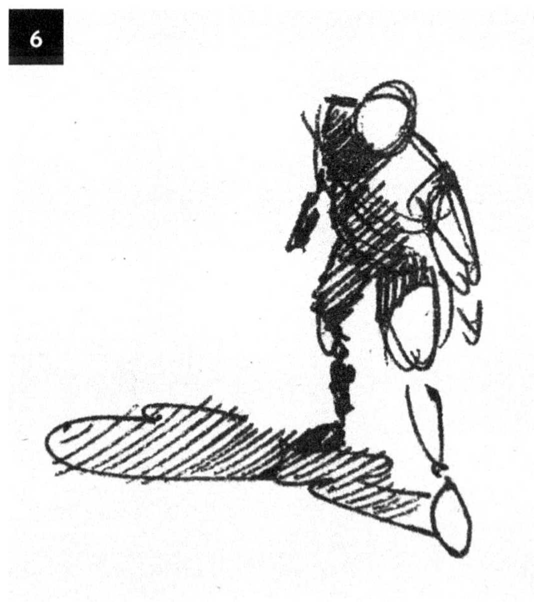

CAPTURING GESTURE

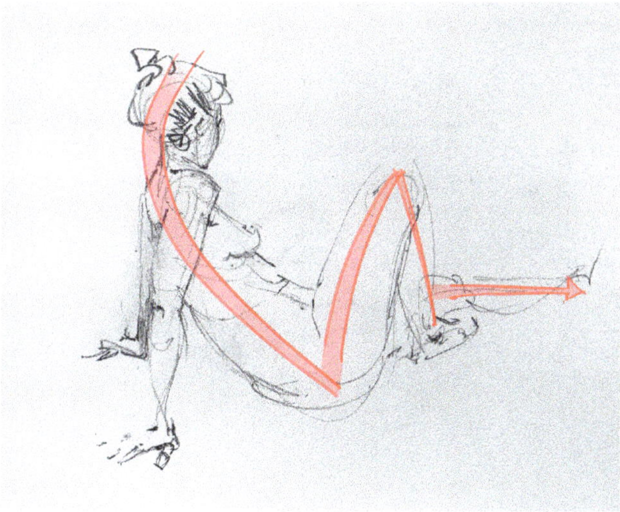

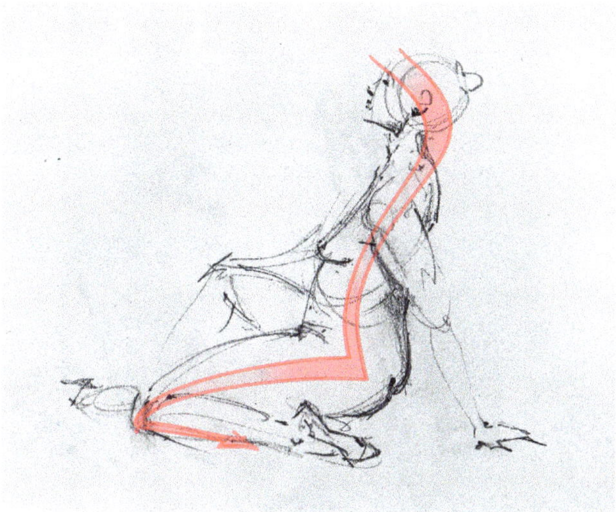

Figure drawing is a wonderful way to practice quickly sketching the human form. Drawing poses in short spans of two to five minutes teaches us to see the gesture of each pose. There's not enough time to get caught up in details, so we concentrate on the general motion and expression.

The directional red lines in these figures represent that most basic motion of a pose. If you can see the gesture and jot this down on your paper as a first step, everything else you add will follow with the same energy.

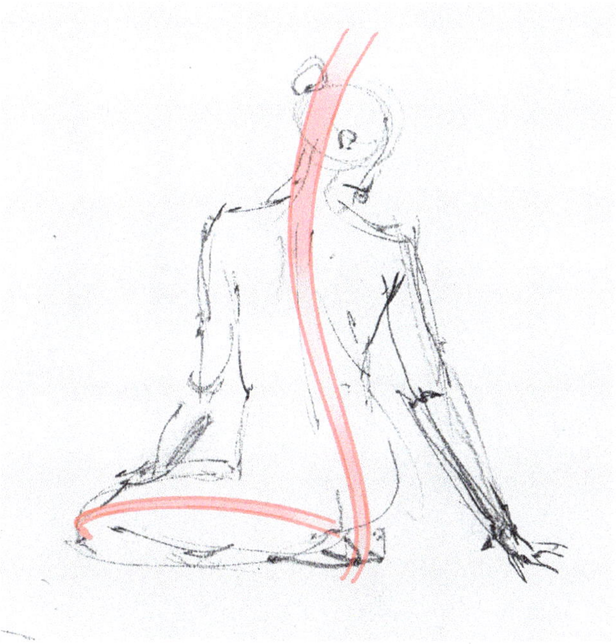

Sketching Process

1 | Draw the gesture with as few lines as possible. Notice the flow of the spine and legs.

2 | Add secondary forms like shoulders and arms.

3 | Begin to add volume to the figure.

4 | Adding details onto this form will maintain the energy and flow of the initial gesture.

1

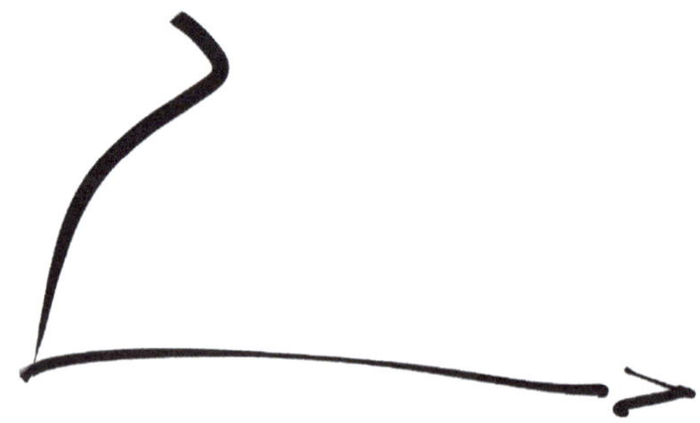

2

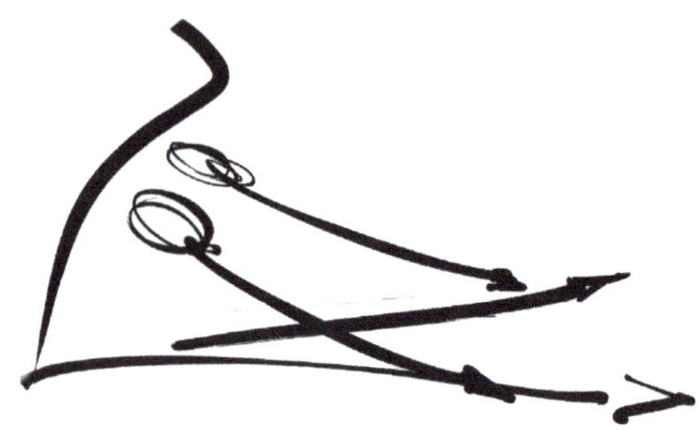

3

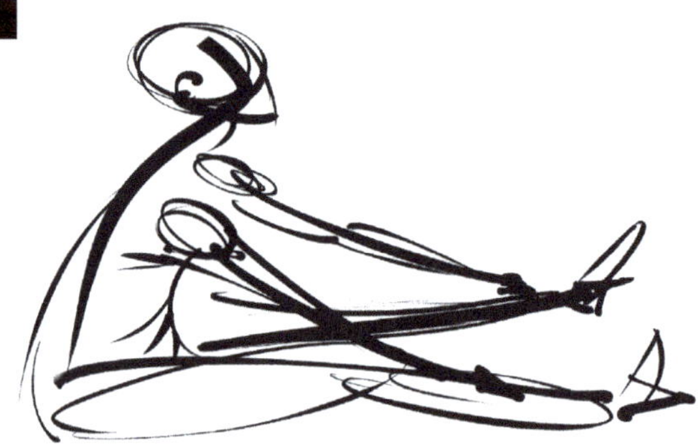

4

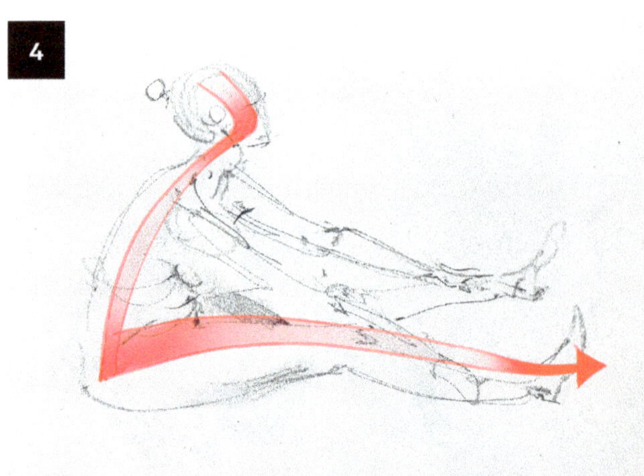

DRAWING FIGURES IN GROUPS

Here are some of my favorite tricks for drawing figures in perspective.

Drawing a group of figures in perspective can seem challenging at first. But, if we are standing while sketching, and we're drawing people who are also standing, then all of the eye lines will match. It doesn't matter how close or far away figures are; if they are standing up, their eye lines will be level. We can draw a straight line connecting everyone's eye line. This line becomes the horizon line for drawing linear perspective.

The same is true while sitting down to sketch, if we are drawing people who are also sitting. Because our eye level is even with everyone else who is sitting, we are able to draw a straight line connecting everyone's eye line. Once again, this line acts as the horizon line for linear perspective.

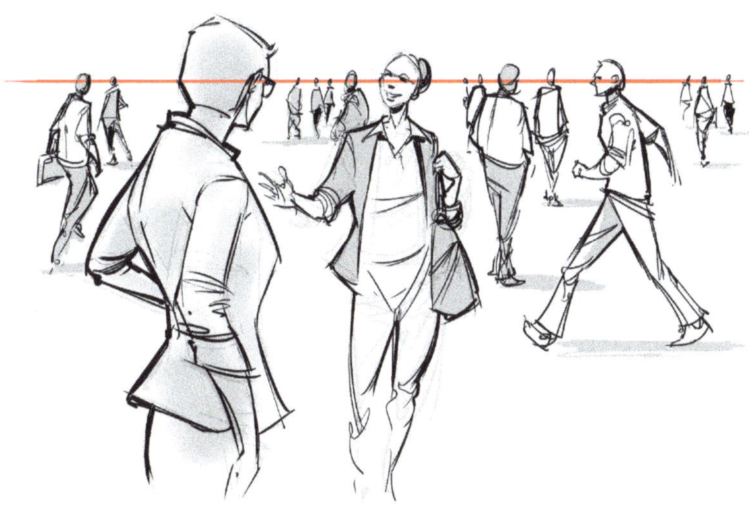

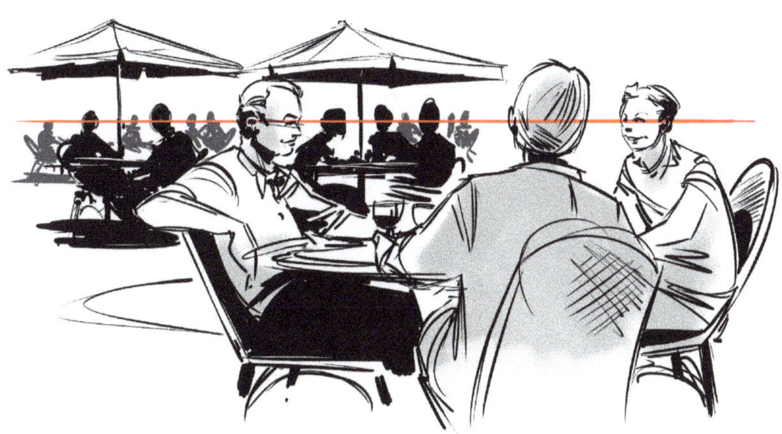

It gets more interesting when we draw some figures who are sitting and others who are standing. These two images are of the same scene, with two figures sitting on a bench in the foreground, and three standing in the background. One image is drawn from the perspective of sitting; the other is drawn while standing.

When we sit to draw, our eye line and the horizon are even with figures who are also sitting. Standing figures will protrude above the horizon.

When we stand to draw the same scene, our eye line is now even with the three standing figures. The seated figures will now be below the horizon.

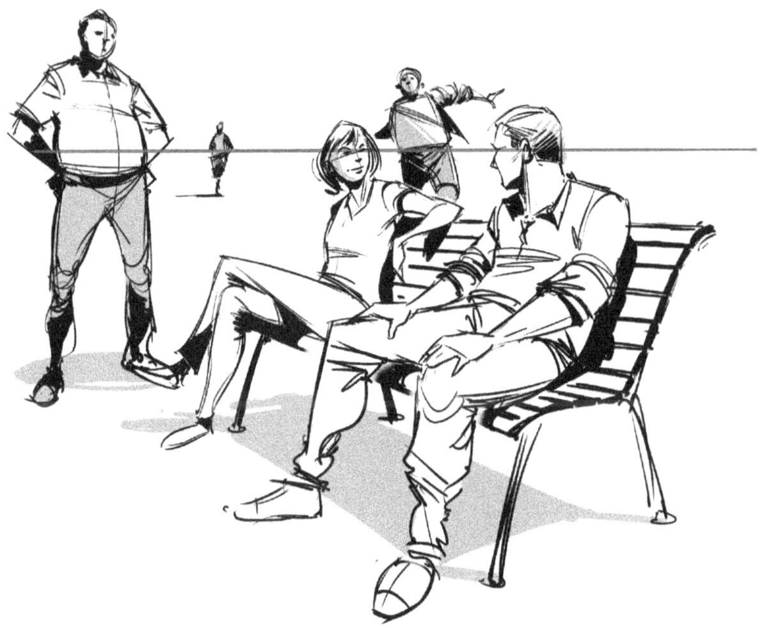

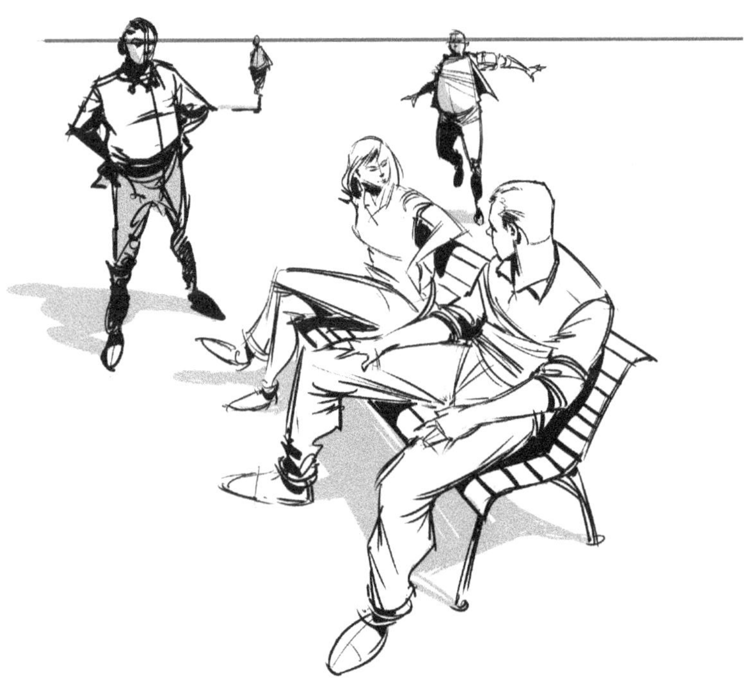

Every Person Tells a Story

When sketching people into a larger scene, we're not just placing stand-ins and extras. These are people with life and history. Each person you draw has a story. Maybe they're rushing home with groceries or strolling to meet a friend. Maybe their bag is heavy, or their feet hurt. Thinking about each figure having a story will add variety to your sketch.

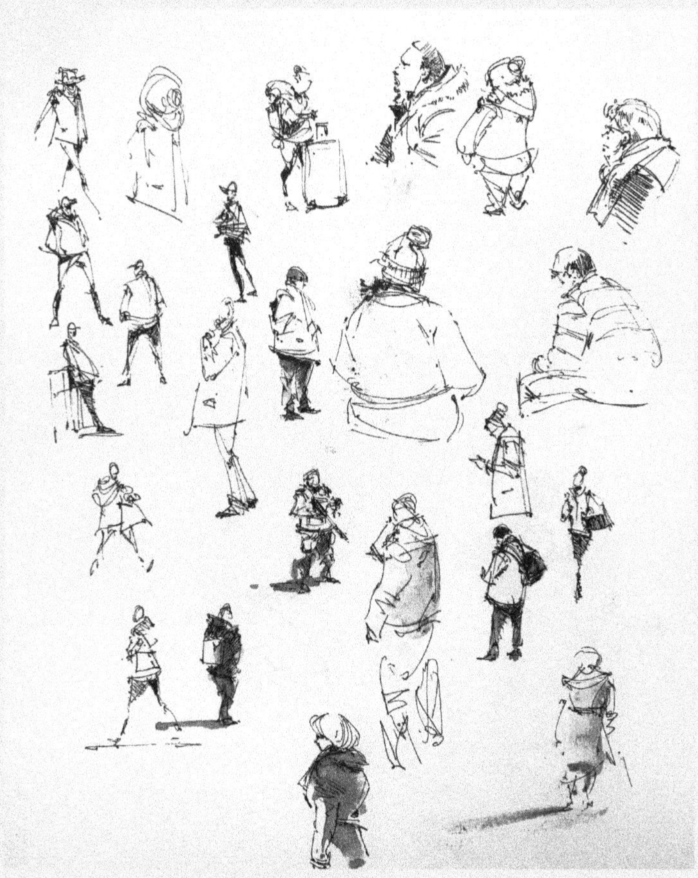

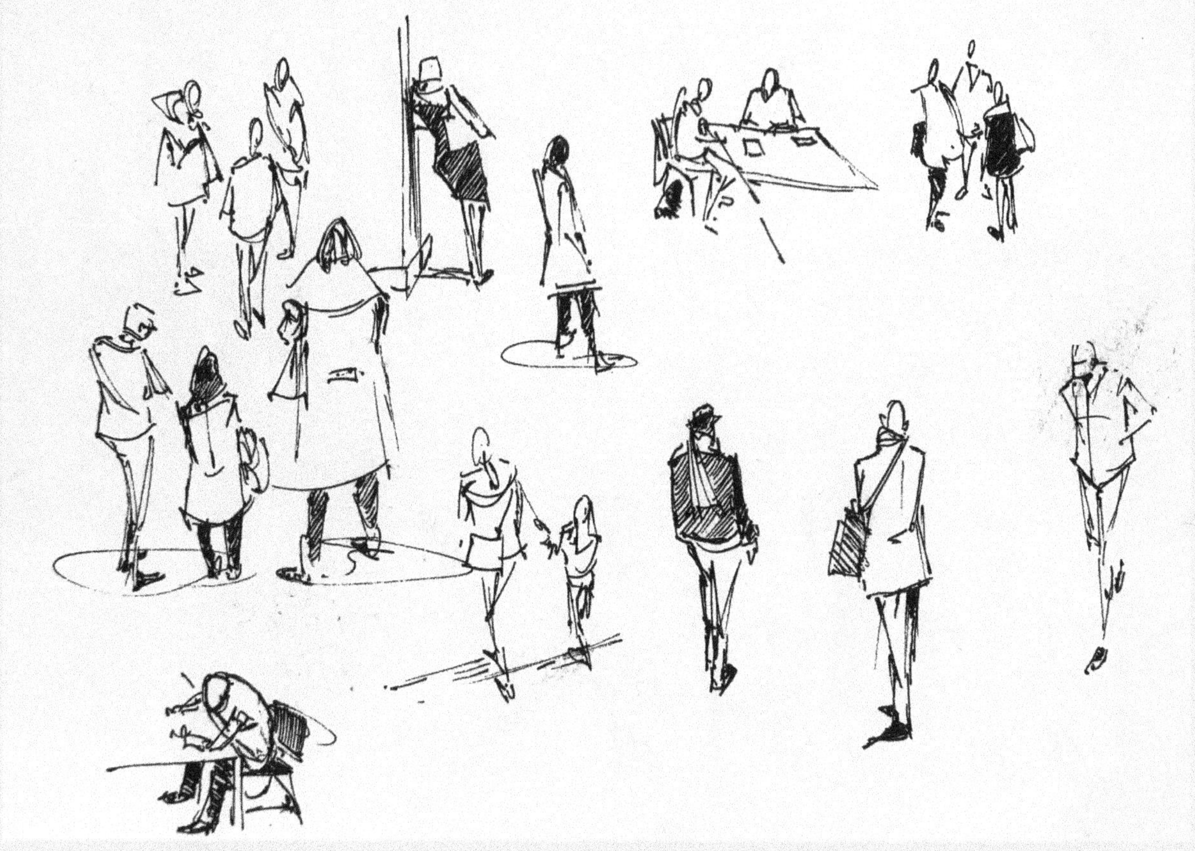

DRAWING THE HEAD

Sketching faces and heads can at first seem intimidating, but once we understand the underlying structure we are free to play.

Sketching Process

DRAWING A FACE STRAIGHT ON

1 | A simple way to sketch the head is by starting with an oval, divided evenly both vertically and horizontally. Eyes will fall on the horizontal line, while the nose sits on the vertical.

2 | Add a circle resting in the top part of this oval. The bottom of this circle gives us the position of the nose.

3 | Facial features such as eyes, nose, and ears will fall on these structural lines. The mouth sits halfway between the nose and the base of the chin.

4 | Adding hair and shading completes the image.

1

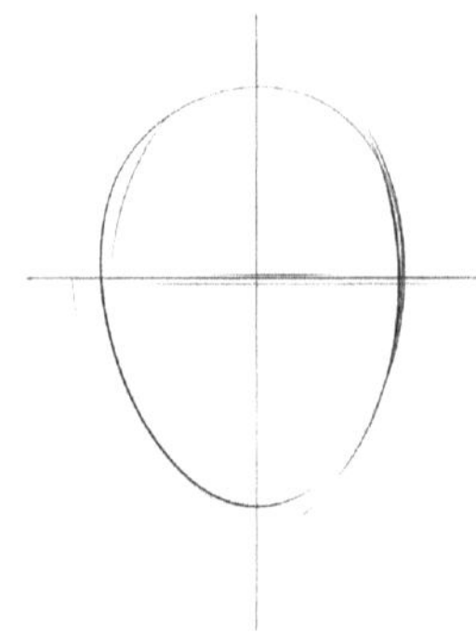

2

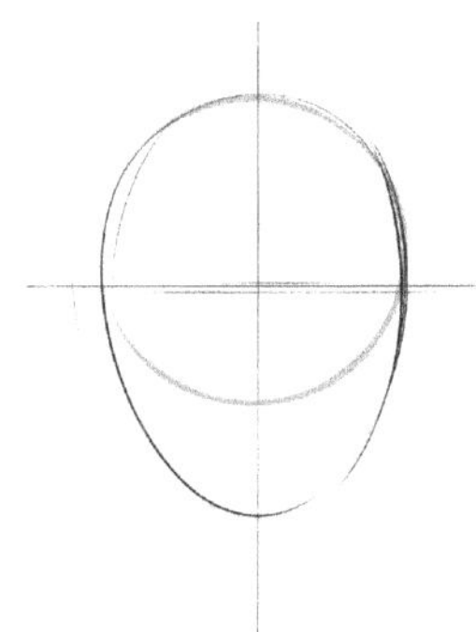

3

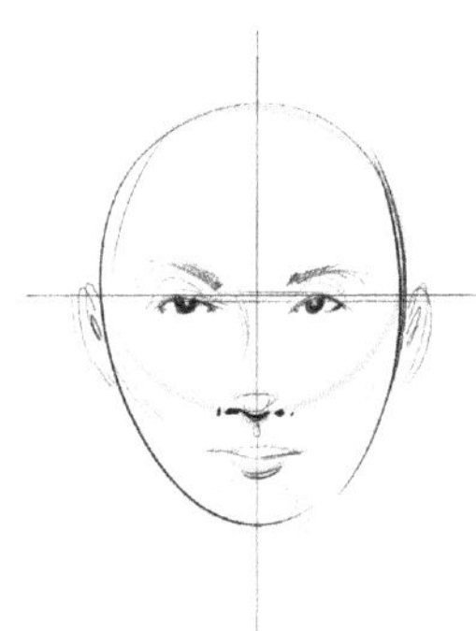

4

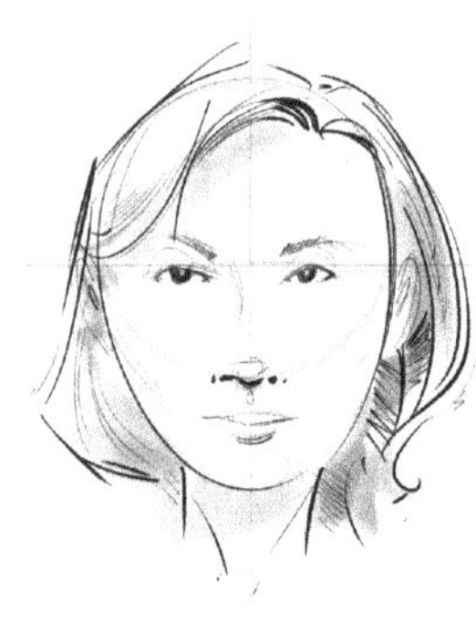

1

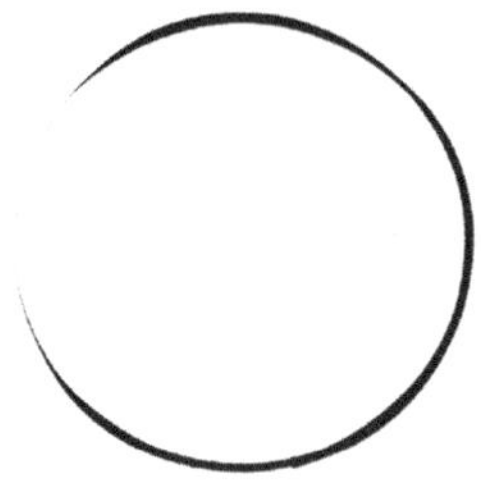

2

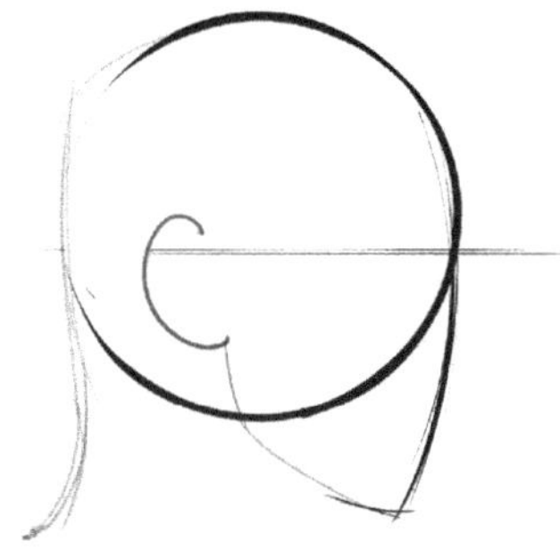

3

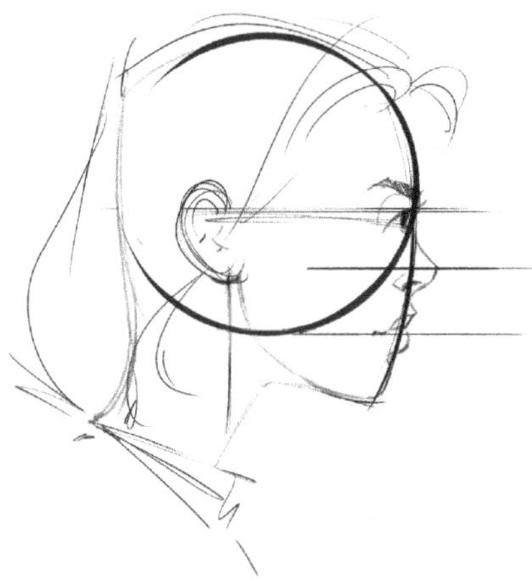

4

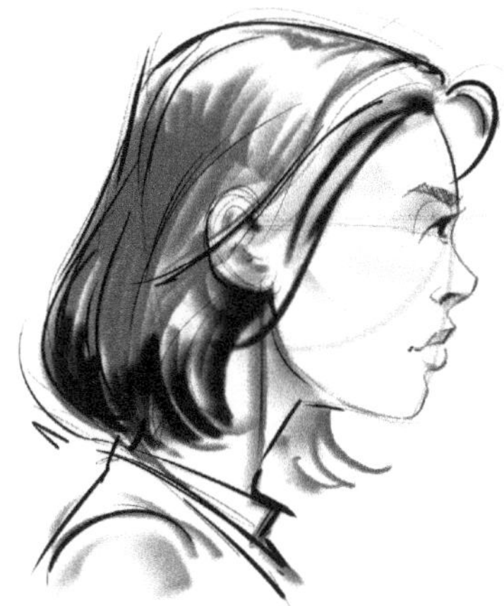

DRAWING A FACE IN PROFILE

1 | To draw a face in profile, start with a circle.

2 | The jaw drops below the front of the circle, while the back of the neck extends down from the back of the circle.

3 | Once again, the eyes sit on a line halfway between the top of the head and the bottom of the chin. The nose and mouth are evenly spaced between eyes and chin.

4 | Once these main features are established, details such as hair and shading can be added.

DRAWING FACES FROM DIFFERENT ANGLES

1 | Practice by filling your page with ovals.

2 | Because we don't always view faces and figures symmetrically from the front, imagine these ovals as three-dimensional eggs, and add horizontal and vertical dividing lines. I like to add ears to anchor these shapes. These eggs are now depicted as tipping and leaning at different angles.

3 | Add details to create faces from interesting angles, looking in different directions, and craning their necks.

1

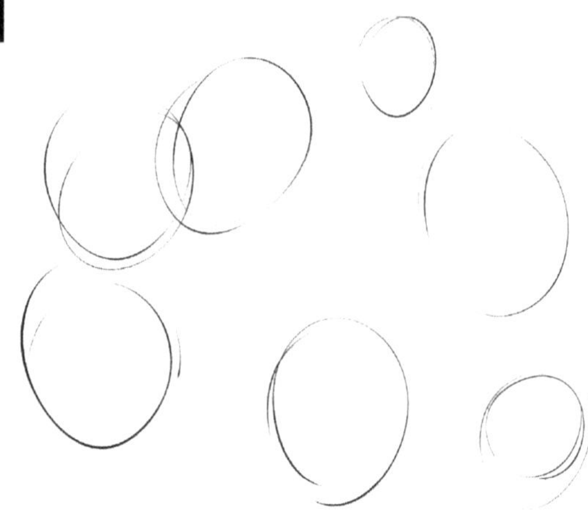

2

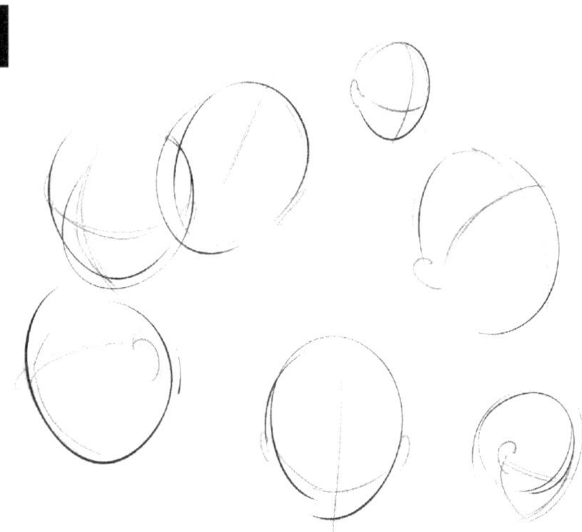

3

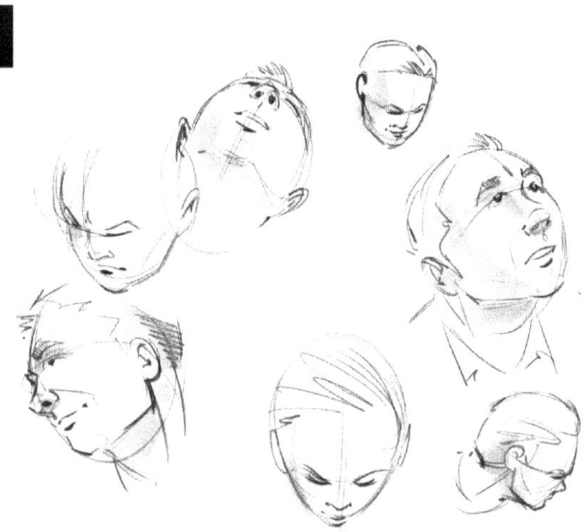

I Never Forget a Face

Everyone's face has unique variations, but these guidelines are a good place to start for accurate proportions. Humans are hard-wired to recognize faces. We're so good at it that we see faces in clouds and random shapes. For sketching, this means that when we draw facial features a little out of place, we notice it immediately. Practice faces until they become second nature.

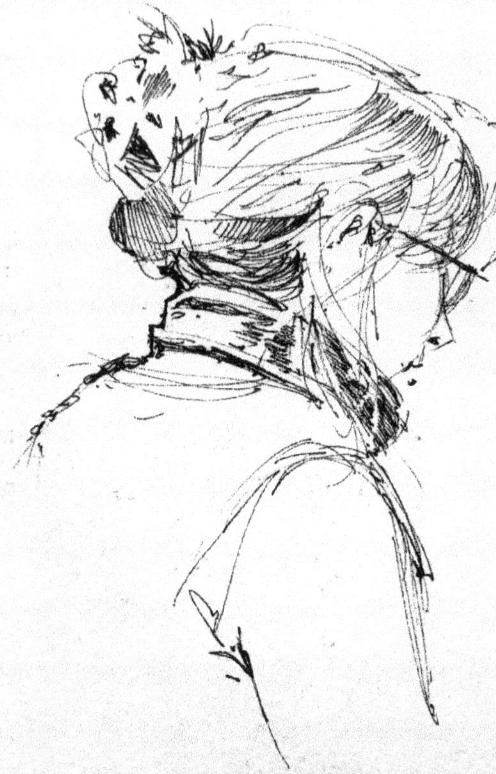

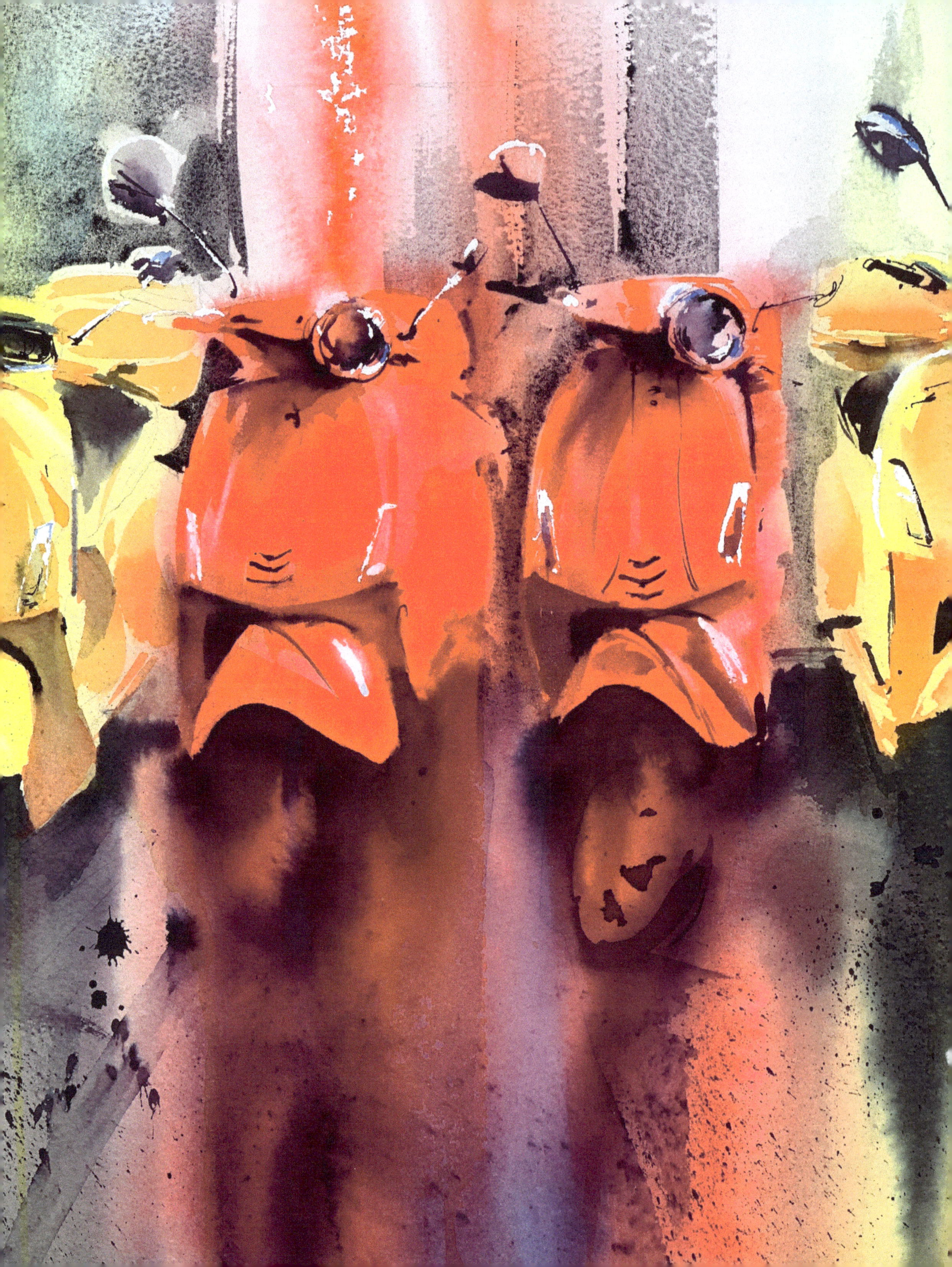

9

WATERCOLOR

A dance is the best analogy I can think of for painting with watercolor. Sometimes we lead, and other times the paint leads us. We are in partnership with the paints. We can guide the process, but we must also listen to the paint, play with the paint, and be ready to adjust if the paint begins to improvise.

DANCING WITH WATERCOLOR

Watercolor is the perfect medium for sketching. It's inexpensive, portable, and easy to get started. A simple set of colors fits in any bag, there are no exotic chemicals needed, and basic materials are readily available. Like the board game Go, watercolor is simple to learn, but it can take a lifetime to master.

Watercolor painting is often described as the hardest medium to master. We can guide the paint, we can cajole it in certain ways, but we're never fully in charge of watercolor. We must never forget we're painting *with* watercolor. It's an act of co-creation. This is the beauty of watercolor. All the mistakes, the times we feel the paint gets away from us and misbehaves, are often the parts of a finished piece with the most life. In this chapter we'll learn to play with the vibrant life of watercolor.

I'll show you some foundational techniques of painting with watercolor, some basic dance steps that can be used in many situations. Music, dance, and paint—for me, these all swirl around each other in the same universe. Just as a musician practices scales before playing jazz, and a dancer practices steps before taking the stage, these are the scales and moves to become familiar with before creating your masterpiece.

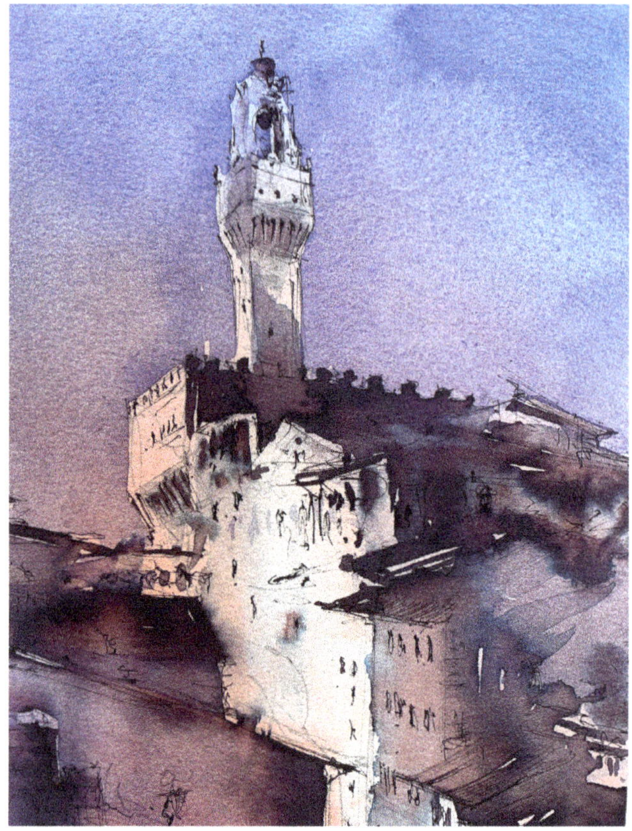

Before sunrise at the Palazzo Vecchio, Florence. Washes of color are perfect for depicting the glow of pre-dawn light and inky darkness.

CREATING MULTIPLE EFFECTS WITH ONE COLOR

One advantage of watercolor is its ability to create immense variety in the way the paint is applied to paper. Each effect becomes a new tool in our kit, a new element to put into practice adding variety and life to our paintings. It's important to break these down into manageable elements.

Here are a few different ways to add texture to your watercolor painting. I'll simplify everything by using just one color.

An Even Wash

The first technique is creating a simple wash of color. An even wash is useful for painting skies and other large areas. Practice this technique until you are comfortable creating consistent results.

1 | Begin by mixing together a large pool of paint in your palette.

2 | Apply the paint to dry watercolor paper with a flat brush. Angle the paper so gravity draws the paint down the page. Begin at the top and make an even line with a flat brush. Continue down the page painting overlapping horizontal brushstrokes. Every two or three strokes reload your brush with paint from your palette to create an even wash all the way down the page.

3 | Once you're done, lay your paper flat. As long as the paper contains moisture, pigment will continue to remain active and on the move. By laying paper flat, the pigment can settle into the fibers of the page. Once dry, the process will have created an even wash of color.

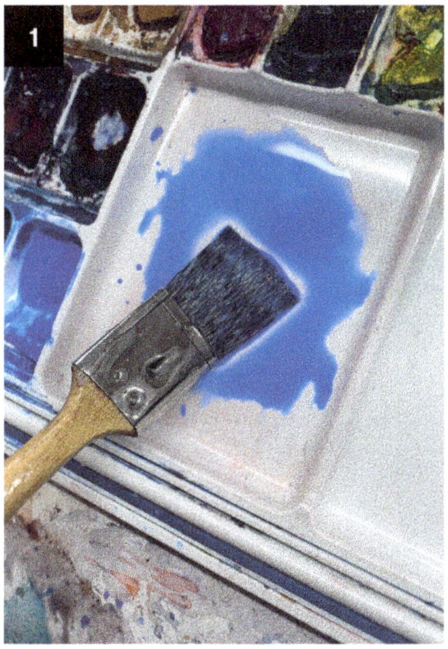

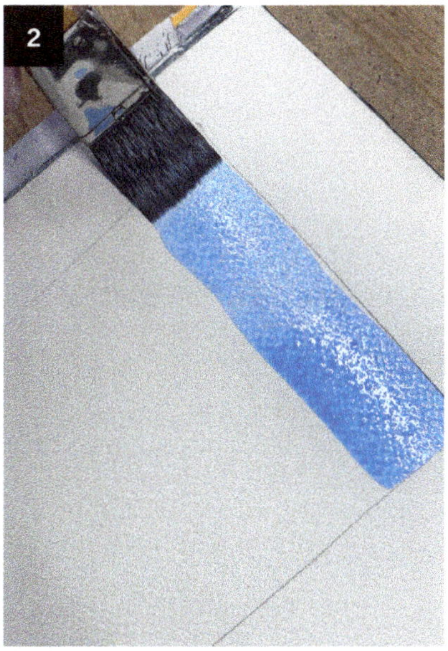

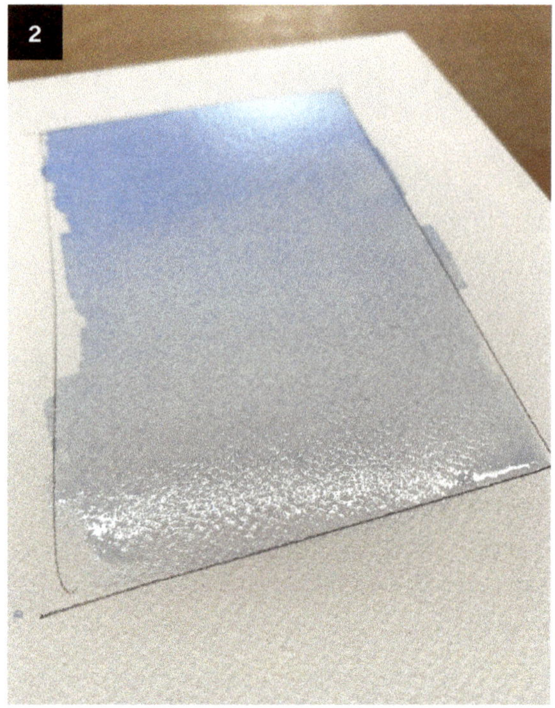

Gradation

The second technique is creating a gradation or a graduated tonality of color. This technique is similar to the even wash, but this time the amount of pigment in the brush will decrease as we go further down the page. The wash will be darker at the top and lighter at the bottom.

1 | Start by applying paint to dry paper, making a couple of brushstrokes with a brush fully loaded with pigment. Next, rinse some of the color from your brush and continue the brushstrokes down the page.

2 | Rinse again a second time and continue to make brushstrokes, so you're now painting with almost entirely clean water.

3 | Lay your paper flat so that the pigment can settle evenly into the paper. Once dry, this will show an even gradation of color from dark to light. This technique is wonderful for painting skies and reflections in water. On a clear day, skies are a deep blue

overhead and gradually lighten closer to the horizon. The opposite is true for water; darker tones are near the bottom of our view and lighten as we approach the horizon.

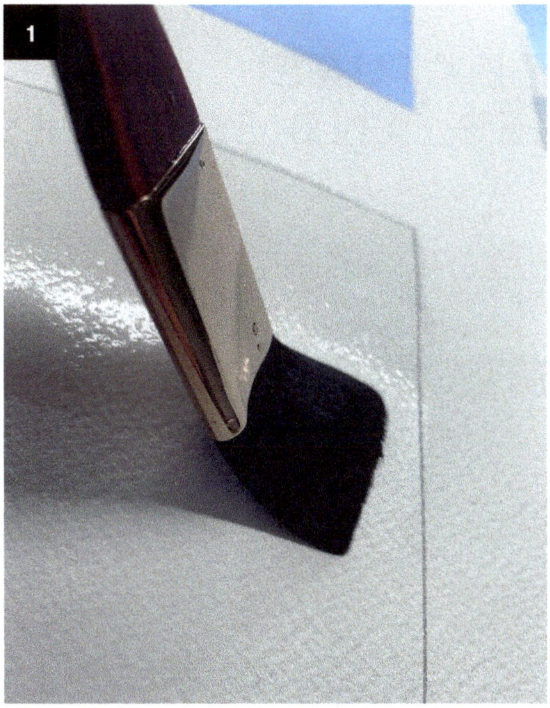

Wet-on-Wet

For the third technique, we will paint wet-on-wet, meaning the paper needs to be wet before we apply paint.

1 | Wet the paper using a flat brush and clean water. Brush horizontally, vertically, and diagonally to make sure the paper is saturated—you want to be sure the water gets into the paper fibers. Judge how damp the paper is by looking at how the paper glistens. Good-quality cotton paper will hold water for a few minutes before slowly drying.

2 | Load your brush with color and hold the wet paper at an angle. Make a single brush-stroke at the top of the page and let the paint flow down the wet page, creating rivulets of color in unpredictable ways. The paint is now in charge. This dynamic combination of paint, water, and paper creates a unique pattern. This is where watercolor comes into its own. Each time you try this, the results will be slightly different, and that's part of the joy.

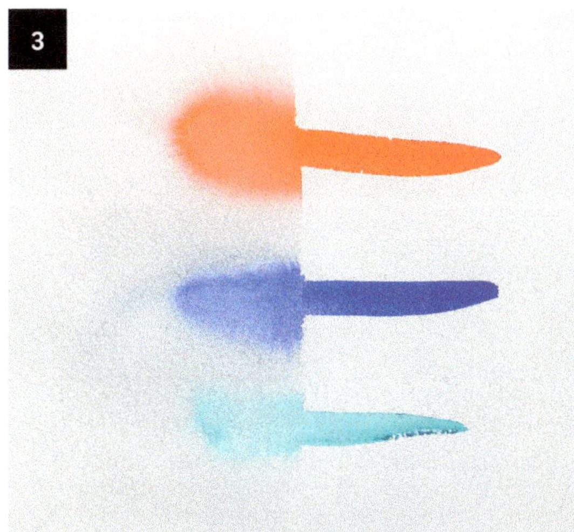

3 | Another way to see the results of the wet-on-wet technique is to brush paper with clean water on the left-hand side and leave the right side dry. Drag a brush loaded with color across the page from right to left. This creates very different results depending on whether the paper is dry or wet.

This wet-on-wet technique has countless applications. I use this method when painting an initial wash of multiple colors. This creates a beautifully fluid underpainting that I can add details to later.

CREATING TEXTURE: SPLATTERS, SPLASHES, AND SCRAPES

To create interesting textures with just one color you can combine all of these steps while throwing in a few others for variety. For this technique, we won't create an even wash of color, but instead create a combination of textures that will be much more messy and playful. This is our chance to see how far we can push our paint and paper and see what we can come up with.

1 | Apply some paint to dry paper and scrub it around with your brush. Add clean water using a second brush and see what this does. Scrape the page with the end of a paintbrush or a fingernail to create lines and scratches. The corner of a credit card or a letter opener also works well.

2 | Flick paint onto the page by tapping your paintbrush. Use a toothbrush to splatter and spray paint. Rub and smudge paint across the page with your fingers. Dab wet paint with a tissue to remove damp pigment.

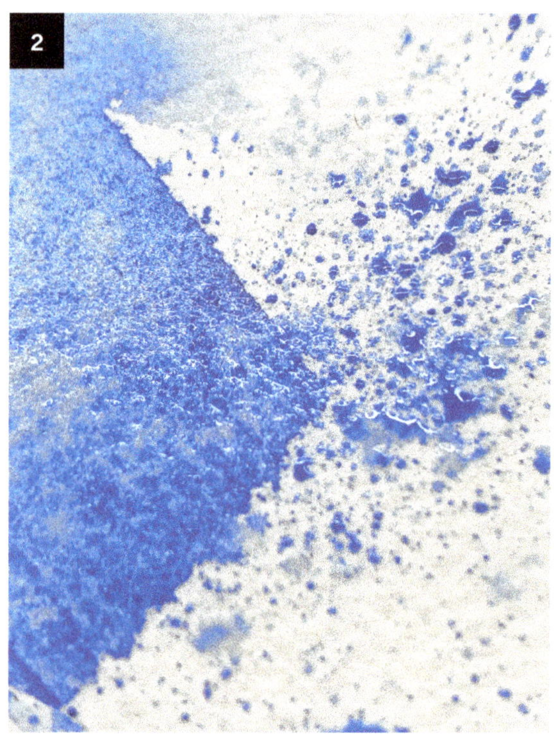

3 | Flick clean water from the brush into a wash of color. This can be done by tapping the brush or using your fingers to flick drops of water. These splatters of clean water repel the pigment already on the page, leaving lighter spots.

3

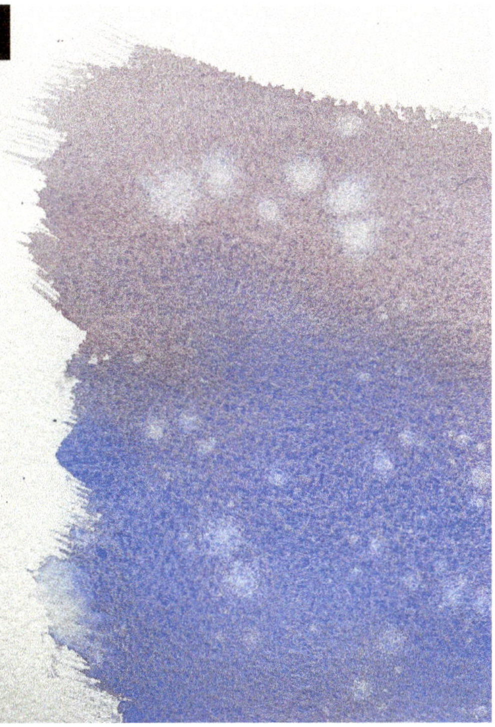

Dry Brush Technique

Dry brushing is that wonderfully scratchy effect created by quickly dragging your brush across the page. Your brush is not bone dry (there must be some water for watercolor to work), but there should be very little moisture in the pigment on your brush, and the paper should be dry. This works best on paper that has some tooth or texture to it.

Dry brush is not unique to watercolor. Similar effects can be achieved with what you have in your sketching bag. An old felt pen creates wonderful dry brush effects. Pencils on rough paper do something similar.

Whether we're painting a clear blue sky, reflections in water, or textured stonework of an old building, we can use these techniques to achieve the illusion of all these multiple textures. The idea is to let the paint do a lot of the work for us.

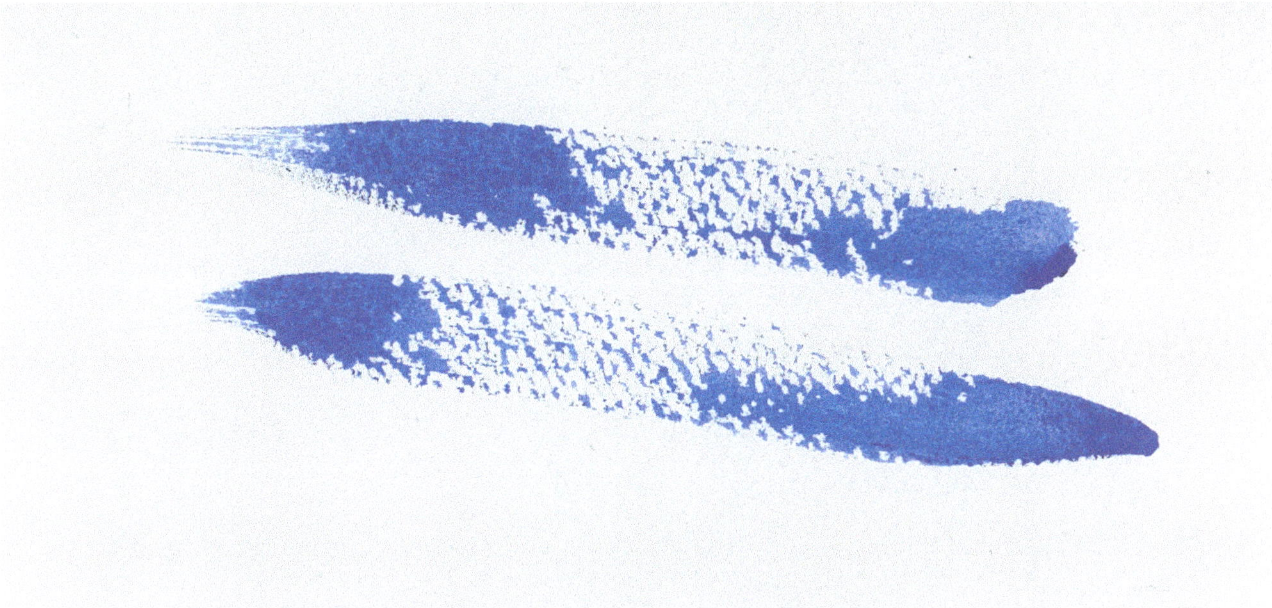

COLOR MIXING

Mixing colors can be done in three main ways. We'll use the same colors in each, but achieve varying results using different processes.

Color Mixing in a Palette

1 | The most straightforward way to mix colors is to blend them in a palette. Create a small pool of cobalt blue in one corner of a palette and a small pool of quinacridone red in the opposite corner.

2 | Swirl them together with your brush. These colors get along very well, and together they create a third color, a beautifully clear lavender.

3 | Once you get the desired color, apply the purple to the page.

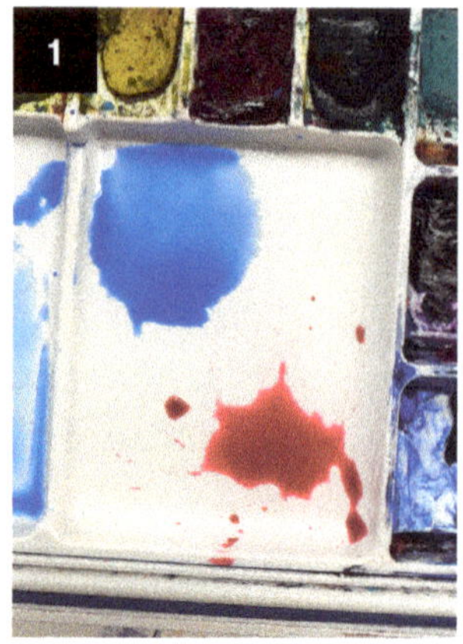

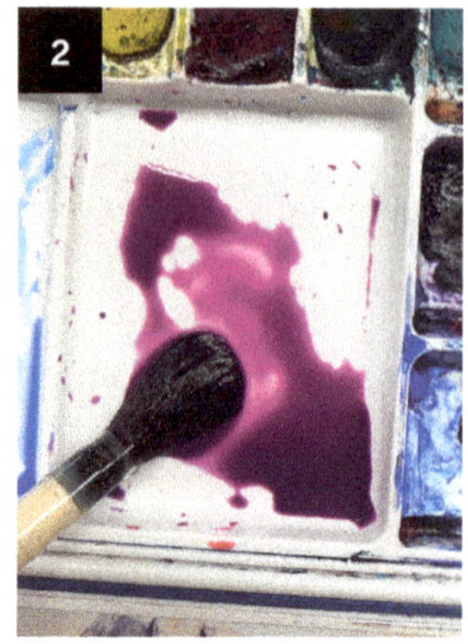

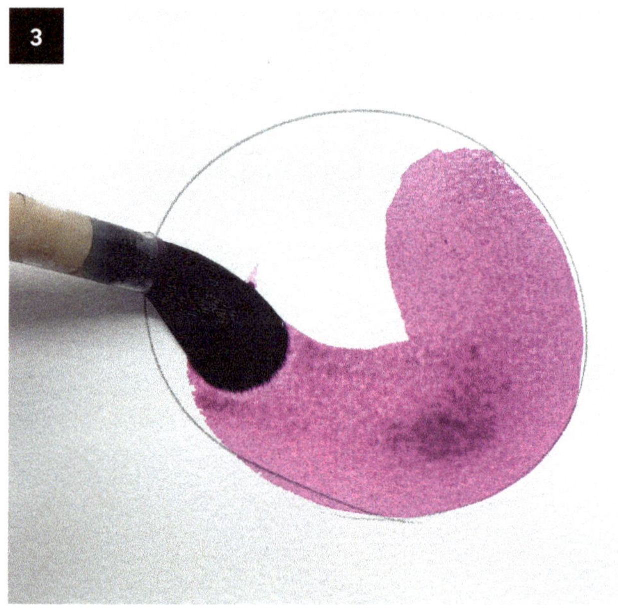

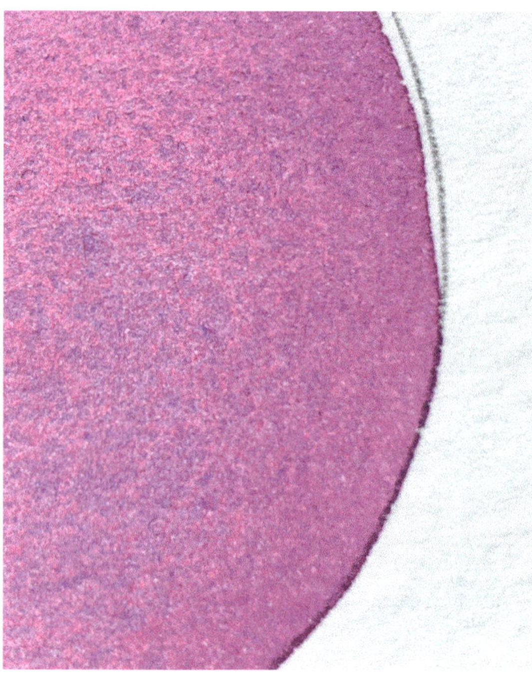

Two colors mixed together in the palette, then applied to the page for an even wash of color.

Glazing

The second way to mix colors is by glazing on paper.

1 | Lay down a single wash of cobalt blue, let it dry thoroughly, then apply a wash of a quinacridone red over the top.

2 | Because watercolor paints are transparent, the blue layer shines through the red layer, and what our eye sees is purple.

Glazing is a wonderful way to build up layers of color that shimmer with intensity. Green trees painted over a yellow background take on a new brightness. Layers of varying blues glazed into skies create added vibrancy.

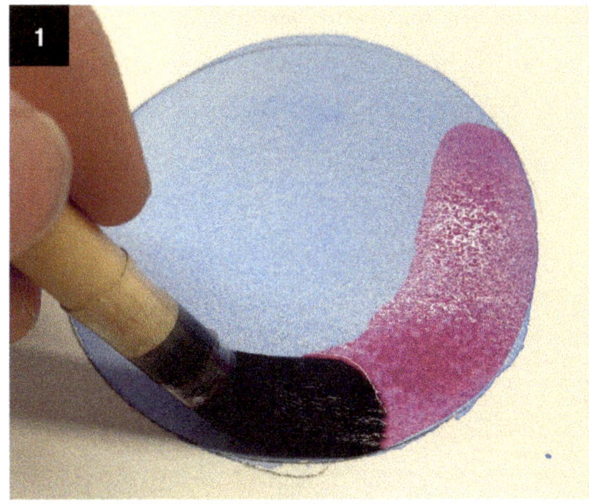

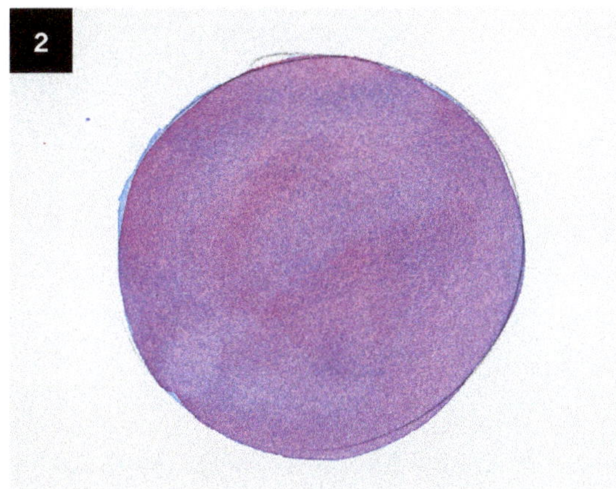

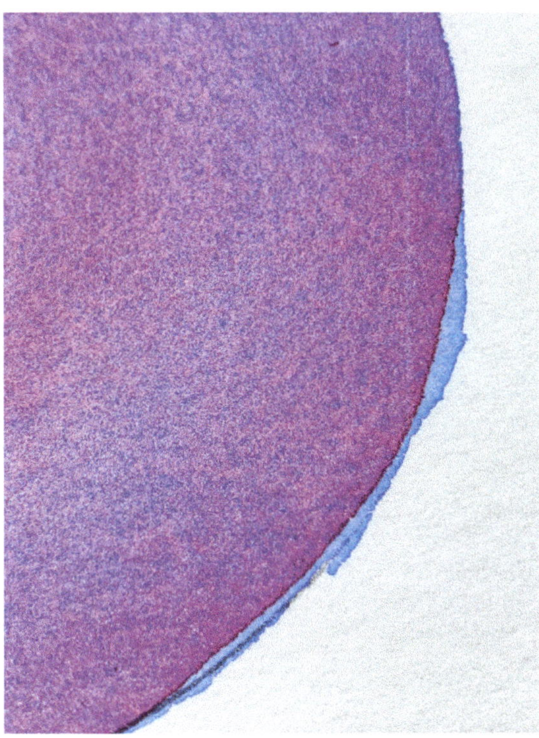

With glazing, light shimmers through the colors and they seem to vibrate in an interesting way.

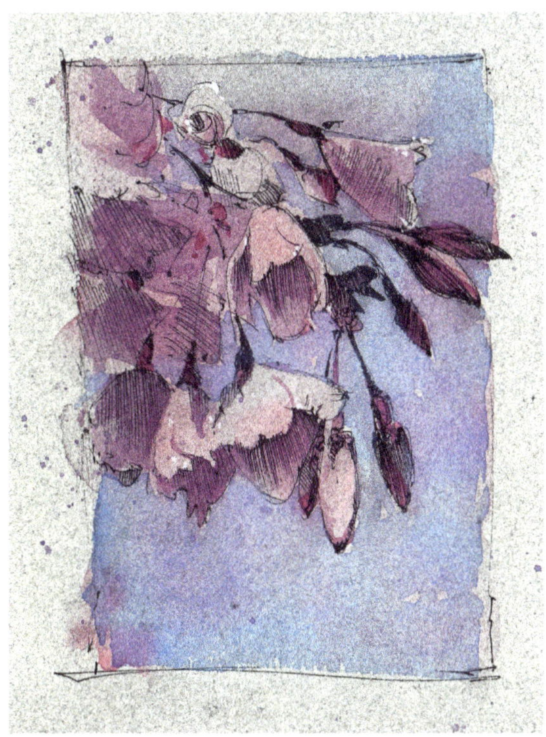

I used the glazing technique with these flowers, layering pinks and blues that glow with light.

Mixing Colors on Paper

The third way to mix paints is by combining them on paper. This is where watercolor really comes into its own. Pigments flow into each other, dancing together in rivulets, pooling, granulating, creating an incredibly dynamic dance.

1 | Start with a lot of pigment and plenty of water. Apply cobalt blue to one area of the paper and quinacridone red to another area, fairly close together. While the paints are still wet, introduce them to each other with your brush.

2 | Hold the paper vertically and tilt it in different directions to allow the colors to flow into each other. This is the most dynamic way to mix colors and is a technique unique to watercolor.

3 | Once you are happy with the way these two colors have blended, return the paper to a horizontal position to stop the flow. The pigments will now settle into the fibers of the paper and begin to dry.

By combining these three color-mixing techniques with the different types of washes, we have the foundational tools of watercolor painting. In any given painting, I use all these techniques together for endless variety.

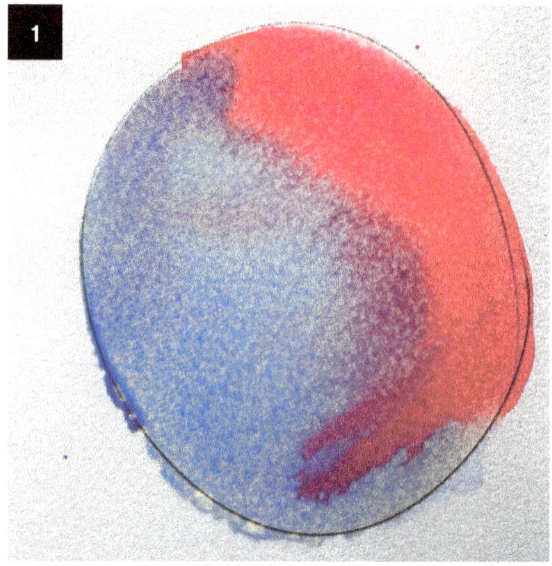

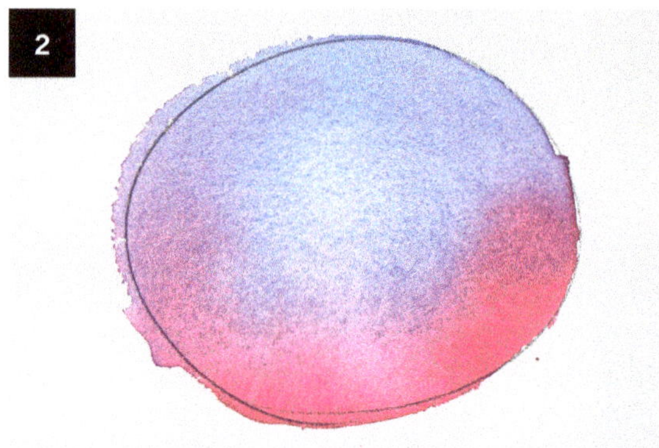

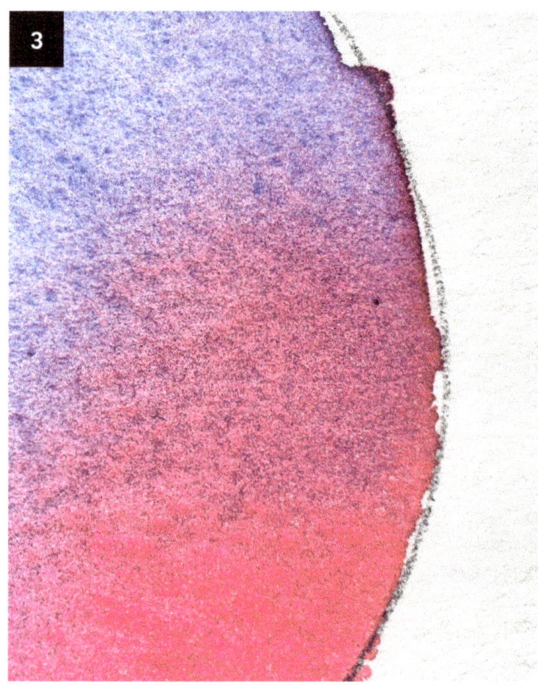

Mixing colors on the page creates an incredibly dynamic dance.

The Perfect Blend

Blending colors on the page is my favorite mixing technique. I use it to create a dynamic underpainting, discussed more later in this chapter in "Stages of a Painting" (page 134). I also mix colors on the page when adding shadow details, allowing me to vary the quality of a color and add variety.

WARM AND COOL COLORS

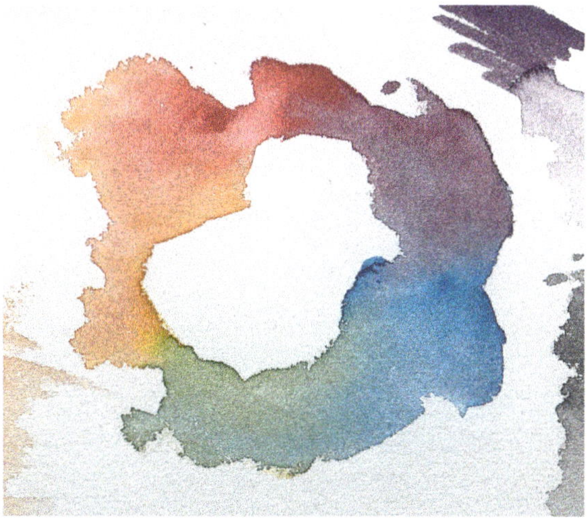

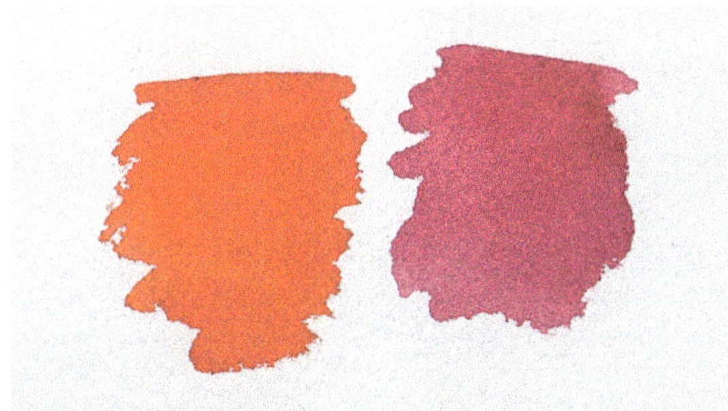

A warm red on the left, pyrrol scarlet, contrasts with a cool red on the right, quinacridone red.

We associate different temperatures with certain colors. We usually think of cool colors as blue, turquoise, and green, and warm colors as red, orange, and yellow. A color wheel can be divided into warm and cool colors.

This loose color wheel (above) shows gradations of color flowing one into the next. Warm colors, oranges and reds, are on the left, while cool purples, blues, and greens, are on the right.

Endless variety exists within this framework. There are warm reds and cool reds, warm blues and cool blues. The juxtaposition of colors often reveals their temperature.

Using warm and cool colors next to each other creates dynamic combinations with real depth. Color temperature is another way to create contrast in a sketch, and contrasts create attention.

Three different temperatures of blue: phthalo blue; cerulean chromium; and cobalt blue.

Push and Pull

Colors can be exaggerated to our advantage. To push a background farther away, make it cooler. And to pull a foreground closer, make it warmer.

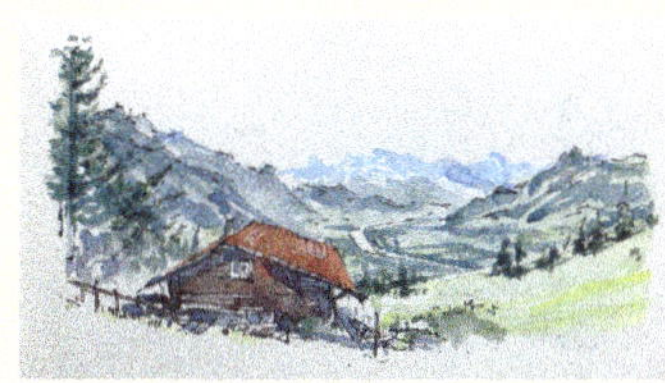

INTENTION IS GOOD, ATTENTION IS BETTER

With sketching and painting, we should have some sort of intention. A clear pencil sketch forms the foundation. We have intentions as to how we'd like things to proceed. But once we touch our tools to the page, our moment-to-moment attention to the process is more important. Our attention to the interplay with our materials becomes more important than any intention we began with.

Painting with watercolor can be such an intricate relationship, part performance, part creation, part mediation. The paints, the paper, the humidity of the day, and the way light and shadows move across a scene all play a part, along with what we bring to the table: our experience and talent, our preparation, our mood, and countless emotions and sensibilities. We need to be open to improvisation.

If you intend to set out to create a masterpiece worthy to hang on a gallery wall, and you fail (in your eyes), you may be frustrated. In the worst case, it might be years before you pick up a brush again. So, I'd like to invite you to play. Play with pencils, play with brushes, and play with watercolor. And pay attention to the process.

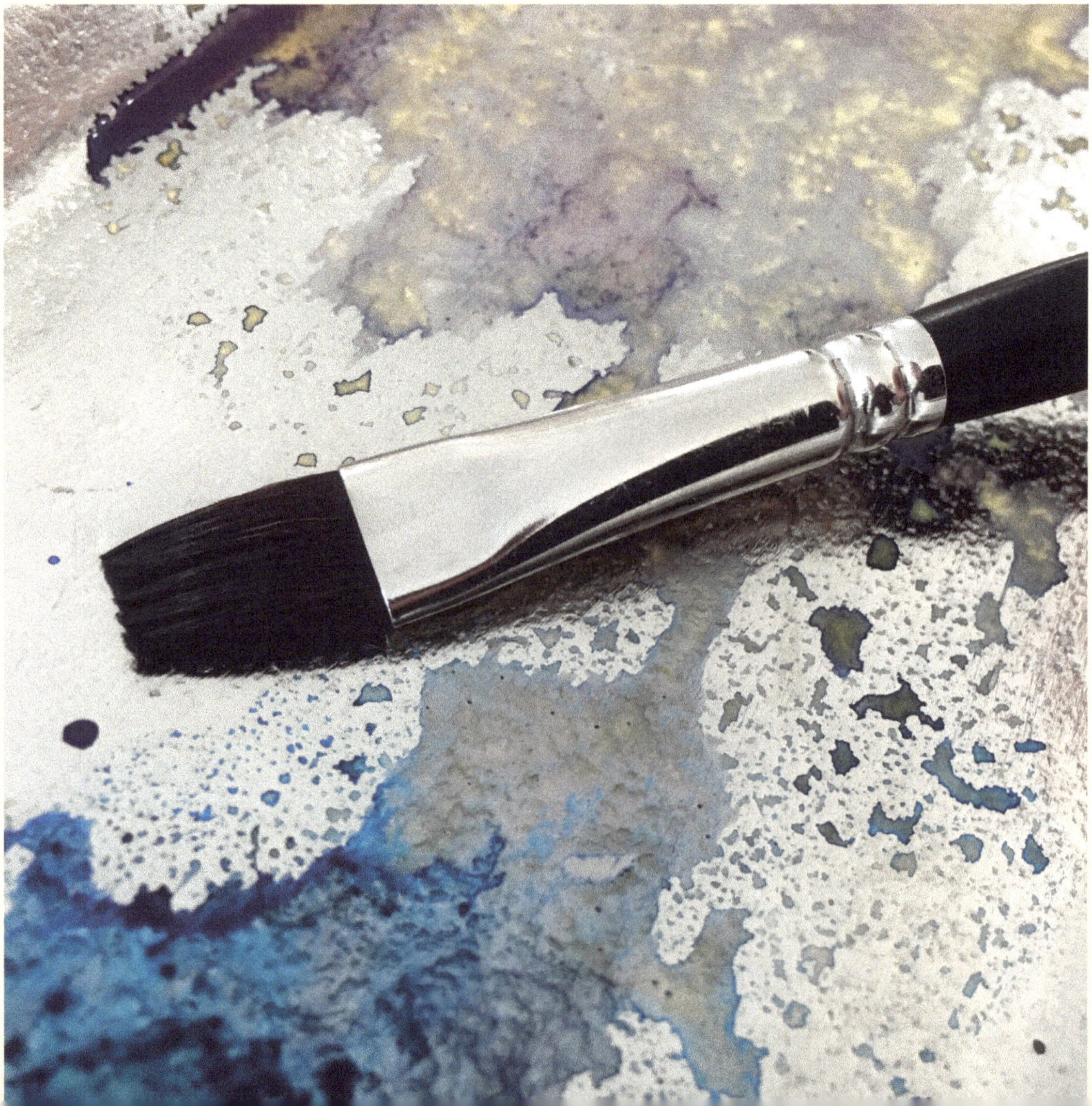

PAINTING WITH A LIMITED PALETTE

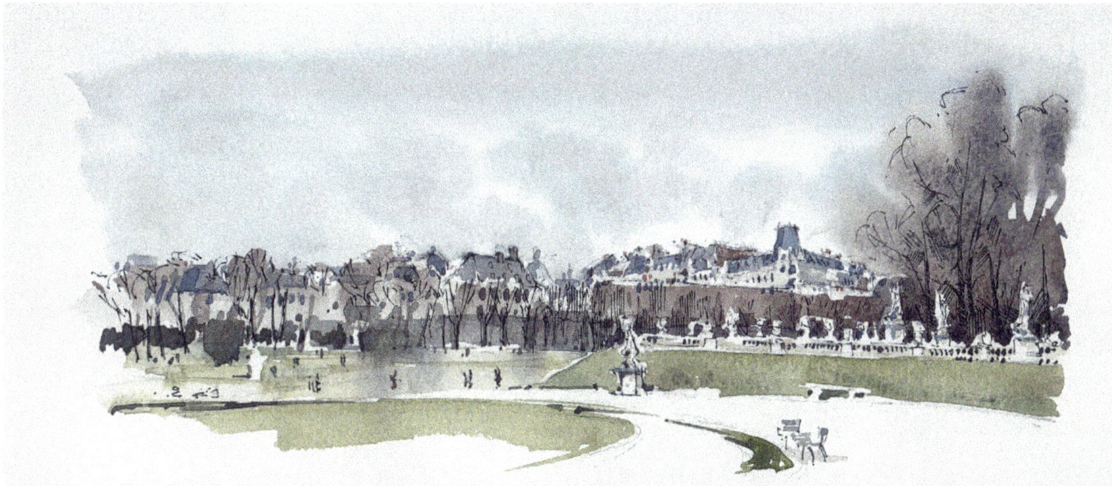

Winter in the Jardin du Luxembourg, Paris. Limiting yourself to just a few colors can yield beautiful results.

Because I sketched for many years using just pencil and ink, color was always a bit of a foreign language. Color intimidated me. When I bought my first set of watercolor paints, I was very hesitant and, as a result, my washes were timid and pale.

I am much more confident now with color, and much bolder with color choices. But I certainly understand how color can be confusing. One solution is purposefully limiting your color palette.

My Six Go-To Colors

Limiting yourself to just six colors can feel like an impossible challenge. Even my smallest travel palette has nine colors, but I've found these are the colors I reach for most often:

- Ultramarine
- Burnt sienna
- Pyrrol scarlet
- Raw sienna
- Quinacridone red
- Phthalo green

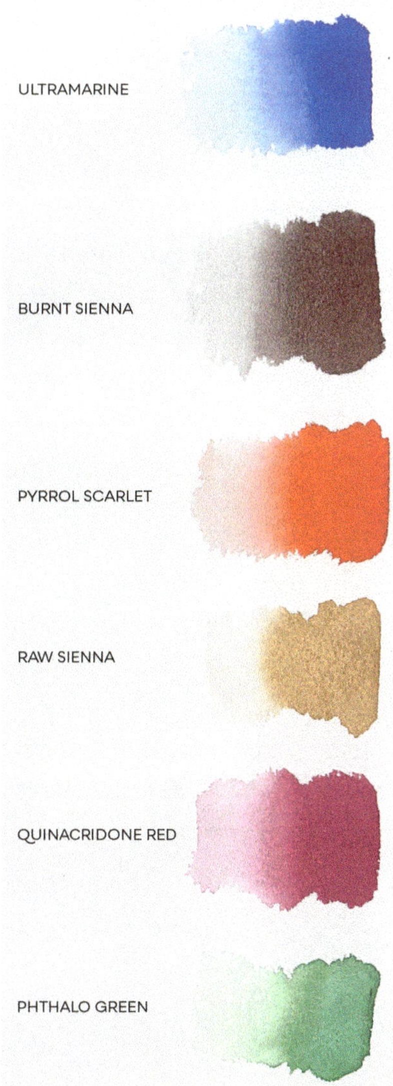

STAGES OF A PAINTING

When I'm doing a more finished painting, I tend to work in three distinct stages. I begin with a pencil sketch, then an ink sketch, and finally, watercolor.

To keep the spontaneity throughout the creation of an entire piece, I move through each of the stages relatively quickly. I want to keep my pencil stroke light and use it to define the overall shape. I make sure I'm happy with the composition, the perspective, and the forms, but I don't want to get bogged down in detail at this stage. I want to move on to the ink stage as quickly as I can.

When I'm sketching my ink lines, I tend to think of them as composing the darkest parts of my composition. Ink is reserved for the deepest shadows, banister railings, window outlines, and only the parts of a composition that contain the darkest of darks.

I don't use ink to outline, for example, every building or every window. The last thing I want to do is create a drawing that I then color in. My philosophy is that each of the stages–pencil, ink, and paint–should play off each other and play well together.

In order to not create a piece laden with details, I will put my pen down before I feel I'm finished. It's easy to get bogged down in detail with a pen and portray too much. Ink can make things too heavy. So, for the style that I have developed, there will be very few ink marks on my page before I reach for my paints. It's much easier to add details later, but harder to take them away.

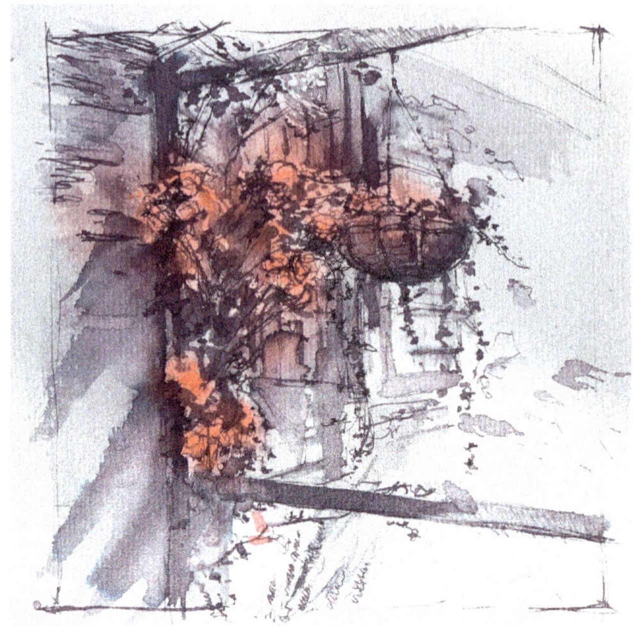

Use dark inks for the deepest of shadows, leaving the white of the paper for bright highlights. Details can remain loosely sketched in. Paper, ink, and paint all work together to complete the image.

Because I love painting light and the way light defines and shapes structures, I find if there's too much ink, it gets in the way of the light. Ink starts to fight with the light and compete with it. I want all these elements to work in harmony.

Painting Process

Once I pick up my paints, I work with an initial wash of color. This is done fairly quickly, often wet-on-wet. The idea is to have colors blend together on the page.

For this style of painting, watercolor likes to be applied with the lightest tones first, then later moving into darker shades. The sky and the sunlit areas are first. The warm colors used to indicate sunlight on stone will mix together, creating variety.

1 | Working wet-on-wet, block in large shapes of color on your sketch. There's no need to color inside the lines at this stage. The paint should be free to flow across the page. Leave some of the white paper shining through. This creates beautiful highlights of sunlight. Using the freedom of wet-on-wet techniques and having colors flow into each other will add spontaneity to your painting. It's okay if your painting looks out of focus. At this stage, your painting is like an orchestra warming up. It's only beginning to find its way.

2 | Once the initial wash is on the page, let it dry completely. When painting outside, this will take only a few minutes.

1

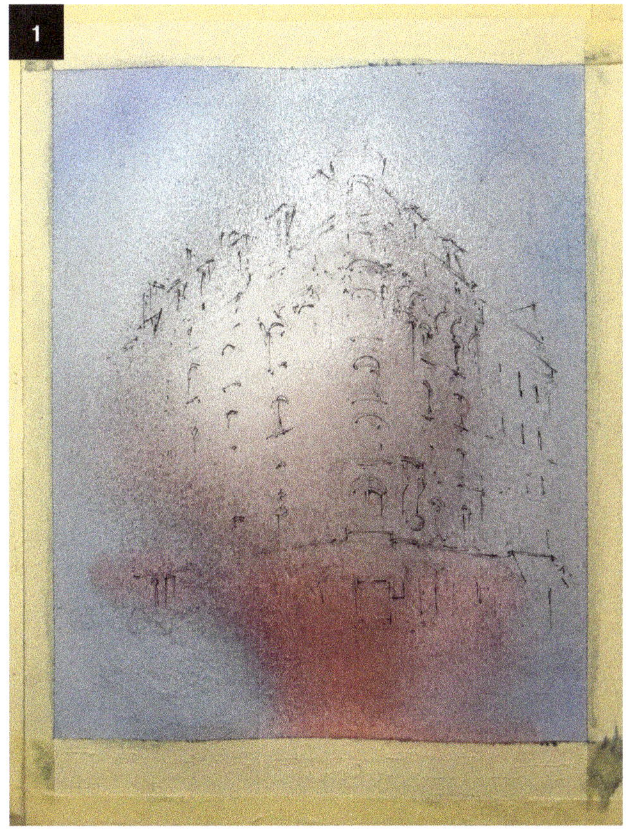

2

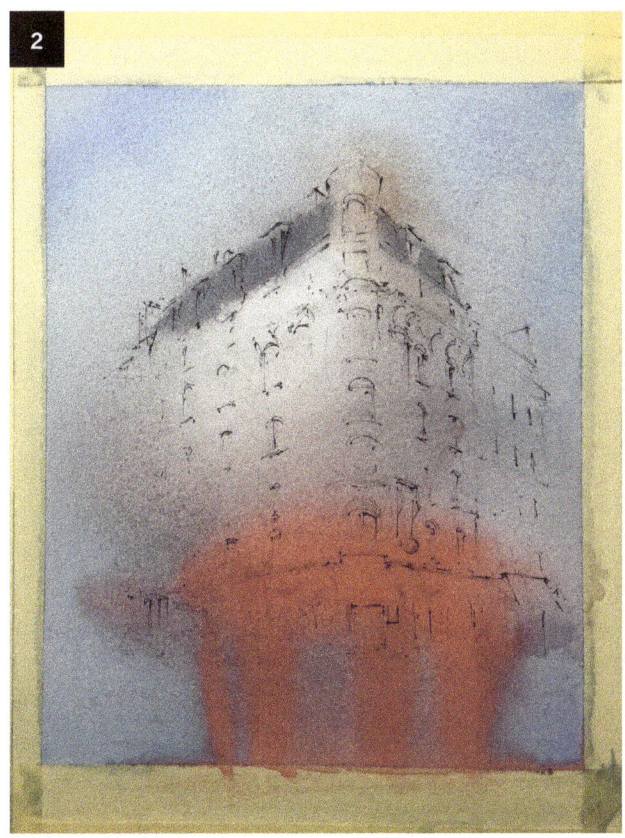

3 | Mix a cool gray for a shadow color. Remember that watercolor dries lighter than when you first apply it, so mix a color that's darker than you think it should be. Wash this color on the page to create bold shadows, deep recesses under café awnings, and streets that hold out shapes for crosswalks.

4 | As a last touch, I will often sketch more details with my ink pen: banister railings, window frames, perhaps some TV antennas. The piece will tell me what it needs.

3

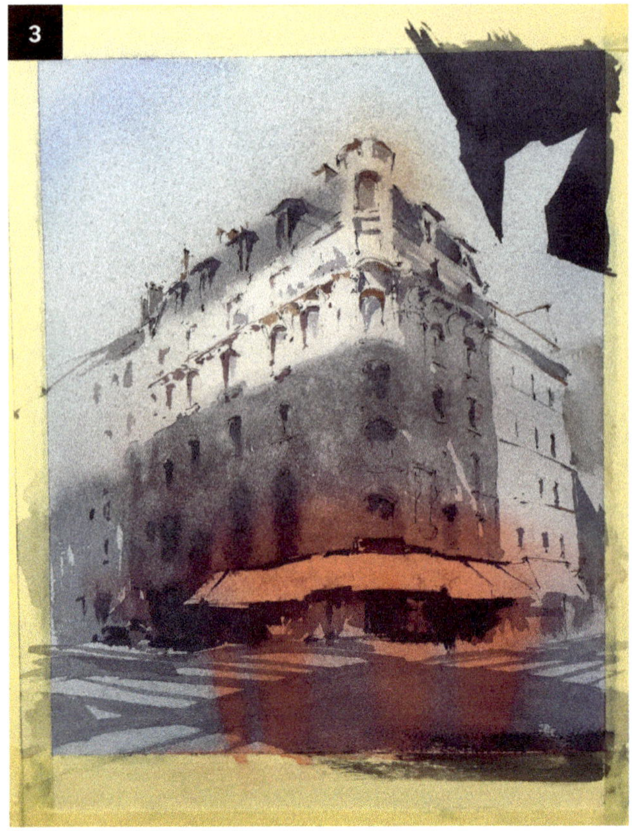

4

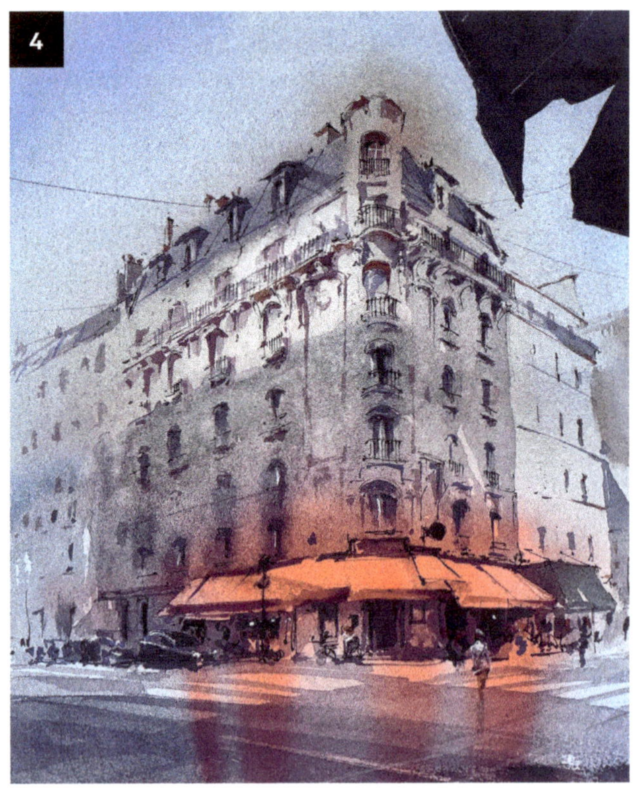

THE COLOR AND CONSISTENCY OF SHADOWS

Varying the colors within your shadows is important. Shadows aren't just one solid wash of color. It's much more interesting to push other colors into them, combining cool and warm colors within the same part of a shadow.

Exaggerating colors is okay. We don't have to be a slave to reality and be dogmatic with our color choices. This can be one area to really play with your sketches. Play with the colors that you're portraying. Push dark colors into a more blue or purple realm. Pull the sunlight out of colors with unexpected oranges and pinks. Push colors to opposite sides of the color wheel, extending the reach of warm sunlight and cool shadows.

We're also not only painting the color of an object. It's one thing to paint a gray roof or a beige chimney, but to paint the light that's reflecting off surrounding objects is much more interesting. To paint the temperature of the day, to paint the mood we want to convey can shift our thinking and add dimension to our work.

To enhance the illusion of depth, we can play with the consistency of shadows. Beyond hard and soft lighting situations, we are free to vary the depth of our shadows. We can increase contrast in some areas and lighten up shadows in others.

Using Light and Shadows to See Beyond the Frame

Paintings and sketches are confined by the borders of our paper, but sometimes it's possible to see beyond the frame. Think of your frame as a window into a larger world. We may be containing something in our view, but it can be wonderful to hint at a lager scene.

In this image of a Paris café on an early Sunday morning (bottom right), there had been a light snow the night before that didn't stick. When I came across the scene, everything glistened. I was drawn to the reflections in the street, and also to the shadows on this building. The sun was still low and the shadows from surrounding buildings were reluctant to leave the scene.

These shadows speak to the presence of surrounding buildings. This is a technique I use to see beyond the frame. Including shadows of other objects like trees, people, or buildings creates a larger scene that refuses to be contained by the page. Even if you're only sketching one building, don't forget you are actually sketching a city.

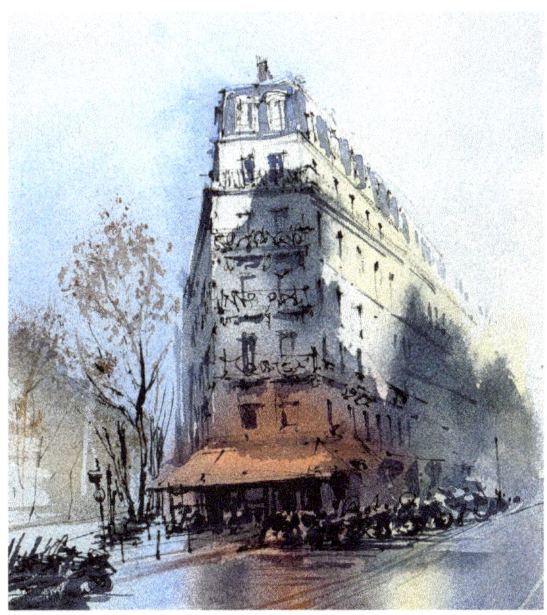

Glistening morning light provides countless opportunities to vary the color and consistency of shadows. These shadows also hint at a larger scene beyond the frame.

CONTRE JOUR

In my work in the film industry I've had the pleasure of collaborating with some of the best cinematographers in the business. Watching these craftsmen and artists work their magic on a film set, it's hard not to pick up a thing or two about lighting. One thing I see time and time again is that subjects are backlit.

Filmmakers didn't invent this technique; they're borrowing it from the Impressionists. Painters Pissarro, Monet, Sorolla, and others, found that by looking into the sun, casting objects in silhouette, bathed their paintings in light.

The term in French is *contre jour*, which means against daylight, and it's a wonderful technique. If something catches your eye and begs to be sketched, take a moment and place the object between you and the sun to create a silhouette. Chances are that this change in the lighting situation will add drama and interest.

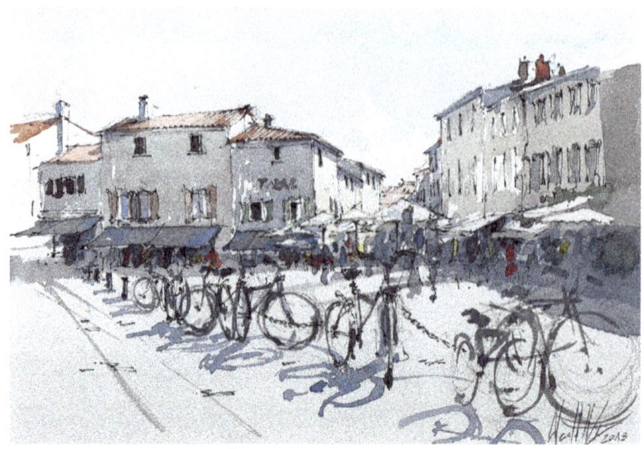

Backlit bicycles create wonderful shadows in this painting from La Flotte, Ile de Ré, France.

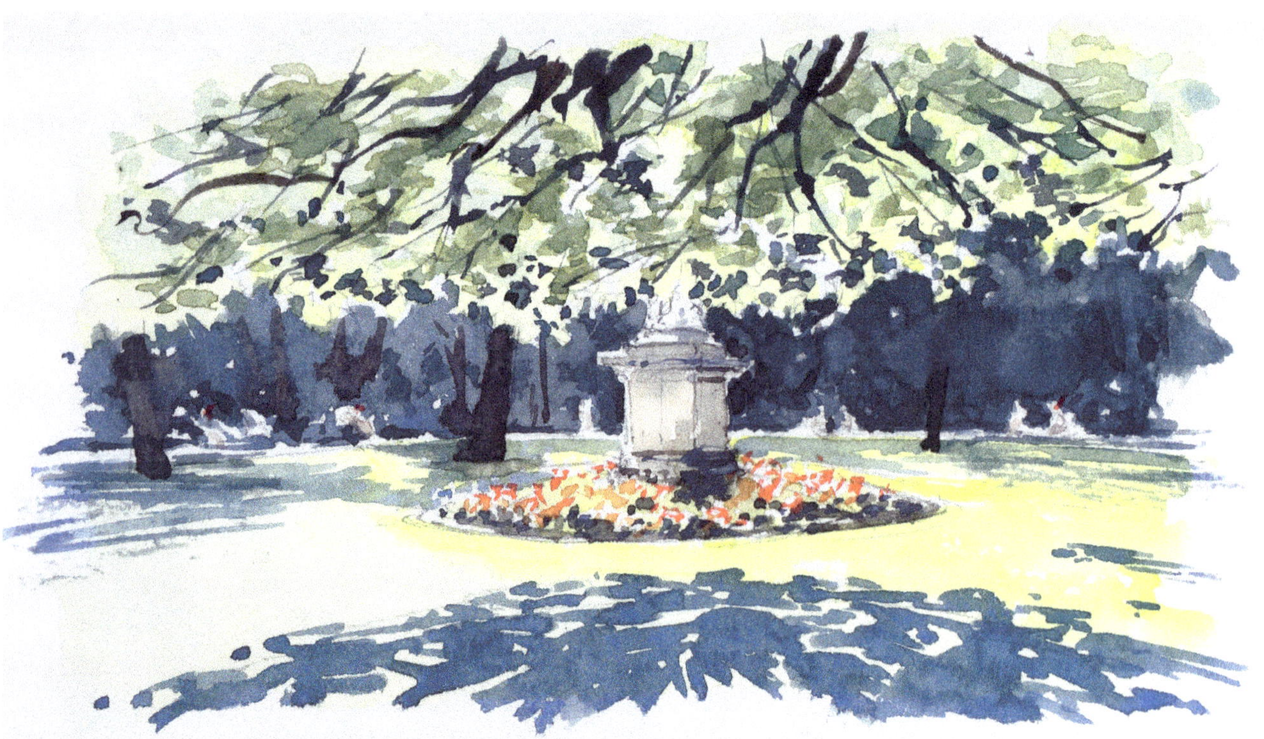

Sunlight illuminates a curtain of leaves in the Jardin du Luxembourg, Paris.

CONCLUSION: KEEP GOING

I hope these pages have provided you with the tips, tools, and inspiration to encourage you on your sketching journey. Like any journey, sketching can provide the joy of reaching new heights as your proficiency increases.

There's a tendency to want each painting to be perfect. There's also the worry that they might not live up to what you see in your head. But remember, the imperfect real is better than perfection imagined. Sketching is less about each individual piece and more about the path your pencil takes over the course of a lifetime.

Take the long view when thinking about your sketches. See your own trajectory of improvement. The key to improving at any skill is to develop the talent for improving technique. Fall in love with the process and the results will take care of themselves.

As Picasso once said, "Inspiration exists, but it has to find you working."

Now you have the tools . . . get out there and play.

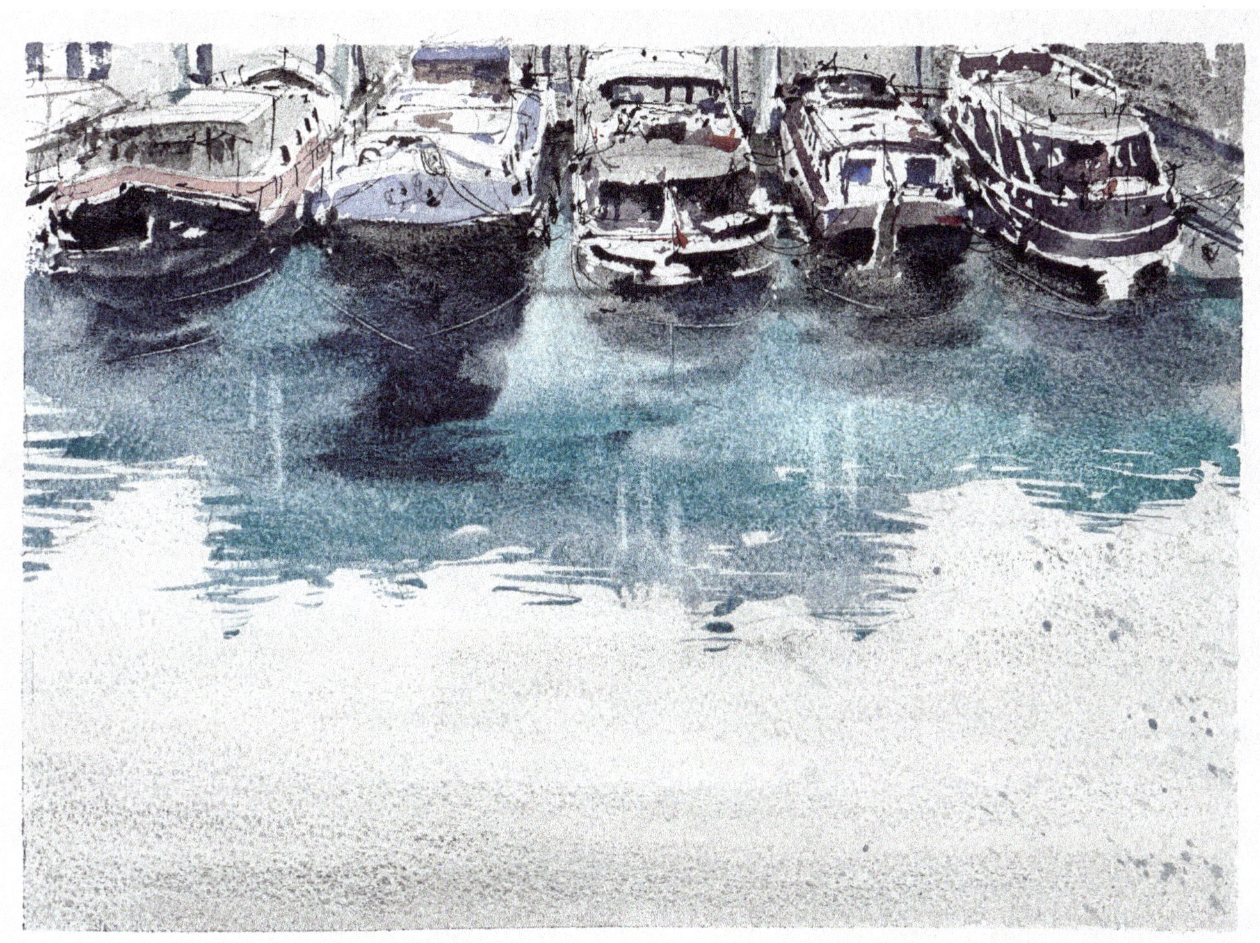

Canal Saint-Martin, Paris.

RESOURCES

Here are some of my favorite brands that make sketching even more enjoyable.

ARCHES: paper
arches-papers.com

Canson: paper
canson.com

Daniel Smith: paints
danielsmith.com

Escoda: brushes
escoda.com

Faber-Castell: pencils, fine liners, and fountain pens
faber-castell.com

Hahnemühle: sketchbooks
hahnemuehle.com

Pigma Micron: fine liners
pigmamicron.com

SMLT: sketchbooks
smltart.com/art

INFLUENCES

Countless artists and teachers have inspired me over the years. Here are some who I always have in mind while sketching and painting.

James McNeill Whistler (1834–1903): Primarily known for his oil paintings. I'm inspired by the etchings that Whistler made late in his life when he visited Venice. Without color, Whistler perfectly captured Venice's shabby magnificence.

J. M. W. Turner (1775–1851): British artist known for his brilliantly atmospheric paintings. I'm drawn to the sketches and watercolors he did while traveling through Luxembourg in 1839.

Félix Ziem (1821–1911): French artist who captured the light of Venice and Istanbul in his paintings. His sketchbooks are a treasure to behold.

ACKNOWLEDGMENTS

A huge thank you to film directors Ben Affleck, Nancy Meyers, Cameron Crowe, Angelina Jolie, Wally Pfister, and cinematographers Roger Deakins, John Toll, Anthony Dod Mantle, Robert Richardson, and Rodrigo Prieto. These visualists and storytellers who I've had the pleasure of working with have given me endless guidance and inspiration. Working alongside them in preparing films for production and watching how they tease a project into existence has been the greatest of schools.

Thanks also to this global community of sketchers, painters, and fellow creatives. We've found each other thanks to social media, and it's your company, conversations, and community that remind me that we are all together. I look forward to more travel and meeting the faces behind the @s and #s.

Un grand merci to the city of Paris, and mes amis ici for allowing my art to blossom. Your colors and personalities have welcomed me with open arms.

And a ginormous thank you to my dear wife, Tiffany. For everything that you do, all your support, and love. I love you.

ABOUT THE AUTHOR

Alex Hillkurtz was born in England and grew up in California, where he was an award-winning film student at Chapman University. He first established himself as a successful illustrator and storyboard artist in Hollywood, working with top studios such as Warner Bros., Marvel, Paramount Pictures, and Universal Studios. He has collaborated with many of the film industry's leading directors and cinematographers.

Currently living in Paris, Alex has turned his focus to a career as a watercolor artist and sketch artist and enjoys discovering the aspects of the city that sketching and painting uniquely allow.

Because of his background, Alex uses the language of cinema to inform his sketched and painted images, moving beyond what is most obvious, and focusing the viewer's eye on what he wants them to see. He believes that in our too-crowded lives, plein air painting moves at a more contemplative pace, revealing a true sense of a place and its stories.

Thinking in cinematic scenes, camera angles, and characters, Alex infuses his work with these discovered and imagined stories and aims to create images that convey the mood and character of a place, just as film scenes do.

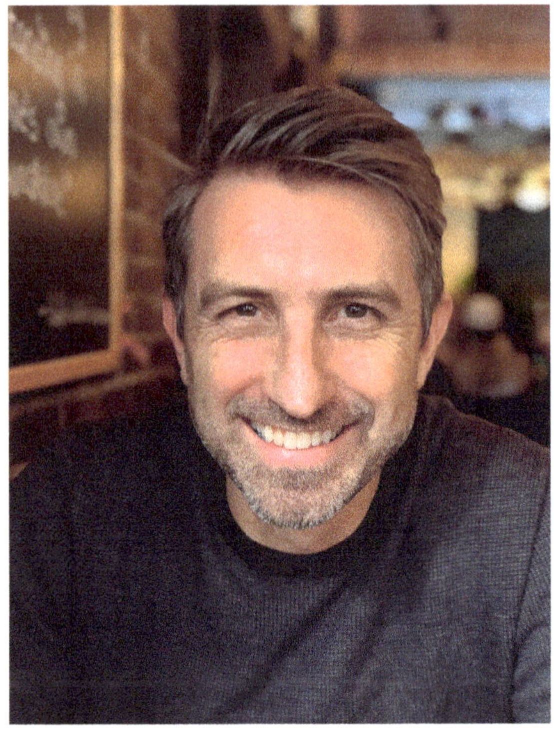

Alex's works have been exhibited in solo and group shows in Europe, the United States, and Russia. He conducts regular workshops and masterclasses on watercolor painting and sketching in Europe and the United States, teaching students of all levels and backgrounds how to infuse their paintings with a marvelous sense of life.

Alex is also active on social media and proud to be part of a wonderful global community of creatives.

Instagram: @hillkurtz
Facebook: AlexHillkurtzArt
Web: AlexHillkurtzArt.com

INDEX

www.ingramcontent.com/pod-product-compliance
Lightning Source LLC
Chambersburg PA
CBHW051711310526
45815CB00007B/8
9781631599231